REFERENCE BOOKS ON FAMILY ISSUES
(VOL. 23)

CHILDREN OF
POVERTY

GARLAND REFERENCE LIBRARY
OF SOCIAL SCIENCE
(VOL. 968)

REFERENCE BOOKS ON FAMILY ISSUES

RESOURCES FOR EARLY CHILDHOOD
An Annotated Bibliography and Guide for Educators, Librarians, Health Care Professionals, and Parents
Hannah Nuba Scheffler, General Editor

PROBLEMS OF EARLY CHILDHOOD
An Annotated Bibliography and Guide
by Elizabeth S. Hirsch

CHILDREN AND DIVORCE
An Annotated Bibliography and Guide
by Evelyn B. Hausslein

STEPFAMILIES
A Guide to the Sources and Resources
by Ellen J. Gruber

EXPERIENCING ADOLESCENTS
A Sourcebook for Parents, Teachers, and Teens
by Richard M. Lerner and
Nancy L. Galambos

SEX GUIDES
Books and Films About Sexuality for Young Adults
by Patty Campbell

INFANCY
A Guide to Research and Resources
by Hannah Nuba-Sheffler, Deborah Lovitky Sheiman, and Kathleen Pullan Watkins

POSTPARTUM DEPRESSION
A Research Guide and International Bibliography
by Laurence Kruckman and
Chris Asmann-Finch

CHILDBIRTH
An Annotated Bibliography and Guide
by Rosemary Cline Diulio

ADOPTION
An Annotated Bibliography and Guide
by Lois Ruskai Melina

PARENT-CHILD ATTACHMENT
A Guide to Research
by Kathleen Pullan Watkins

RESOURCES FOR MIDDLE CHILDHOOD
A Source Book
by Deborah Lovitky Sheiman
and Maureen Slonim

CHILDREN AND ADJUSTMENT TO DIVORCE
An Annotated Bibliography
by Mary M. Nofsinger

ONE-PARENT CHILDREN, THE GROWING MINORITY
A Research Guide
by Mary Noel Gouke and
Arline McCarthy Rollins

CHILD ABUSE AND NEGLECT
An Information and Reference Guide
by Timothy J. Iverson and Marilyn Segal

ADOLESCENT PREGNANCY AND PARENTHOOD
An Annotated Guide
by Ann Creighton Zollar

EMPLOYED MOTHERS AND THEIR CHILDREN
by Jacqueline V. Lerner and
Nancy L. Galambos

CHILDREN, CULTURE, AND ETHNICITY
Evaluating and Understanding the Impact
by Maureen B. Slonim

PROSOCIAL DEVELOPMENT: CARING, HELPING, AND COOPERATING
A Bibliographic Resource Guide
by Alice Sterling Honig and
Donna Sasse Wittmer

HISPANIC CHILDREN AND YOUTH IN THE UNITED STATES
A Resource Guide
by Angela L. Carrasquillo

FAMILY ADDICTION
An Analytical Guide
by Douglas H. Ruben

CHILDREN OF POVERTY
Research, Health, and Policy Issues
edited by Hiram E. Fitzgerald, Barry M. Lester, and Barry Zuckerman

CHILDREN OF POVERTY

Research, Health, and Policy Issues

Edited by
Hiram E. Fitzgerald
Barry M. Lester
Barry Zuckerman

GARLAND PUBLISHING, Inc.
NEW YORK & LONDON / 1995

Library of Congress Cataloging-in-Publication Data

Children of poverty : research, health, and policy issues / edited by
Hiram E. Fitzgerald, Barry M. Lester, and Barry Zuckerman.
p. cm. — (Reference books on family issues ; vol. 23)
(Garland reference library of social science ; vol. 968)
Includes bibliographical references and index.
ISBN 0-8153-1738-7
1. Poor children—Services for—United States. 2. Poor children—
Health and hygiene—United States. 3. Poor children—Research—
United States. I. Fitzgerald, Hiram E. II. Lester, Barry M.
III. Zuckerman, Barry S. IV. Series: Reference books on family
issues ; v. 23. V. Series: Garland reference library of social
science ; v. 968.
HV741.C53616 1995
362.7'1'0973—dc20   94-11694
                                                                          CIP

Printed on acid-free, 250-year-life paper
Manufactured in the United States of America

Contents

v

Preface

Proceedings of a Society for Research in Child Development Round Table

In agreeing to sponsor the 1993 Society for Research in Child Development (SRCD) round table discussions, "Children of Poverty," we at the Irving B. Harris Foundation knew that the way had been cleared for a formidable process to begin. As Hiram Fitzgerald, the program's organizer, wrote to me, the intent of the round tables was "to help chart the course for child development research, health care, and public policy for the next ten years." We believe the papers presented and the round table discussions, along with their broader distribution in this volume, do indeed offer useful insights and powerful guidance to researchers, policy makers, and practitioners and interventionists with a vast range of professional training.

Importantly, this work constitutes a charge to SRCD and its membership to respond to the plight of children of poverty by redoubling its commitment to sound research, taking into account the myriad methodological proposals and issues of perspective touched on in this text. Moreover, it is a call for more attention to the impact of research in the realms of practice and policy. Some people believe that it is foolhardy to address this awesome problem. Nonetheless, we can all agree that confronting poverty is critical, particularly because it affects so many children. Its ramifications are alarming, and I would argue that it is equally foolhardy for us to ignore the cycle of poverty and to go blithely about our lives thinking the problem will solve itself. Researchers must cooperate, as Lerner suggests, not only with program staff but with community members to understand the context in which efforts to ameliorate poverty operate, and to emphasize longitudinal research spanning decades. They must also take into account the persistently disproportionate representation of African Americans, Hispanics, and other minority groups among the poor, examining not only how their experiences differ from those of the majority, but studying within-group variation and how the *same mechanisms* which are at work in *all* families differentially affect the poor. The papers presented here point the way for increasingly interdisciplinary, methodologically integrated, and contextually-based research. They set an agenda for the decade to come.

However, as round table participants began to realize, good research alone is not enough. It is bound inextricably with an interest in the dissemination and use of the results for children's well-being. It seems to me that the actualization of this phenomenon, as implicitly or explicitly addressed in the present work, involves activity in three primary areas: program development and evaluation, training, and public policy. Each of these merits further illumination.

Developmental research can be of great use to intervention programs, in guiding their development and evaluating their effectiveness. Researchers must exercise caution, however, in responding to the need for evaluations. They must offer their wisdom about appropriate methodology, scope, and timing while remaining sensitive to the needs of those served as well as those paying for programs. Based on my own experience in the philanthropic community, I have realized that there seems to be some law ordained in heaven requiring most foundation trustees (and most government funding agencies as well, I suspect) to favor innovative projects which they can fund for one to three years. After that, the program by their definition is no longer innovative and is presumably old enough to replicate or abandon as a bad idea. Most new programs with which I have been associated are lucky if, in their third year, they are beginning to operate more or less in the way they were originally planned. It takes at least another three years from that point forward for such programs to stabilize so they can be intelligently evaluated. The community of SRCD can provide another voice in the call for thoughtful, timely, and cost-efficient rather than cost-cutting, evaluation that recognizes but does not bend to the will of politics.

A second area for SRCD to consider is the necessity for training good staff. Our nation is very, very slow in the training of sorely needed public health nurses, nurse practitioners, early childhood development people, social workers, occupational therapists, and paraprofessionals in all of these categories. As a consequence, even if we had all the money necessary to mount huge programs, it would take us at least ten years to rev up and train the needed personnel. Researchers in child development could be of significant practical assistance by contributing their knowledge to the generation of effective training programs. More importantly, they can work closely with future social scientists to help them learn as much about asking questions as answering them. They can foster, by example, a willingness to integrate their work with that of scholars from other disciplines, thereby amplifying our understanding of complex issues like poverty. Finally, they can help young academics see how their piece of the poverty puzzle fits with those of other professionals such as interventionists, advocates, and policy makers. In fact, as Houston suggests in this volume, we might even train our graduate students to write for audiences such as policy makers as well as other scholars.

Communicating with the policy community represents, perhaps, the most exciting and challenging aspect of the work outlined here. The number of poor is growing faster than the population as a whole. Any sensible person must realize we cannot just wait for the problem to correct itself. If doing nothing can be called a policy, then that has been our national policy. I think of it as "Let's not rock the boat—let's just sink quietly." Today, however, with heath care reform and welfare reform both on the national policy agenda, we have a choice opportunity to rock the boat in support of poor children. Barnard and Morisset, as well as others in this volume, have a clear notion of where to start.

> The ultimate answer to changing the lives of children at risk due to poverty and inadequate parenting are intervention strategies that provide preventive interventions that begin in pregnancy and continue

through the early years of the child's life. It is not enough
to help the parent or child alone. These interventions must
address the family as a whole and integrate health,
behavioral, vocational, and educational services. There
must be a new attention to relationships in all these service
systems, particularly for the socially at-risk client.
Additionally, neighborhood and community contexts
must be considered. Parents and children cannot thrive
where family and community violence are a fact of daily
life. Only by reducing the risk factors (poverty, stress, etc.)
and increasing resilience through supportive services can
we stop stealing developmental competence and health
from our nation's children. Poverty of the individual is
compounded by poverty of the neighborhood and
community. (pp. 189–190, this volume)

Their question is whether we will find the social will to act on
this knowledge.

I would assert that we *must* find the will because *it is not
only the poor who are in trouble. We are all in trouble.* We are at risk
of losing our Social Security benefits through the inadequate
development of society's human capital invested in its children.
We should all join in and ask *why* so many poor African
Americans, poor Hispanics, and poor whites have to live lives of
despair, only to end up in hospitals, welfare lines, prisons, and
morgues. When we know the answers it will become clear to
those who read the chapters which follow that "the larger point
is about honesty: Children fare better in some circumstances
than others, and no decent society will remain silent when it
comes to pointing out which circumstances are which" (Chester
Finn, former assistant secretary of education under William
Bennett, quoted in Harris, 1990).

Now is the time for the Society for Research in Child
Development to accept this obligation to share its collective
knowledge about "Children of Poverty." Participants in this
round table discussion outlined several action steps for
consideration including recognizing and promoting a variety of
research strategies, training the next generation of its members,
requiring its members to consider the policy relevancy of their
work as part of the publication process, and condensing and

crystallizing findings for policy makers. I look forward to seeing their results in the coming decade.

We in the larger society have an obligation as well. We must support their efforts and be strong advocates for children of poverty. We must reinforce their messages about the long-term, resource-intensive, and integrated strategies necessary to make a real difference in the lives of children and families. What appears costly now is but a pittance compared with the costly ramifications of neglecting our children. As Kliman and Rosenfeld put it in their book, *Responsible Parenthood*, "It makes a real difference to *you* whether *my* child turns out to be, say, a dedicated teacher or a narcotics peddler. If my child is retarded or delinquent, you—without any vote in the matter—help foot the bill or could be one of his or her victims. All children are everyone's children . . ." All of us share responsibility for our children. At the Irving B. Harris Foundation, we are pleased to support the work of the Society as it takes action.

Irving B. Harris

Introduction

By the year 2000, the population of the United States is estimated to be 275 million, and by the middle of the 21st century, demographers project a population of 375 million. In 1991, 35.7 million people (roughly 14% of the population of the United States) had incomes below the federally defined poverty level. Assuming no change in the percent of the population falling below the poverty level, by the end of the century the number of people living in poverty will be 38.5 million, and by 2050 it will exceed 50 million.

The National Center for Children in Poverty's (NCCP) analysis of 1990 census data indicate that 14 million of America's poor are children, with approximately 5 million of these under the age of six years. In 1989 the ten worse cities for children under six years of age had poverty rates ranging from 52.4% (Detroit, Michigan) to 44.8% (Laredo, TX). The Children's Defense Fund's analysis of 1990 census data indicate that among minority children living in large urban areas, "...42.1 percent of blacks, 35.3 percent of Latinos, 34.4 percent of Native Americans, and 22.9 percent of Asian Americans were poor." (CDF Reports, Aug. 1992, p. 8). According to the NCCP, Erie, PA ranked first among the ten worse cities in the United States for poverty among African American children (62.0%) and for Latino children (68.5%). In addition, the 1990 census data indicate that:

- 23% of all children under six years of age live in poverty.
- Children under six are more likely to be poor than any other age group.
- Roughly 25% of all poor children under six live with a single parent who worked full-time, or with married

parents who combined worked the equivalent of one full-time job.

- 58% of poor children are minorities, although only 33% of all children under six are minorities.
- Children under six living with single parents are 5 times more likely to be poor than are children living with two parents.
- The United States has the highest rate of child poverty among the world's industrialized nations.
- The proportion of full-time workers whose wages are too low to bring a family of four out of poverty now comprises 18% of the work force.
- The age group of women most likely to bear and rear children (18 to 34 years), experienced a shift in the proportion paid low wages from 29% in 1979 to 48% in 1990.

In the Fall of 1992, the Society for Research in Child Development (SRCD) published a "Social Policy Report" in an effort to inform its members about the crisis of child poverty. That publication painted a gloomy picture about America's resolve to eradicate child poverty. In contrast to powerful stereotypes and myths about child welfare, the facts suggest that America's children receive fewer benefits than any other age group. According to Strawn (1992), "The federal government spent an average of $11,350 per elderly person in 1990— compared to just $1,020 in federal spending per child under age 18." (p. 18).

This volume then, addresses the topic of poverty. It is the first in a series of studies involving children that will focus on the research, health care, and public policy issues that must be addressed by developmentalists as the twentieth century draws to a close and as society begins to articulate its agenda for the twenty-first century. Crime, substance abuse, child abuse, divorce, adolescent pregnancy, racism, infant mortality and morbidity, childhood communicable diseases, chronic illness, depression, and hopelessness visit every socioeconomic class. However, it is becoming increasingly clear that in highly industrialized, technologically sophisticated societies, these uninvited visitors aggregate in lower socioeconomic groups and exacerbate risk for poor developmental outcomes.

If American society in the year 2050 believes that it will be able to contain 50 million poor people, it does not understand the notion of critical mass. Early childhood education specialists often refer to "sleeper effects" to describe long term positive outcomes of early interventions. In other words, although early interventions may not show immediate positive outcomes, it does not preclude such outcomes appearing later in the life cycle. For example, an early intervention may not significantly raise the preschool age child's cognitive level of functioning, but it may be directly responsible for that child's decision to remain in school rather than drop out, thereby leading to long-term gains in skilled performance and cognitive functioning. However, sleeper effects are not exclusively linked to positive outcomes. Violence among teenage youth has increased 25% since 1980; homicide is the second leading cause of death among all 15–24 year olds in the United States; over 3 million children annually witness parental abuse; and hundreds of thousands of guns and knives are taken to school each day in the United States. Are these the sleeper effects of poverty? It is no longer meaningful or relevant to describe 35 million people in terms of a percentage of the population. Poverty affects people, not percentages.

How does the scientific community deal with these issues? Some scientists believe that social problems are government's problems. Others believe that the scientific community must become actively involved in attempts to resolve social problems. That is to say, scientists have an obligation to generate knowledge, but they also have an obligation to see that knowledge generation leads to knowledge application. To this end, an interdisciplinary group of applied developmental scientists met in New Orleans, one day prior to the 1993 meeting of the Society for Research in Child Development, to discuss research, health care, and public policy issues as they impact on children of poverty. Each participant's ten minute presentation was followed by a roundtable discussion. This volume contains expanded versions of each presentation, along with the discussion that followed the original presentations. The roundtable discussions that follow each chapter are direct transcriptions from audiotapes recorded at the time of the meeting. Chapters 5 and 8 are completely new for this volume. For each of these chapters, two members of the roundtable were asked to provide questions for response by the authors. These answers are presented as Roundtable Commentaries, rather than as Roundtable Discussions. Although one of the roundtable participants choose not to prepare a chapter, we did include this colleague's contributions during the roundtable discussions.

In addition to the roundtable participants, 53 observers attended the day long session. Opportunities were provided for observers to participate in the discussion. We had intended to include their comments in this volume. However, the audiosystem we used was not sufficient to provide clear copy of their comments. Our apologies to Ed Tronick, Michael Salomon-Weiss, George S. Morrison, Harriet McAdoo, John McAdoo, Gary Resnick, and Nancy Thomas. Each of these colleagues were members of the audience and each offered valuable comments during the round table discussions. Our promise to include their comments in these proceedings is, therefore, a promise unfulfilled. We will do better next time.

Finally, we would like to thank the members of the SRCD Executive Committee for sponsoring the Roundtable, in part, via the SRCD Liaison to Pediatrics program. We are especially grateful for the financial support provided by the Irving B. Harris Foundation, and are delighted that Irving Harris has contributed introductory comments to the volume. Plans are underway for the next two roundtables, Children of Color and Children of Addiction.

Hiram E. Fitzgerald
Barry M. Lester
Barry Zuckerman

Contributors

Round Table participants are indicated in bold.

Kathryn E. Barnard, R.N., Ph.D.
Mail Stop WJ-10
Child Development and Mental
    Retardation Center
University of Washington
Seattle, WA 98195

Francine S. Brem, R.N., Ph.D.
Rhode Island College
Department of Nursing
600 Mt. Pleasant Avenue
Providence, RI 02911

Jeanne Brooks-Gunn, Ph.D.
Center for the Study of Young
    Children & Families
Teachers College, Columbia
    University
5255 W. 120th Street, Box 39
New York, NY 10027

Cynthia García-Coll, Ph.D.
The Stone Center
Wellesley College
106 Central Street
Wellesley, MA 02181-8268

Greg J. Duncan, Ph.D.
Survey Research Center
Panel Study on Income Dynamics
University of Michigan
Ann Arbor, MI 48109

Hiram E. Fitzgerald, Ph.D.
Department of Psychology and
    Institute for Children, Youth,
    and Families
Michigan State University
East Lansing, MI 48824-1117

Vivian L. Gadsden, Ph.D.
National Center on Adult
    Literacy
University of Pennsylvania
3910 Chestnut St.
Philadelphia, PA 19104-3111

Irving B. Harris
Irving B. Harris Foundation
2 North La Salle Street
Suite 605
Chicago, IL 60602-3703

xix

Aletha C. Huston, Ph.D.
Department of Human
  Development
4001 Dole Human Development
  Center
University of Kansas
Lawrence, Kansas 66045

Pamela Klebanov, Ph.D.
Center for the Study of Young
  Children & Families
Teachers College, Columbia
  University
5255 W. 120th Street, Box 39
New York, NY 10027

Milton Kotelchuck, Ph.D., MPH
School of Public Health
Department of Maternal and
  Child Health
University of North Carolina
CB #7400, Rosenau Hall 201H
Chapel Hill, NC 27599-7400

Gontran Lamberty, Ph.D.
Maternal Child Health Research
  Program
MCHB, Parklawn Building,
  Room 18A55
5600 Fishers Lane
Rockville, MD 20857

Richard M. Lerner, Ph.D.
Institute for Children, Youth, and
  Families
2 Paolucci Building
Michigan State University
East Lansing, MI 48824-1110

Barry M. Lester, Ph.D.
Brown University Program in
  Medicine
Departments of Psychiatry and
  Pediatrics
1011 Veterans Memorial Parkway
E. Providence,RI 02915

Fong-ruey Liaw, Ph.D.
Department of Child
  Development
Taiwan Normal University
Taiwan

Sara G. Mattis, M.A.
Virginia Polytechnic Institute and
  State University
Department of Psychology
Blacksburg, VA 24061

Margaret M. McGrath, DNSc.
University of Rhode Island
College of Nursing
Kingston, RI 02881

Vonnie McLoyd, Ph.D.
Department of Psychology and
  Center for Human Growth and
  Development
300 N. Ingalls, 10th Level
University of Michigan
Ann Arbor, MI 48109-0406

Colleen E. Morisset, Ph.D.
Child Development and Mental
  Retardation Center
Mail Stop WJ-10
University of Washington
Seattle, WA 981985

Suzanne Randolph, Ph.D.
Department of Family Studies
University of Maryland
1204 Marie Mount Hall
College Park, MD 20742

Craig T. Ramey, Ph.D.
Departments of Psychology,
  Pediatrics, Public Health
  Science, and Sociology
Civitan International Research
  Center
1719 Sixth Avenue South
University of Alabama at
  Birmingham
Birmingham, AL 35294-0021

Arnold J. Sameroff, Ph.D.
Center for Human Growth and
  Development
300 N. Ingalls, 10th Level
University of Michigan
Ann Arbor, MI 48109-0406

Ronald Seifer, Ph.D.
Department of Psychiatry and
  Human Behavior
Brown University
Bradley Hospital
1011 Veterans Memorial Parkway
East Providence, RI 02915

Mary C. Sullivan, MSM, R. N.
College of Nursing
University of Rhode Island
Kingston, RI 02881

Heidie A. Vázquez García, B.A.
The Stone Center
Wellesley College
106 Central Street
Wellesley, MA 02181-8268

Robert A. Zucker, Ph.D.
Departments of Psychology and
  Psychiatry
Alcohol Research Center
400 East Eisenhauer Parkway,
  Suite A
University of Michigan
Ann Arbor, MI 48104

Barry Zuckerman, M.D., F.A.A.P
Department of Pediatrics
Boston University School of
  Medicine
Boston City Hospital
818 Harrison Avenue, T214
Boston, MA 02118

PART ONE

Research Agenda

CHAPTER 1

Toward an Understanding of the Effects of Poverty upon Children

Jeanne Brooks-Gunn, Pamela Klebanov, Fong-ruey Liaw, and Greg Duncan

Living in poverty exacts a toll on children and families. Research on the dimensions of the untoward effects of poverty is accumulating at a rapid pace, as witnessed by several edited volumes, notably *Children in poverty* (Huston, 1991), *Escape from poverty: What makes a difference for children?* (Chase-Lansdale & Brooks-Gunn, in press), and *Effect of Neighborhoods upon Children and Families* (Duncan, Brooks-Gunn, & Aber, in press), as well as special journal issues of *Child Development* (Huston, Garcia-Coll, & McLoyd 1993, in press), *Journal of Clinical Child Psychology* (Culbertson, in press), *American Behavioral Scientist* (1991), and *Children and Youth Services Review* (Danziger & Danziger, in press).

Current work tells us that we need to be concerned about poor children and their families. However, it does not inform us as to either the pathways by which poverty exerts its effects on children or on the relative importance of various dimensions of poverty in influencing children.

In this manuscript, we first look at how poverty is measured and how various measurement schemes alter interpretations of poverty effects. Absolute and relative indices of poverty are discussed; then, several recent attempts to use basic needs budgeting as a means to construct the income necessary to insure minimum levels of well-being are reviewed.

Next, we consider how various dimensions of poverty and income influence children's well-being. Our premise is that the multiple dimensions of poverty are rarely considered, rendering it difficult to provide much understanding of how poverty effects children. Both family and neighborhood poverty are considered in this chapter. Examples are given based on data from two sets of large longitudinal studies—the Infant Health and Development Program (IHDP)[1] and the Panel Study of Income Dynamics (PSID).[2]

Then, possible pathways through which poverty might exert effects on children are presented. The first set of pathways focuses on models derived from more macro-oriented disciplines—sociology, demography, epidemiology, and economics. Parental resources, including time, income, and emotional, cognitive, and social capital, are often the constructs underlying this work. The second set of pathways is derived from more micro-oriented approaches, those typically encountered in developmental psychology, psychiatry, and pediatrics. Risk and protective models are often used in developmental approaches. Several examples of additive risk, cumulative risk and double jeopardy models are presented, to see how family processes and risk factors play out in the context of poverty. A brief section considers a more complete model, attempting to marry the different disciplinary approaches (Brooks-Gunn, Phelps, & Elder, 1991; Duncan, 1991). This model is presented in more detail elsewhere (Brooks-Gunn, in press a).

What Is Poverty?

Official Poverty Threshold

The official poverty level is established by the federal government. It is based on the estimated cost of an "economy food budget" or shopping cart of food, multiplied by three. The multiplier was based on the premise that food accounted for about one-third of a family's after-tax income (Orshansky, 1965; Fisher, 1992). The poverty level is adjusted for family size, the age of the head of the household, and the number of children under age 18. Annual adjustments to the poverty index are made for the cost of living based on the Consumer Price Index. In 1991, U.S. poverty thresholds for families of three, four, and five persons were $10,860, $13,924, and $16,460, respectively. These thresholds are based on incomes before taxes.

One of the advantages of an absolute poverty level such as the U.S. thresholds is that comparisons may be made on an annual basis. Estimates of the number of persons living below the poverty threshold have been made yearly since 1959 by the U.S. Bureau of the Census (Hernandez, 1993). The comparative usefulness of the poverty threshold is illustrated in Figure 1, which presents the percentage of elderly persons and children in poverty for the past 20 years. As can be seen rates of poverty for the elderly have declined over the time period. In contrast, poverty rates for children have increased during this time period (although rates dropped between 1959 and 1969, not shown in Figure 1). Rates were in the mid-teens during the 1970s, and then rose to about 20% in the 1980s. The percentage of children who were poor continues to be 20% or even higher in the 1990s (currently 23%).

Much has been written about the causes of the increases in poverty rates for children; causes include (a) structural changes in the economy, including reduction of unskilled and semi-skilled jobs, stagnation of the economy (unemployment rates and wage rates), movement of jobs from inner cities, (b) changes in federal programs, including the failure of government benefits for poor people (e.g. AFDC) to keep up with inflation (eroding the impact of income transfers on families and on the movement of families above the poverty line), and increases in inequalities between the affluent and the poor (in part due to tax changes), and (c) structural changes in the family (increases in childbearing outside of marriage, increases in single parent households due to divorce, increases in maternal employment without the assurance of adequate child care). See Brooks-Gunn and Maritato (in press); Danziger and Stern (1990); Danziger and Weinberg (1986); Duncan (1991); Ellwood (1988); Garfinkel and McLanahan (1986); Hernandez (1993); Palmer, Smeeding, and Torrey (1988); Wilson (1987).

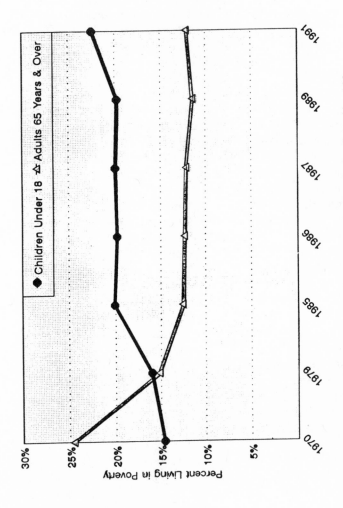

Source: U. S. Bureau of the Census, Current Population Reports, Series P-60, No. 168.

FIGURE 1. Percentage of Elderly and Children in Poverty over the Past 20 Years

Poverty as a Relative rather than an Absolute Concept

As just stated, the United States uses an absolute standard of poverty, based on what is believed to be necessary for a family's basic needs (or was believed to be necessary in 1959). While this measure is adjusted for the cost of living, it is based on a standard, which allows for comparisons over time as to how many individuals are poor or not poor.

Relative measures of poverty are not based on a standard. Instead, they are relative to the entire population's income, and as such change over time. The argument for relative measures has to do with the fact that minimum standards, as viewed by the society, are not static. As incomes rise, standards may also rise. Rainwater (1974, 1992) has presented data pursuant to this line of reasoning very persuasively. For example, public opinion polls from the 1930s through the 1960s have asked questions about how much income families need to "get along" and what income level is low or inadequate. Generally, these polls indicate that about 50% of the median for family income is defined by the population as necessary for basic needs.

Some countries, such as Canada, define poverty relative to the median income of the population. Using such a definition, in the United States, the "absolute" poverty line was .46 of the median income in 1965, and it was .41 of the median income in 1983 (Duncan, 1991; Huston, 1991). Clearly, the number of families categorized as poor would be higher if we used a relative standard such as Canada does.

In a recent volume by Hernandez of the U.S. Bureau of the Census (1993), relative poverty rates were calculated based on having less than 50% of the median family income for each year, following the work of Rainwater (1974). Relative poverty rates are about 37% higher than the official poverty rates for children.

Poverty Rates and Federal Programs

Another indicator of poverty involves the needs standards set for eligibility for various federal programs. Typically, families are eligible for programs if their family incomes are 150% or 185% of the poverty threshold for their family size (eligibility criteria vary by program). If children who live in families within 150% of the poverty threshold are included as poor (often the group between 100% and 150% is labeled "near poor"), the percentage of children age six and younger who would be classified as poor would be over 40%, not just over 20% (National Center for Children in Poverty, 1991).

Basic Need Budgets

The food basket approach to defining poverty thresholds, while easy to understand, is limited. Reasons include the following—food today accounts for about one-fifth of a family's expenditures (housing costs having increased substantially since 1959), the official poverty level only includes cash income (excluding in-kind transfers such as food stamps and medical care), and the current level does not take into account regional variation in living costs (with housing and transportation being two costs that vary greatly).

The food basket approach estimates what a family requires to meet its basic needs (by using a multiplier). Recently, several economists have built basic needs budgets in a slightly different way than Orshansky did (Ruggles, 1990; Watts, 1993). Watts terms the food basket approach the gross-up approach and the basic needs budget approach the category standard approach. Expenditure norms are derived for a small number of categories, usually food, housing, transportation for employed adults, health care, child and dependent care, clothing and clothing maintenance, personal care and miscellaneous. The budgets are, as Watts says, *lean*. They do not include what developmental psychologists would call learning or stimulating experiences (no books or other reading material, no recreation, no educational expenses). They do not take into account the cost of obtaining quality child care or moving to neighborhoods with high quality schools. They do not include what we might call "start up" costs (furnishing an apartment). Even so, in the Ruggles (1990) calculation, the number of single parent families living below the poverty line in 1989 would be 39% using the official poverty threshold and 47% using their basic needs budget (rates for children would be 48% vs. 56%).

It is clear that there is no consensus as to whether the poverty level should be determined by a method other than the food basket by three method, whether it should be adjusted for regional variations in cost of living, whether it should be based on expenditures, rather than income, or whether it should include in-kind transfers. However, this brief discussion does illustrate the difficulty that today's family at the poverty line or slightly above it has in making ends meet.

Life below the Poverty Threshold

We have still not confronted what it means to live below the poverty threshold. First, it is clear that individuals below the poverty line cannot meet basic expenses. Our colleague, Ann Doucette-Gates, has provided an estimate of basic income needs for a family of four in New York City. She includes housing (rent), food, basic needs, and taxes. Estimates of income are made for a family on AFDC, a family where one individual works a 40-hour week at minimum wage ($4.25 an hour), and a family where one individual works a 40-hour week at $10 an hour. The family with an employed adult is below the poverty line, as is the family on AFDC. These two families bring in over $350 less than what their basic expenditures are (not including health care and child care costs). The family where the wage earner brings home $10 an hour just about breaks even.

The poverty threshold makes no distinction between receipt of income from AFDC, from employment, or from both. Debates centering on the possible existence of a welfare culture and on the inadvisability of requiring poor mothers to enter the work force would benefit from such information (Smith, in press; Zill et al., in press; Wilson, Ellwood, & Brooks-Gunn, in press). It also makes no distinction between families who are close to the poverty threshold and those who are way below it.[3]

Estimates of effects of poverty upon children are often made looking at income, rather than focusing on "a" poverty line. However, unless non-linear models are employed to see if income effects are more pronounced at the bottom of the income distribution or if a disjuncture in income effects occurs around 150% or 185% of the poverty line, then using income as a proxy for poverty provides little specific information on poverty *per se.* Instead, only the more general statement, "more income is beneficial for children" may be made.

Using the IHDP age 5 outcomes, we find linear and non-linear effects of income upon child outcome (based on income-to-needs ratios derived using poverty thresholds; see Brooks-Gunn, Duncan, et al., 1993; Duncan, Brooks-Gunn & Klebanov, in press, for a discussion of the income and poverty measures and the sample). Another approach to the premise that income effects may be discontinuous is to make comparisons between the poor and not poor. A variant on this theme involves looking at poor, near poor, and not poor, to see if the near poor are more similar to the poor or to individuals who are not poor. Again, using the IHDP data set, we first look at a few family characteristics of families categorized based on income-to-needs ratios. We divide the sample into poor (100% or less of the poverty threshold), near poor (101% to 150% of the poverty threshold), not poor (151% to 200% of the poverty threshold) and affluent (over 200% of the poverty threshold).

First we take a look at familial characteristics—structural variables—(household density and maternal education), maternal characteristics (maternal depressive symptomatology, categorical beliefs about childrearing), and parenting behavior (provision of learning experiences and warmth). These data suggest that poor and near poor families are not similar to one another except on depression, and that near poor families are more similar to the not poor on household density, warmth, and beliefs about childrearing. All groups are dissimilar on learning environment and maternal education (Figure 2).

Looking at child's IQ scores at age 5 as an outcome provides data similar to the familial characteristic data presented. The unadjusted mean IQ scores of children who are poor and near poor are quite similar to one another and are much lower than those for children who are not poor. Adding maternal education and single-parent household variables as

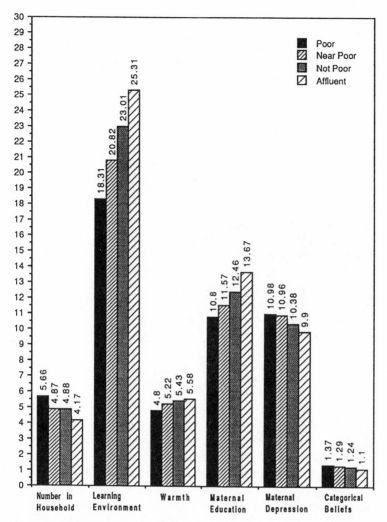

Source: IHDP
Note: Adjusted for site, treatment, gender, birth weight, and ethnicity.

FIGURE 2. Adjusted Means for Number in Household, Home Environment, and Maternal Characteristics at Age 3 by Four Income Groups

covariates alter the adjusted means somewhat (i.e., about a 4 point difference), but the income group differences still exist. Findings are somewhat different for behavior problems (Brooks-Gunn, in press a).

Poverty in Developmental Analyses

Family Poverty

Relatively little information exists in developmental literature vis-à-vis the effects of poverty upon children. Four of the most critical dimensions (and issues) are outlined here. These include: (a) the use of income versus social class measures; (b) the use of poverty measures which do not consider duration of poverty; (c) the use of poverty measures which do not consider the timing of poverty in children's lives; and (d) the use of poverty measures which do not consider the ecology in which children reside (see Brooks-Gunn, in press; Duncan, Brooks-Gunn, & Klebanov, in press, for a review of literature on these points).

Neighborhood Poverty

Few developmental studies include measures of neighborhood poverty, either, even though the contexts in which children live are of great interest, and are not limited to those involving the family. Sociologists and economists are more likely to study neighborhood income influences, as well as to detail some of the ways in which neighborhoods possibly influence behavior (Jencks & Mayer, 1990; Jencks & Petersen, 1992; Wilson, 1987).

Exceptions to this statement are provided by the Social Science Research Council's Committee on the Underclass. A working committee on Neighborhoods, Families, and Children has commissioned five data sets to attach geo-code Census Tract information. A volume on this endeavor is forthcoming (Duncan, Brooks-Gunn & Aber, in press). Our group has used the IHDP and PSID to investigate the effects of neighborhood poverty upon child and adolescent outcomes. Summaries of our results for child outcomes at ages three and five and for maternal outcomes and parenting behavior at the 3-year assessment point may be found in Brooks-Gunn, Duncan, et al. (1993), Duncan, Brooks-Gunn, and Klebanov (in press), and Klebanov, Brooks-Gunn, and Duncan (in press). These analyses are based on the framework provided by Wilson (1987, 1991) on how structural and family level processes in neighborhoods influence individual outcomes. Also, Jencks and Mayer (1990) have presented several possible models which might explain how neighborhoods might influence children's well-being. We have attempted to test the usefulness of these models in the IHDP and PSID. The models that have received the most support in our work are based on the premise that affluent neighbors, or the absence of poor neighbors, have positive influences on children. One is a "contagion" model, in that peers engaging in certain problem behaviors are likely to spread problem behavior. Another includes a set of "collective socialization" models, which focus on the benefits of role models and monitoring within neighborhoods. Wilson (1987, 1991), in his analysis of the structural changes in post-industrial society that contributed to an increase in the number of poor and jobless people in inner-city neighborhoods, provided insight into how "contagion" and "collective socialization" models might operate.

Taking this work as a starting point, we have begun to look for possible effects of neighborhood income upon children's well-being in the IHDP and PSID samples. The outcomes of interest are age-five IQ scores and behavior problem scores in the IHDP (sample size is 895 of the 985 children for whom we have enough information to geocode addresses; approximately 10% of the sample was Latino, and 55% African-American, and one-third white). The outcomes in the PSID were teenage childbearing (defined as having a birth prior to both the 20th birthday and first marriage) and high school drop-out (defined as having neither a high-school diploma nor a GED at the time competed schooling was measured, typically when the young women were in their early 20's). The PSID sample that we used included 1132 African-American and 1214 white women between ages 14 and 19. The oldest cohort in the sample was age 14 in 1968 (and 19 in 1973) while the youngest cohort was 14 in 1980 (and 19 in 1985).

The two indicators of the socioeconomic composition of the neighborhood are the fraction of families in the Census tract with incomes under $10,000 ("low income") and the fraction of families with incomes over $30,000 ("affluent"). In regression equations, these are compared to the fraction of families defined as middle income families ($10,000 to $30,000).

In the IHDP, age-five IQ scores were associated with the presence of affluent neighbors, but not the absence of poor neighbors (the omitted category, to which both are compared, is the presence of middle class neighbors). Neighborhood residence also influences externalizing behavior problems at age five; the presence of low income neighbors increases the likelihood of behavior problems (see Brooks-Gunn, Duncan et al., 1993; Duncan et al, in press). In the PSID, the presence of affluent neighbors is associated with a lower rate of high school drop-out and out-of-wedlock teenage births. This effect is found after controlling for ethnicity, maternal education, and single parenthood.

These data suggest that collective socialization may be operating, in that the absence of affluent neighbors confers risks to both young children and adolescents. Whether this effect is due to the presence of role models, the absence of planful or efficacious families, or other mechanisms, is not known.

Familial Resources and Poverty

Poverty often co-exists with low levels of other parental resources. Research is necessary to describe not only the frequency and patterning of co-occurrence, but the ways in which lack of various resources may heighten children's vulnerability. Parental resources focus on family income and time available to engage in parenting activities (Hill & Stafford, 1985; Lazear & Michael, 1987).

Time and Income as Resources

Time and income are often associated within families in complex ways. For example, children in single parent households often have only one parent with whom to interact on a daily basis. Single parents, especially if working, have little time to spend with their children. This issue is not limited to single parent families. As more mothers enter the labor market, less time is presumably spent with their children. Little is known about how and whether increased material well-being through the mother's employment offsets possible negative effects of increased mother absence from the home. As another example, the birth of a sibling alters the time available to spend with older children; the addition of a family member also probably alters the distribution of financial resources in the home and perhaps even the overall level of resources, if a parent chooses to leave the work force or reduce the number of hours worked (which is more likely to occur with the birth of a second than a first child).

Family structure, maternal employment, familial income, density of children to adults, and maternal education may all be considered parental resources. These five factors contribute to the human and social capital available to families and their children. The structure of a family in terms of single versus two-parent families has direct consequences for the monitoring of child behavior. Mother-headed families often experience a reduction in the time a mother has to spend with her children due to time spent in paid employment and increased responsibilities for sole maintenance of the household (Hill & Stafford, 1980; Nock & Kingston, 1988; Brooks-Gunn, in press c; Thomson et al., 1992). The presence of a co-residing grandmother or other extended family member may provide some support. Maternal employment may provide material benefits that offset the reduction in time spent with children. Additionally, working mothers may experience an increase in their sense of self-worth which may enhance their parenting skills (Hoffman, 1989).

Differential Effects of Resources in Poor and Not Poor Families

Such factors may have different effects in poor than in not poor families. Take, for example, maternal employment and child care (Baydar & Brooks-Gunn, 1991; Desai, Chase-Lansdale, & Michael, 1989). Using the Children of the NLSY, grandmother care in the first year of life offsets the slightly negative impact of maternal employment in poor white families upon three- and four-year-olds' cognitive and behavior scores. In contrast, non-relative baby-sitter care has negative effects, perhaps because of the inability to purchase high quality care when income is low and the cost of child care is proportionately much higher. Non-relative baby-sitter care did not have negative effects in not poor white young children.

Not only are single parent households and the transition from father presence to father absence the focus of much work, but so are the effects of multigenerational households as a response to single parenthood and the cost of rearing children alone, issues of direct relevance to those studying poverty. Studies in the past have focused on the normative role of the grandmother in providing emotional support, help during times of crisis, and nondisciplinary interactions with grandchildren (Cherlin, in press; Tinsley & Parke, 1984); while newer studies are beginning to examine the quality of grandmother parenting (Chase-Lansdale, Brooks-Gunn, & Zamsky, in press). A second adult in the household may provide additional resources, and may be particularly important when more than one child resides in a household, given that parental time must be allocated among children. While fathers and grandmothers have been studied vis-a-vis their effects on children, it is possible that the more important dimension is density of children to adults, rather than the specific adult figure (Baydar, Brooks-Gunn & Senior, in press; Furstenberg, 1976; Furstenberg et al., 1987; Lee et al., 1990). This model is typically not tested specifically (either the focus is on father-absent households, or grandmother-present households; Brooks-Gunn & Chase-Lansdale, 1991). In one study where it was tested, father and grandmother presence had similar beneficial effects on African-American infants (Baydar et al., in press).

While a great deal is known about each of these four resource factors, little is known about their relative effects, their interactive effects, their timing, or their duration. For example, the effect of parental transitions such as having the father move out of the household between the child's second and fifth birthday has significant negative effects on child IQ at age five, which disappears once family income-to-needs is controlled. However, marital transition continues to exert a negative effect on behavior problems even after controlling for family income (Duncan, Brooks-Gunn, & Klebanov, in press).

Change in Parental Resources

Research has not adequately addressed the issue of how a *change* in parental resources influences children's outcomes or a *change* in children's outcomes (see, as examples of exceptions, Cherlin, in press; Furstenberg, Brooks-Gunn, & Morgan, 1987; Elder, 1974; Baydar, 1988). Studies also have not looked at possible interactions among parental resource characteristics. For example, low family income may be more devastating for children when mothers have little education (i.e., high school drop-outs) than when they have completed high school (although no work on this exists). Maternal employment during the first few years of a child's life may be more detrimental in low income families than in high income families (Wilson, Ellwood, & Brooks-Gunn, in press).

Risk Models

Several complementary frameworks have been used to study associations between poverty or poverty risk factors and child outcomes. These include additive risk, cumulative risk, and double jeopardy models. (However, many scholars include elements of all frameworks when considering effects of risks on children. Hence, the current separation of frameworks may appear somewhat artificial and may not do justice to other researchers' formulations. These frameworks are considered separately since it is our interest to see which of several possible mechanisms are most helpful in explaining the ways in which risk factors are associated with child outcomes.)

The *additive* model of risks posits that the reason that poor children do less well is that they have more poverty risk factors than children who are not poor (Huston, 1991; McCormick & Brooks-Gunn, 1989; Parker et al., 1988), and that these risk factors have an additive or synergistic effect on child outcomes (see Sameroff & Chandler, 1975). Children living in poverty are likely be subject to other biological and environmental risks, such as low birth weight, low maternal education, female headship, unemployment, maternal depression, low social support, stressful life events, or inadequate parenting (Elder, 1974; Huston, 1991; Klerman, 1991; Liaw & Brooks-Gunn, 1993; McLanahan, 1988; McLoyd, 1990). These risk factors have been termed "poverty co-factors" (McCormick & Brooks-Gunn, 1989), and have been associated with adverse child outcomes (Chase-Lansdale & Brooks-Gunn, in press; Cochran & Brassard, 1979; Conger et al., 1992; Crnic, Greenberg, Ragozin, Robinson, & Basham, 1983; Culbertson, in press; Danziger & Danziger, in press; Hunt, 1983; Institute of Medicine, 1985; Huston, García-Coll, & McLoyd, 1993, in press).

A different model has been proposed, in which development is determined, not simply by the single risk factors, but more by the interplay between the child and the environmental characteristics (Sameroff & Chandler, 1975). This model focuses on the transactions between children and their caretaking environment as the mechanism to break or maintain the linkage between earlier insults and later disorder. Studies to date have focused primarily on biological risks to test this premise. One of the best samples is a two-decade study of the children of Kauai. Werner and colleagues report an interaction between perinatal problems and SES, such that perinatal problems were associated with much lower scores at ages 2, 10, and 18 in low SES than high SES families (Werner, Bierman, & French, 1971; Werner & Smith, 1982). Other studies with low birth weight infants also support the mediating effect of the childrearing environment, such that significantly poorer developmental outcomes would occur when children with biological or perinatal risks were reared in an adverse environment (Beckwith & Cohen, 1984; Cohen & Parmelee, 1983; Escalona, 1982; Sameroff & Chandler, 1975).

Following the transactional perspective of child development, the *cumulative* risk model posits that it is the accumulation of risks, rather than the individual risk factors, that accounts for developmental delays seen in some young children (Liaw & Brooks-Gunn, 1993, in press; Sameroff et al., 1987; Werner & Smith, 1982). The premise is that as risks increase, effects on children become more pronounced. This framework would account for the fact that some children in poor families do well, since not all poor families experience multiple negative events in addition to poverty; and some children in more advantaged families do not do well, since some of these families may experience multiple negative events. The best example to date is a study conducted by Sameroff and colleagues (Sameroff et al., 1987, 1993) which looks at the cumulative effects of social-environmental risk factors in predicting children's IQ scores at ages 4 and 13. This study finds that as the number of risks increases, IQ scores decrease at both ages, with a steep drop with three or more risk factors.

The third framework has been termed "*double jeopardy*" (Parker, Greer, & Zuckerman, 1988). This model posits that children from poor families experience more risks than children from families who are not poor, and that the consequences of the risks are more severe for poor than for not poor children (Brooks-Gunn, 1990a; Huston, 1991; McCormick & Brooks-Gunn, 1989; Parker, Greer, & Zuckerman, 1988).

We have used these three different frameworks to examine the contribution of additive risk, cumulative risk, and double jeopardy models to child outcomes *in the context of poverty*. Additionally, we have considered protective factor models as well. Our outcomes are IQ and behavior problem scores at age 3 (IHDP, over 700 low birth weight premature children included in these analyses). We separated children into those whose families were poor and those who were not poor at the 12-month assessment point (1986), based on federal guidelines for poverty standards using family income and family size data (Brooks-

Gunn, Klebanov, & Liaw, submitted; Liaw & Brooks-Gunn, 1993). Poverty was defined as being 150% or less of the poverty line. About half of this sample is poor.

Following Sameroff and colleagues (1987, 1993), we identified a variety of risk factors. In the analyses to be presented here,[4] these included one biological characteristic (very low birth weight), family structural and resource characteristics (unemployment, father absence, family density, low maternal education, and low maternal cognitive ability [Peabody Picture Vocabulary Test-Revised; Dunn & Dunn, 1981]), and life events and parenting measures (categorical as opposed to perspectivistic views of childrearing [Concepts of Childrearing Questionnaire; Sameroff & Feil, 1985], maternal depression [General Health Questionnaire, Goldberg, 1978], social support [6 social support vignettes: Cohen & Lazarus, 1978; McCormick, Brooks-Gunn et al, 1987], stressful life events [see Liaw & Brooks-Gunn, in press for a listing], poor home environment [HOME, Bradley & Caldwell, 1984]). In all analyses, the following variables were entered as covariates—child gender, child neonatal health (length of stay in neonatal nursery adjusted for birth weight and standardized to a mean of 100 and a SD of 16; Scott et al., 1989), ethnicity, mother's age (in years), and clinical site (two dummy variables, based on average family income, ethnic composition, and mother's educational attainment at each of the sites). Three sites were relatively high SES (Boston, Seattle, New Haven), four sites were relatively low SES (Bronx, New York City; Miami, Philadelphia, and Dallas), and one site was between these two groups (Little Rock, Arkansas).

Additive Risk Model

Table 1 presents some of the findings of these analyses by comparing the group that was high risk to that which was low risk vis-à-vis 3-year IQ scores. A significant difference between the high-risk and low-risk groups for the poor families was found for 5 of the 11 risk factors—employment, maternal verbal ability, childrearing beliefs, home environment, and social

TABLE 1

Unadjusted Mean Scores of High-Risk and Low-Risk Children's Stanford-Binet IQ Scores and Behavior Problems (N = 785)

Risk Variable	Stanford Binet IQ				Behavior Problems			
	Poor		Not Poor		Poor		Not Poor	
	Low	High	Low	High	Low	High	Low	High
Employment	80.5	75.6*	97.8	87.8*	47.8	51.7	40.6	53.8**+
Father presence	79.9	77.3	99.3	84.6***	47.5	50.7	40.5	48.6*
Family density	79.1	75.7	97.8	82.4**	49.8	48.8	41.1	52.7*
Mother's education	79.9	76.4	98.5	85.8**	45.3	54.4**	41.6	44.1
Mother's PPVT-R	83.9	75.9***+	102.6	83.5***+	45.0	51.5*	39.0	48.5**
Birth weight	78.9	76.7	97.8	92.6	48.8	51.6	41.4	44.1
Mother's depression	78.7	77.0	97.0	94.9	46.8	56.5***+	39.8	52.9***
Mother's belief of child development	80.4	75.6*	98.5	86.0**	48.1	51.4	40.7	49.4*
HOME at 12 months	79.9	74.2*	98.3	79.9***	49.0	51.0	41.1	50.8*
Stressful life events	78.8	76.3	96.1	101.3	46.9	59.1**	41.4	47.1
Social support	80.1	75.3*	96.4	97.6	48.6	51.1	39.9	49.0**
Largest difference between low- and high-risk groups	8.0		19.1		9.7		13.2	

*p < .05;   **p < .01;   *** p < .001.

support. Significant differences also were found between the high-risk and low-risk groups for 7 factors—employment, father presence, family density, maternal education, verbal ability, childrearing beliefs, and home environment.

Ordinary least-squares multiple regressions were conducted to see if risk factors had an additive effect on children's IQ scores. When we ran separate regressions for poor and not poor children, the risk factors were much less likely to contribute to poor children's IQ scores than they were to not poor children's IQ scores. The proportion of variance accounted for the two groups is quite different (6% for the poor and 16% for the not poor groups).

More behavior problems (higher scores on the Child Behavior Check List; Achenbach et al., 1987, as reported by mothers when the children were age 3) were seen in poor children with the following characteristics— low maternal education and verbal ability, high depression, and more stressful life events. And behavior problems were associated with 8 of the 12 risk factors in the children who were not poor— unemployment, father absence, high family density, low maternal PPVT-R score, maternal depression, categorical view of child development, poor home environment, and low social support (see Table 1).

The multiple regression analyses for behavior problems as the outcome, conducted separately for the poor and not poor families, are more similar that those for IQ as the outcome. Low maternal verbal ability and high maternal depression were associated with more behavior problems in both groups. The percentage of variance accounted for was 18% in the poor children's behavior problem scores and 25% in the not poor children's scores.

Cumulative Risk Model

As the number of risks increased, so did low IQ scores and high behavior problem scores. This was true for poor and not poor children (see Liaw & Brooks-Gunn, in press). The mean IQ difference between the lowest- and highest-risk groups was twelve IQ points in the poor children, and twenty-nine IQ points in the not poor children. These differences were larger than the mean differences seen for individual risk factors (see Table 1). The same is true for behavior problems.

Double Jeopardy Model

As expected, poor families were much more likely to have more risk factors; in terms of individual factors, all were more likely in poor families with the exception of the biological characteristics (and, of course, the IHDP only included low birth weight children and the sample was stratified in terms of birth weight; Brooks-Gunn, Klebanov, Liaw, & Spiker, 1993; Infant Health & Development Program, 1990).

Risk factors were more frequent even after controlling for ethnicity. Such analyses are critical since ethnic minority families are much more likely to be poor, to be persistently poor, and to live in poor neighborhoods, as seen in nationally representative samples (Duncan, Brooks-Gunn, & Klebanov, in press; Duncan, 1991; Smeeding & Torrey, 1988). This is also true in the IHDP (Brooks-Gunn, Duncan, Klebanov, & Sealand, 1993).

The IQ scores of poor children were always lower than those of not poor children across number of risks. However, a significant interaction of multiple-risks by poverty status indicates that when many risks were present, the IQ scores of the poor and not poor children began to converge. That is, the slope of the regression line was steeper for the not poor children than the poor children (see Liaw & Brooks-Gunn, in press, for a discussion of treatment effects).

Summary

Taken together, these results suggest that each of the models is useful in describing the ways in which individual and cumulative risks might operate and whether risks have different effects in poor and not poor children. We caution that these models were not set-up to test differences in the predictive power of these models. Clearly, though, the cumulative risk model is highly predictive of IQ delays and behavior problems, and this is true for poor and not poor children. At the same time, the double jeopardy model also found support, as poverty was a powerful predictor of child outcome over and above the number of cumulative risks. The children whose families were not poor had much higher mean IQ scores when none or few risk factors were present. As risks accumulated, however, these children's scores were similar to those of the multiproblem poor families.

The additive model, as expected, provides information as to how individual risks operate. Our data suggests that risk factors contribute to child outcomes somewhat differently in children who are from poor and not poor families. That is, poverty itself, being highly associated with all of the risk factors, may really be accounting for links between separate risk factors and child outcomes as reported in previous studies that have either not controlled for poverty status or looked at predictors of child outcome in poor samples and not poor samples (Brooks-Gunn, McCormick & Heagarty, 1988).

Combining Parental Resource, Cumulative Risk, and Protective Factor Models

Parental resources, cumulative risk, and protective factor models each are only a part of the story in understanding the mechanisms by which poverty influences children's well-being. Models need to be built that incorporate all of these possible contributors to well-being and, with respect to poverty, all of the pathways by which poverty might influence children. Such a model has been developed by our group (see Brooks-Gunn, in press b).

Models need to take into account the fact that children influence parental behavior, characteristics, and resources, so that reciprocal effects often operate (Bronfenbrenner, 1986; Lewis & Rosenblum, 1974; Maccoby, 1992; Maccoby & Martin, 1983). These bi-directional effects might be different in families who are poor and those who are not.

Models also need to address the fact that parental behavior and family processes may influence child outcomes directly or indirectly, in part dependent on child characteristics. For example, the ability to find and hold a job provides the family economic resources which may influence the child by the quality of schooling and child care received, or the neighborhood in which the family resides, all of which affect child well-being (Baydar & Brooks-Gunn, 1991; Brooks-Gunn et al., 1993). However, an event like having a low birth weight child or a developmentally delayed child may impact on parent work decisions. Mothers with low birth weight infants enter the work force somewhat later than mothers with normal birth weight infants (Mott, 1991). Even within the low birth weight category, mothers with lighter low birth weight infants enter the work force later than those with heavier low birth weight infants (Brooks-Gunn, McCormick, et al., in press). Mothers who are poor may find it more difficult to obtain adequate child care for their vulnerable low birth weight child, limiting their work options more than those of mothers who are not poor (and have more financial resources available).

Poverty and Ethnicity

What has been missing from our discussion, except for a fleeting reference or two, is the association between ethnicity and poverty. Children from ethnic minority families are much more likely to grow up in poor families, with rates being double or triple that for non-minority families. Even these figures greatly *underestimate* the differences in the life situations of white children and African American and Hispanic American children. Basing poverty rates on one year of family income does not provide estimates of the persistence of poverty. African American children are much more likely to be poor for multiple years than are white children (Duncan, 1991). And African American children are much more likely to be living in poor neighborhoods (defined by the number of poor individuals residing in a Census Tract or Enumeration District) than are white children (see Table 2 in Duncan et al., in press).

We find that these ethnic differences in family and neighborhood poverty account for a significant portion of the variance in ethnic differences in IQ and behavior problems

(Brooks-Gunn, Duncan, et al., 1993; Brooks-Gunn et al., in press). Since so many developmental studies do not include measures of poverty, ethnic differences in child outcome may be over-estimated.

The differences in life experiences go deeper than just poverty. For example, using the data from the IHDP presented in the section on cumulative risk of this chapter, we calculated the presence of each of the twelve risk factors for the children who were poor by ethnic group (keeping in mind that our sample of Hispanic-American children is quite small). As can be seen in Table 2, African American and Hispanic American poor children were more likely to live in families where the head of the household was unemployed, the father was absent, mothers had low verbal ability scores, mothers had categorical views of child development, HOME scores were low, and social support was less available than for white children who were poor.

The lives of poor ethnic minority children also differ from those of poor white children in that the former have to contend with discrimination. Their parents must decide how to prepare their children for discrimination. They must also decide how to provide socialization experiences that are culturally-sensitive (Spencer, Brookins, & Allen, 1985; García-Coll, 1990; Connell, Spencer, & Aber, 1994). Regrettably, our data sets do not contain the measures of the relevant constructs.

Given the potential impact of ethnicity on the lives of poor children, we have controlled for maternal ethnicity in the analyses presented here. We realize that this is only one way, and perhaps the least theory-driven way, to address ethnicity.

Another strategy is to examine separately possible differential effects of biological and environmental char-acteristics upon outcomes of different ethnic groups. We have looked at differential effects by ethnicity using interaction terms in some of our analyses (Brooks-Gunn, Duncan, et al., 1993; Duncan et al., 1994). Given our use of covariates such as female headship, low maternal education, and low income-to-needs (factors for which minority families show more disadvantage), interactions have tended not to be significant (see, as an exception, the analyses of neighborhood effects on teenage childbearing as a single parent using the PSID; Brooks-Gunn, Duncan, et al., 1993).

TABLE 2

Percentage of Poor Follow-Up Children Who Experienced Risk Factors in the Infant Health and Development Program

Risk Factor	Black	Hispanic	White	Total
Unemployment of head of household	52.5*	53.8	19.6	46.1
Father absence	74.1*	53.8	39.1	64.8
High family density (child-adult ratio > 2)	27.8	23.1	19.6	46.1
Low maternal education (< 12th grade)	47.5	65.4	39.1	47.8
Low maternal PPVT-R (< 81)	77.8*	88.5	37.0	70.9
Very low birth weight (< 1500 grams)	29.7	30.8	21.7	28.3
High depression	25.3	26.9	37.0	27.8
Categorical view of child dev.	50.8*	50.0	23.9	44.8
Low HOME score	38.0*	19.2	6.5	29.6
High stressful life events	19.0	23.1	28.3	21.3
Low social support	41.1*	53.8	19.6	38.3

*indicates ethnic group differences were significant, $p < .01$.

Conclusion

We need more refined research methods and analyses focusing on the measurement of poverty, the dimensions of family poverty, the inclusion of neighborhood poverty measures, links between poverty and other familial resources, and links between poverty and parenting characteristics.

Acknowledgments

This paper was presented at a Roundtable on Children of Poverty, sponsored by the Society of Research in Child Development and the Irving B. Harris Foundation (New Orleans, March, 1993). We wish to thank Ann Doucette-Gates, Marie McCormick, and Cecelia McCarton for their help in thinking through conceptual issues, Ruth Gross in her role as director of the IHDP, and Virginia Marx for her support. We also wish to thank Educational Testing Service, Division of Policy Research, for their continued support as well as for the post-doctoral fellowships held by Dr. Klebanov and Dr. Liaw. This work has been funded by the National Institute for Child Health and Human Development (NICHD), the NICHD Child and Family Well-being Research Network, the Pew Charitable Trusts, the Russell Sage Foundation, and the March of Dimes Foundation. We appreciate their support.

NOTES

1. The Infant Health & Development Program (IHDP) is a multisite clinical trial designed to test the efficacy of providing family and early childhood intervention services to low birth weight (LBW) premature children in order to reduce developmental delays. Services were provided to families randomized into the intervention group from discharge from the neonatal nursery until age 3 (home visits, center-based schooling, and parent support groups). The sample was stratified according to site (eight medical centers) and birth weight (lighter LBW 2000 grams or less and heavier LBW 2001 to 2500 grams). See Infant Health and Development Program (1990); Brooks-Gunn et al. (1993); Brooks-Gunn, McCormick, et al. (in press); Gross et al. (1992); McCormick et al. (1992); Ramey et al. (1992); Kraemer & Fendt (1990).

2. The Panel Study of Income Dynamics (PSID) is an ongoing longitudinal survey of U.S. households begun in 1968 (Survey Research Center, 1984). By following all members of its sample over time,

including children as they leave their parent's homes, the PSID maintains a representative sample of the non-immigrant U.S. population (which means that Hispanic-American families are under-represented). Low-income families were over-sampled.

3. In the IHDP, when only children whose families are below the poverty line are included in analyses, no income effect is seen on age five IQ. However, the income distribution for those families below the poverty threshold is truncated.

4. The analyses presented here differ somewhat from those to be found in Liaw and Brooks-Gunn (in press) and Brooks-Gunn, Klebanov, and Liaw (submitted). Specifically, these analyses include poor home environment, as measured by the HOME at the 12-month assessment, while the other two articles do not include this measure (given their focus on HOME-learning as an outcome at the 36-month assessment). Also, neonatal health (length of stay in the neonatal nursery adjusted for birth weight) and teenage parenthood were not included as risk factors in these analyses. Finally, in these analyses, ethnicity was included as a covariate, not a risk factor. This chapter presents the data by model, an approach not taken in the two journal articles.

REFERENCES

Achenbach, T. M., Edelbrook, C., & Howell, C. T. (1987). Empirically based assessment of the behavioral, emotional problems of 2- and 3-year old children. *Journal of Abnormal Psychology*, 15,(4), 629–658.

American Behavioral Scientist, 34, (4) [Special issue]. (1991).

Baydar, N. (1988). Effects of parental separation and re-entry into union on the emotional well-being of children. *Journal of Marriage and the Family*, 50, 967–981.

Baydar, N., & Brooks-Gunn, J. (1991). Effects of maternal employment and child-care arrangements in infancy on preschoolers' cognitive and behavioral outcomes: Evidence from the Children of the NLSY. *Developmental Psychology*, 27(6), 932–945.

Baydar, N., Brooks-Gunn, J., Senior, A. M. (in press). How do living arrangements affect the development of Black infants? *Family Relations*.

Beckwith, L., & Cohen, S. E. (1984). Home environmental and cognitive competence in preterm children during the first 5 years. In deA. Gottfried (Ed.), *Home environmental and early cognitive development* (pp. 235–271). New York: Academic Press.

Bradley, R. H., & Caldwell, B. M. (1984). The HOME inventory and family depression. *Developmental Psychology*, *38*, 315–320.

Bronfenbrenner, U. (1986). Ecology of the family as context for human development: Research perspectives. *Developmental Psychology*, *22*, 723–742.

Brooks-Gunn, J. (1990a). Identifying the vulnerable young child. In D. E. Rogers & E. Ginzberg (Eds.), *Improving the life chances of children at risk* (pp. 104–124). Boulder, CO: Westview Press.

———. (1990b). Promoting health development in young children: that educational interventions work? In D. E. Rogers & E. Ginzberg (Eds.), *Improving the life chances of children at risk* (pp. 104–124). Boulder, CO: Westview Press.

———. (in press a). Growing up poor: Context, risk and continuity in the Bronfenbrenner tradition. In P. Moen, G. H. Elder, & K. Lusher (Eds.), *Linking lives and contexts: Perspective on the ecology of human development*. Washington, DC: American Psychological Association.

———. (in press b). Opportunities for change: Effects of intervention programs on mothers and children. In P. L. Chase-Lansdale & J. Brooks-Gunn (Eds.), *Escape from poverty: What makes a difference for children?* New York: Cambridge University Press.

———. (in press c). Research on step-parenting families: Integrating discipline approaches and informing policy. In A. Booth & J. Dunn (Eds.), *Step-parenting families with Children: Who benefits and who does not?* Hillsdale, NJ: Erlbaum.

Brooks-Gunn, J., & Chase-Lansdale, P. L. (1991). Children having children: Effects on the family system. *Pediatric Annals*, *20*(9), 467–481.

Brooks-Gunn, J., Duncan, G. J., Klebanov, P. K., & Sealand, N. (1993). Do neighborhoods influence child and adolescent behavior? *American Journal of Sociology*, *99*, 353–395.

Brooks-Gunn, J., Klebanov, P. K., & Liaw, F. (in press). The provision of learning experiences in the contest of poverty: The Infant Health and Development Program. *Children and Youth Services*.

Brooks-Gunn, J., Klebanov, P. K., Liaw, F., & Spiker, D. (1993). Enhancing the development of low birth weight, premature infants: Changes in cognition and behavior over the first three years. *Child Development, 64*(3), 736–753.

Brooks-Gunn, J., McCanton, C., Casey, P., McCormick, M., et al. (in press). Early intervention in low birthweight, premature infants: Results through age 5 from the Infant Health and Development Program. *Journal of the American Medical Association*.

Brooks-Gunn, J., McCormick, M., Shapiro, S., Benasich, A. A., & Black, G. (in press). Effects of early education intervention on maternal employment, public assistance, and health insurance. *American Journal of Public Health, 86,* 926–931.

Brooks-Gunn, J., Phelps, E., & Elder, G. H. (1991). Studying lives through time: Secondary data analyses in developmental psychology. *Developmental Psychology, 27*(6), 899–910.

Brooks-Gunn, J., & Smith, J. (forthcoming). Dimensions of income poverty. Paper to be presented at conference on Income Poverty. J. Brooks-Gunn & G. Duncan (Organizers).

Chase-Lansdale, P. L., & Brooks-Gunn, J. (Eds.). (in press). *Escape from poverty: What makes a difference for children?* New York: Cambridge University Press.

Chase-Lansdale, P. L., Brooks-Gunn, J., & Zamsky, E. S. (in press). Young multigenerational families in poverty: Quality of mothering and grandmothering. *Child Development, 65,* 373–393.

Cherlin, A. J. (in press). Child care and the Family Support Act: Policy issues. In L. Chase-Lansdale, & J. Brooks-Gunn (Eds.), *Escape from poverty: What makes a difference for children?* New York: Cambridge University Press.

Cochran, J., & Brassard, J. (1979). Child development and personal social networks. *Child Development, 50,* 601–616.

Cohen, S. E., & Parmelee, A. H. (1983). Prediction of five-year Stanford-Binet scores in preterm infants. *Child Development, 54,* 1242–1253.

Cohen, J. B., & Lazarus, R. S. (1978). *Social support questionnaire.* Berkeley, CA: University of California.

Connell, J. P., Spencer, M B., & Aber, J. L. (1994). Educational risk and resilience in African-American youth: Context, self, action, and outcomes in school. *Child Development, 65,* 493–506.

Conger, R. D., Conger, K. J., Elder, G. H., Jr., Lorenz, F. O., Simons, R. L., & Whitbeck, L.B. (1992). A family process model of economic hardship and adjustment of early adolescent boys. *Child Development, 63,* 526–541.

Crnic, K. A., Greenberg, M. T., Ragozin, A. S., Robinson, N. M., & Basham, R. B. (1983). Effects of stress and social support on mothers and premature and full-term infants. *Child Development, 54,* 209–217.

Culbertson, J. L. (Ed.). (in press). *Journal of Clinical Child Psychology,* [Special issue: Poverty and children].

Desai, S., Chase-Lansdale, L., & Michael, R. T. (1989). Mother or market? Effects of maternal employment on cognitive development of 4-year-old children. *Demography, 26*(4), 545–561.

Danziger, S. K., & Danziger, S. (Eds.). (in press). *Children and Youth Services Review, 50* (5) [Special issue: Child poverty and social policies].

Danziger, S., & Stern, J. (1990). The causes and consequences of child poverty in the United States. *Innocenti Occasional Papers (No. 10 Special Subseries, Child Poverty in Industrialized Countries).* Florence, Italy: International Child Development Centre.

Danziger, S., & Weinberg, D. (1986). *Fighting poverty: What works and what doesn't.* Cambridge, MA: Harvard University Press.

Duncan, G. J. (1991). The economic environment of childhood. In A. Huston (Ed.), *Children in poverty: Child development and public policy.* Cambridge: Cambridge University Press.

Duncan, G. J., Brooks-Gunn, J., & Aber, L. (in press). *Neighborhood poverty: Context and consequences for development.* New York: Russell Sage Foundation.

Duncan, G. J., Brooks-Gunn, J., & Klebanov, P. K. (in press). Economic deprivation and early-childhood development. *Child Development 65,* 296–318.

Dunn, L. M., & Dunn, L. M. (1981). *Peabody picture vocabulary test-revised.* Circle Pines, MN: American Guidance Services.

Elder, G. (1974). *Children of the great depression.* Chicago: University of Chicago Press.

Ellwood, D. T. (1988). Poverty among single-parent families. In D. T. Ellwood (Ed.), *Poor support: Poverty in the American family* (pp. 128–158). New York, NY: Basic Books.

Escalona, S. K. (1982). Babies at double hazard: Early development of biological and social risk. *Pediatrics, 70*(5), 670–676.

Fisher, G. (1992). *How the statistical poverty thresholds were developed*. Unpublished manuscript.

Furstenberg, F. F. Jr., Brooks-Gunn, J., & Morgan, P. (1987). *Adolescent mothers in later life*. New York: Cambridge University Press.

Furstenberg, F. F. Jr. (1976). *Unplanned parenthood: The social consequences of teenage childbearing*. New York: The Free Press.

Garfinkel, I., & McLanahan, S. (1986). *Single mothers and their children: A new American dilemma*. Washington, DC: Urban Institute Press.

García-Coll, C. T. (1990). Developmental outcome of minority infants: A process-oriented look into our beginnings. *Child Development, 61*(2), 270–289.

Gross, R. T., Brooks-Gunn, J., & Spiker, D. (1992). Efficacy of comprehensive early interventions for low birth weight, premature infants and their families: The Infant Health and Development Program. In S. L. Friedman & M. D. Sigman (Eds.), *The psychological development of low birth weight children: Advances in applied developmental psychology* (pp. 411–433). Norwood, NJ: Ablex Publishing Corp.

Goldberg, D. P. (1978). *General health questionnaire*. Berks, England: FFER Publishing Company.

Hernandez, D. J. (1993). *America's children: Resources from family, government, and the economy*. New York: Russell Sage Foundation.

Hill, C. R., & Stafford, F. P. (1985). Parental care of children: Time diary estimates of quantity, predictability and variety. In F.T. Juster & F.P. Stafford (Eds.), *Time, goods, and well-being* (pp. 415–437). Ann Arbor, MI: Survey Research Center, Institute for Social Research, University of Michigan.

Hoffman, L. W. C. (1989). Effects of maternal employment in the two-parent family. *American Psychologist, 44*(2), 283–292.

Hunt, J. V. (1983). Environmental risks in fetal and neonatal life as biological determinants of infant intelligence. In M. Lewis (Ed.), *Origins of Intelligence: Infancy and Early Childhood* (2nd ed.) (p. 255–384). New York: Plenum Press.

Huston, A. (Ed.). (1991). *Children in poverty: Child development and public policy*. Cambridge, MA: Cambridge University Press.

Huston, A. C., García-Coll, C. & McLoyd, V. C. (Eds.). (1993, in press). *Child Development* [Special issue on Children and Poverty].

The Infant Health and Development Program Staff (Brooks-Gunn as member of Research Steering Committee). (1990). Enhancing the outcomes of low birthweight, premature infants: A multisite randomized trial. *Journal of the American Medical Association*, *263*(22), 3035–3042.

Institute of Medicine. (1985). *Preventing low birthweight*. Washington, DC: National Academy Press.

Jencks, C., & Mayer, S. (1990). Is the American underclass growing. In C. Jencks & P. Petersen (Eds.), *The urban underclass*. Washington, DC: The Brookings Institute.

Jencks, C., & Petersen, P. (Eds.). (1992). *The urban underclass*. Washington, DC: The Brookings Institute.

Klebanov, P. K., Brooks-Gunn, J., Duncan, G. J. (submitted). Does neighborhood and family affect mother's parenting, mental health, and social support.

Klerman, L. V. (1991). The association between adolescent parenting and childhood poverty. In A. C. Huston (Ed.), *Children in poverty: Child development and public policy*. Cambridge: Cambridge University Press.

Kraemer, H. C., & Fendt, K. H. (1990). Random assignment in clinical trials: Issues in planning (Infant Health and Development Program). *Journal of Clinical Epidemiology*, *43*(11), 1157–1167.

Lazear, E. P., & Michael, R. T. (1988). *Allocation of income within the household*. Chicago, IL: University of Chicago Press.

Lee, V., Brooks-Gunn, J., Schnur, E., & Liaw, T. (1990). Are Head Start effects sustained? A longitudinal comparison of disadvantaged children attending Head Start, no preschool, and other preschool programs. *Child Development*, *61*, 495–507.

Lewis, M., & Rosenblum, L. (Eds.) (1974). *The effect of the infant on its caregiver: The origins of behavior* (Vol. 1). New York: Wiley.

Liaw, F. R., & Brooks-Gunn, J. (1993). Patterns of low-birthweight children's cognitive development and their determinants. *Developmental Psychology*, *29* (6), 1024–1035.

————, (in press). Cumulative familial risks and low-birthweight children's cognitive and behavioral development. *Journal of Clinical Child Psychology*.

Maccoby, E. E. (1992). The role of parents in the socialization of children: An historical overview. *Developmental Psychology*, *28*,(66), 1006–10017.

Maccoby, E. E., & Martin, J. A. (1983). Socialization in the context of the family: Parent-child interaction. In P. H. Mussen & E. M. Hetherington (Eds.), *Handbook of child psychology: Socialization*, *personality, and social development* (pp. 1–102). New York: John Wiley & Sons.

McCormick, M. C., & Brooks-Gunn, J. (1989). Health care for children and adolescents. In H. Freeman & S. Levine (Eds.), *Handbook of medical sociology* (pp. 347–380). Englewood Cliffs, NJ: Prentice Hall.

McCormick, M. C., Brooks-Gunn, J., Workman-Daniels, K., Turner, J., & Peckham, G. (1992). The health and developmental status of very low birth weight children at school age. *Journal of the American Medical Association, 267*(16), 2204–2208.

McLanahan, S. (1988). Family structure and dependency: Early transitions to female household headship. *Demography, 25*(1).

McLoyd, V. C. (1990). The impact of economic hardship on black families and children: Psychological distress, parenting, and socioemotional development. *Child Development, 61,* 311–346.

Mott, F. L. (1991). Developmental effects of infant care: The mediating role of gender and health. *Journal of Social Issues, 47,* 139–158.

National Center for Children in Poverty. (1990). *Five million children: A statistical profile of our poorest young children.* New York: School of Public Health, Columbia University.

Nock, S. C., & Kingston, A. W. (1988). Time with children: The impact of couples' work-time commitments. *Social Forces, 67,* 59–85.

Orshansky, M. (1965). Counting the poor: Another look at the poverty profile. *Social Security Bulletin, 26* (July), 3–29.

Palmer, J., Smeeding, T., & Torrey, B. B. (Eds.). (1988). *The vulnerable.* Washington, DC: Urban Institute Press.

Parker, S., Greer, S., & Zuckerman, B. (1988). Double jeopardy: The impact of poverty on early child development. *The Pediatric Clinics of North America, 35,* 1227–1240.

Rainwater, L. (1974). *What money buys: Inequality and the social meanings of income.* New York: Basic Books.

———. (1992). Poverty in American eyes. *Koelner Zeitschrift fuer Sozilogie und Sozialpsychologie.*

Ramey, C. T., Bryant, D. M., Wasik, B. H., Sparling, J. J., Fendt, K. H., & LaVange, L. M. (1992). The Infant Health and Development Program: Program elements, family participation, and child intelligence. *Pediatrics, 3,* 454–465.

Ruggles, P. (1990). (1992). *Drawing the line—Alternative poverty measures and their implications for public policy*. Washington, DC: The Urban Institute Press.

Sameroff, A. J., & Chandler, M. J. (1975). Reproductive risks and the continuum of caretaking causality. In F.D. Horowitz, M. Hetherington, S. Scarr-Salapatek, & G. Siegal (Eds.), *Review of child development research* (Vol. 4) (pp. 187–244). Chicago, IL: Society for Research in Child Development.

Sameroff, A. J., & Feil, L. A. (1985). Parental concepts of development. In I. Sigel (Ed.), *Paternal belief systems: The psychological consequence for children* (pp. 83–105). Hillsdale, NJ: Erlbaum.

Sameroff, A. J., Seifer, R., Barocas, R., Zax, M., & Greenspan, S. (1987). Intelligence quotient scores of 4-year-old children: Social environmental risk factors. *Pediatrics, 79*, 343–350.

Sameroff, A. J., Seifer, R., Baldwin, A., & Baldwin, C. (1993). Stability of intelligence from preschool to adolescence: The influence of social and family risk factors. *Child Development, 64*, 80–97.

Scott, D. T., Bauer, C. R., Kraemer, H. C., & Tyson, J. (1989). A neonatal health index for preterm infants. *Pediatric Research, 24*, (4/2), 263a.

Smeeding, T. M., & Torrey, B. B. (1988). Poor children in rich countries. *Science, 242*, 873–877.

Smith, S. (in press). Two generation models: A new intervention strategy. In P. Chase-Lansdale & J. Brooks-Gunn (Eds.), *Escape from poverty: What makes a difference for children*. New York: Cambridge University Press.

Spencer, M. B., Brookins, G. K., & Allen, W. R. (1985). *Beginnings: The social and affective development of black children*. Hillsdale, NJ: Erlbaum.

Survey Research Center. (1984). *User guide to the PSID*. Ann Arbor, MI: ICPSR.

Thomson, E., Mclanahan, S., & Curtin, R. B. (1992). Family structure, gender, and parental socialization. *Journal of Marriage and Family, 54*, 368–378.

Tinsley, B. J., & Parke, R. D. C. (1984), Grandparents as support and socialization agents. In M. Lewis & L. Rosenblum (Eds.), *Social connection: Beyond the dyad* (pp. 161–194). New York: Plenum Press.

Watts, H. W. (1993, March). *A review of alternative budget-based expenditure norms*. Paper prepared for Panel on Poverty

Measurement of the Committee of National Statistics, NAS/NRC.

Werner, E. E., Bierman, J. M., & French, F. E. (1971). *The children of Kauai: A longitudinal study from the prenatal period to age 10*. Honolulu: University of Hawaii Press.

Werner, E. E., & Smith, R. S. (1982). *Vulnerable but not invincible: A longitudinal study of resilient children and youth*. New York: McGraw Hill.

Wilson, J. B., Ellwood, D. T., & Brooks-Gunn, J. (in press). Welfare to work through the eyes of children: The impact on parenting of movement from AFDC to Employment. In P. L. Chase-Lansdale & J. Brooks-Gunn (Eds.), *Escape from poverty: What makes a difference for children?* New York: Cambridge University Press.

Wilson, W. J. (1987). *The truly disadvantaged*. Chicago, IL: University of Chicago Press.

———. (1991). Studying inner-city social dislocations: The challenge of public agenda research. *American Sociological Review*, *56*(11), 1–14.

Zill, N., Moore, K. A., Smith, E. W., Stief, T., & Coiro, M. J. (in press). The life circumstances and development of children in welfare families: A profile based on national survey data. In P. L. Chase-Lansdale & J. Brooks-Gunn (Eds.), *Escape from poverty: What makes a difference for children?* New York: Cambridge University Press.

* * *

Round Table Discussion

Lamberty. Did you consider race and ethnicity in your analyses?

Brooks-Gunn. In all the analyses that I showed here, I've controlled for ethnicity. So these are all adjusted means. We have some analyses looking at the difference between black and white children on IQ scores. We started with the premise that the largest effect is the fact that Blacks are so much more likely to be poor, and they are so much more likely to be persistently poor. It turns out that if you look at neighborhood poverty, minority young children are much more likely to live in neighborhoods with high concentrations of poverty. And it turns out that of

Black children in America, only 15 to 20 percent escape either having their family be poor or living in a poor neighborhood.

Lamberty. So that emphasizes the role that race plays in most of what you have been talking about. And the thing that is incomprehensible to me is that most of the research, as well as most of the conceptual framework on which research is based, completely avoids dealing with that.

Brooks-Gunn. Your point is well taken. Let me finish my comment on the IQ difference, though. When I put family income, duration of poverty, and neighborhood income into the equation, the standard deviation difference drops by three-quarters. And then when I put in female headship and maternal education, it drops a bit further. And when I put in provision of learning experience from the home, basically the race difference disappears. That's for IQ. When I look at behavior problems and enter everything into the equation, Black children actually have fewer behavior problems than the White children. But the important thing is I think that it is very hard to separate out ethnicity and poverty because the poverty rates are so different for minority and non-minority children.

Ramey. I want to go back to the issue of definition for a moment, because I think we've made a serious mistake in adopting this relativistic perspective, which I believe has gotten us into serious trouble in public policy arenas, because we've defined the problem in such a way that it is never solvable. If we do median income, then clearly we're in a cycle where, as the Biblical saying goes, the poor will always be with us. I think we really want to find out what it functionally takes to rear children to some minimally acceptable standard. And of course setting that standard is going to be a very politically charged event in itself. The relationships between affluence or poverty and outcomes are probably not likely to change. So, it seems to me that we need to go beyond an index, whether it's the food basket index or whether it's tied to median household incomes. We need to clarify in a way that the American public will understand what it takes to live in this country in a reasonably decent fashion. I know that you are involved in trying to work on various aspects of this and I wonder if you might want to comment on how it's going.

Brooks-Gunn. Obviously, it's not clear where the academy is going to go, and obviously, I can't say even if the committee had decided. But I can say that several economists have been developing what they call "basic needs budgets" to try to decide what it does take to live, exactly Craig's question. And we've had several of these people come to the committee to talk. There are several papers that have just come out, one in *Journal of Human Resources*, for example, where they've looked at basic needs budgets and put several things into those budgets. What's interesting is that basic needs budgets, before the new iteration that has occurred in the last year, never included health care or child care. I've got something we did just for New York. What we were interested in showing is that even at the minimum wage an individual can't make it. Even at $10 an hour one is going to have trouble making it in New York. When we did our needs budgets, we didn't put in health care or child care to start with, even though I feel that they ought to be included. When health care is entered, the welfare family is in better shape than the family on minimum wage, because the welfare family will probably be getting health care, whereas the family on minimum wage will not. The neat thing is that the economists who have done these new basic needs budgets, have actually put health care and child care into the budgets for the first time. So what's really interesting to me, from my developmental perspective, is that economists are trying to grapple with the child care issue. Actually, what they put in for child care wasn't the amount that most of us think would be needed annually to purchase high-quality child care, but it wasn't as low as I thought it would be.

Ramey. The problem with an index is that most people don't understand it. And if they do understand it, they'll discount it. So if we say it takes $400 a month to feed a family, someone will be able to say, "Well, I can actually do it on less than that, if you made meals . . ." I think what this does is to force all of us to take this functional perspective and to look at the different dimensions that we must be concerned with. So, I think this is the direction in which we should be going.

Kotelchuck. I was interested in hearing a little more on neighborhood poverty. There's a lot of movement of social class differentiation in the African American community. This speaks actually against the homogeneity of neighborhoods, I would think. I'm just curious how you might respond to that or think about that.

Brooks-Gunn. What's the best way to respond to that? What the research has done is come up with four different theories to explain neighborhood effects, some of which do have to do with a mix of affluent and non-affluent neighbors in one neighborhood, some of which really speak more to just having as many affluent neighbors as you can. In terms of policy the research is pretty clear: living in a neighborhood where many residents are poor and few are affluent, middle class families have left inner cities *en masse*, which translates into negative outcomes for children and youth. So the question is how to change this situation. One solution is to bring back middle-class families, another is to increase employment opportunities, and yet another is to increase university resources. If there aren't jobs for high-school graduates or non-high-school graduates or there's no transportation out to where the jobs are in the suburbs, and the unemployment rate stays high, it's going to be very hard to get middle-class families to move back. Many policy scholars have come down on jobs and transportation to jobs if the jobs have left the community.

Kotelchuck. It's just a two-edged sword. You can make many positive arguments about things that need to change, but it is a very mixed finding. The last thing I'd say about it is that there are probably more sophisticated analyses yet to come, as people are developing the power of their neighborhoods in these models. There might be other ways of defining neighborhood poverty.

Brooks-Gunn. The measure we're using is bad as an income measure in a strange way. It is kind of like a static measure, and all of us are developmentalists who want to get at process. And there are people who are starting to look much more at process in neighborhoods, which is really exciting work.

Lerner. This is more of a comment. It strikes me that we really haven't dealt with what I think is the import of Dr. Lamberty's comment. That is, given the lack of equality about who is likely to become poor, and the fact that we have our developmental analyses, we may not understand the causal linkages between being poor and child outcomes. It's not just an issue of race. I think that any of us who think that the solution lies just in developmental psychology, or just in economic analysis, will fall short of the mark. Unless we deal with the pervasive issues of racism—it's not just race, it's racism—and unless we build that into our analyses, we will fail. Moreover, we talked about the need for subjective definitions, obviously we also need subjective or qualitative analyses. We need to begin bringing the voices of the people who are living under racism and poverty into the mix. We don't need more sophisticated analyses alone, although I certainly as a quantitative psychologist would argue for that, but we also need more sophisticated qualitative analyses in which we work with our quantitative skills using the voices of the people who are actually living under the conditions of persistent and pervasive poverty and suffering, for generation after generation. We need to get that onto the table.

CHAPTER 2

African American Infants: Contributions and Concerns

Suzanne M. Randolph

This is a discussion of issues regarding research on African American infants that have both contributed to and limited our understanding of their development and child development more generally. The title of my paper derives from my experience working with a project at Howard University, which we referred to as the Newborn Study (Rosser & Randolph, 1989). Over 100 African American infants and their mothers were followed from birth to age three to examine their physical, socioemotional, and cognitive development. The impetus for this research came from reviews of literature published between 1930 and 1980 on child development, and, in particular, from literature on black children (McLoyd & Randolph, 1984, 1986). I should note that I use the term "black" as inclusive of African American children as well as other children of African descent (Caribbean, Nigerian, etc.). A number of reviews revealed that through 1980 much of the literature on black children's development had been written from a deficit perspective. Many of the studies reviewed painted black children as being deficient as compared to other children or as being at risk for detrimental developmental outcomes in their childrearing environments. Rarely were factors that contributed to optimal outcomes studied; however, there was some evidence that many children in these environments do indeed perform optimally (i.e., survive and even thrive). Also these literature reviews suggested that the study of black children has contributed to our understanding of developmental phenomena more generally.

In our research, we attempted to address a number of aspects of previous research that contributed to the one-sided, deficit picture of black children's development. In the Newborn Study, we attempted to address one aspect of previous research which was of concern to us—the use of convenience samples that limited the opportunity to obtain optimal samples—because, in my opinion, many of the samples of black children are drawn from settings to which researchers have easy access (public hospitals, low income populations participating in a publically funded program, etc.). And within these samples, children at risk for poor developmental outcomes may be disproportionately represented. Also, we are provided little demographic or background information about the infants other than their race/ethnicity and weight. There is virtually no information about the prenatal care or labor and delivery experiences of the mother. Even so, researchers proceed in comparing the performance of these infants with that of other infants, usually white middle class infants from more optimal environments, and conclude that the black children's development was less optimal, without much discussion about the validity of these findings or the lack of generalization (McLoyd & Randolph, 1986).

In the Newborn Study we also used a convenience sample, newborns at Howard University Hospital, because we were located in a Department of Pediatrics and Child Health that was responsible for the neonatology unit. However, in order to avoid the pitfalls of studies that simply enrolled a consecutive, convenience sample of largely low income infants, we selected infants based on standard pediatric criteria that defined an optimal newborn (e.g., weight, Apgar scores, gestation, prenatal care, and type of delivery). In addition, because the hospital served primarily African Americans (of all income groups) in the Washington, D.C. metropolitan area, we were able to recruit a sample that included families of all income levels. Even in this city which is consistently listed among the nation's highest with respect to infant mortality and low birth weight incidence, we were able to recruit 80 mothers and their infants into our optimal group (full term healthy). In addition, we recruited 40 pre-term infants in order to investigate differences in developmental outcomes between the healthy infants and infants at risk because of their birth status. These included 20 preterm healthy infants who met all the standard pediatric criteria except they were born at lower weight and 34–36 weeks gestation, and 20 preterm sick infants, who had shorter gestation (34–36 weeks), lower Apgar scores (7–9), weight, and respiratory distress syndrome, but no other medical complications. In essence, both a "normative sample" and an "at risk" sample of African American infants were included in the same sample. This research provided an opportunity to generate baseline data with an African American sample against which the at risk sample could be compared, so as to correct the deficit perspective of previous research that compared low income African Americans to middle income whites.

Another concern with previous research has been the collection of outcome data without attention to process or cultural (childrearing) factors that may contribute to these outcomes. In the Newborn Study we used standard developmental assessment tools and techniques such as the Brazelton Neonatal Behavioral Assessment Scale (BNBAS), the Bayley Scales, Carey's Temperament Scales, the Home Observation for Measurement of the Environment (HOME), the Ainsworth Strange Situation, and a variety of other standard measures, repeated over time. However, we supplemented these measures, which largely assess outcomes, with study of specific instruments that captured mothers' expectations for children's milestone accomplishments, as well as their childrearing attitudes and practices. This supplemental information was valuable in interpreting changes in developmental outcome that might be due to childrearing practices rather than maturational changes (Winborne & Randolph, 1992). For example, changes in infants' self-quieting ability on the BNBAS from two days to one month seemed due to: (1) mothers' expectations that finger sucking should be discouraged from birth; and (2) their operationalization of that belief by covering the infants' fingers in terry cloth hand covers on the end of their sleepers and continuously pulling children's fingers/hands down from their mouths, as we observed at one month in their homes. We also found using the developmental expectations scale we developed specifically for this study, that at one month, mothers of boys differed from mothers of girls in terms of their expectations for the ages at which various self-help skills would be accomplished (Rosser & Randolph, 1989). Collection of such data may prove beneficial at later ages when children's developmental data are analyzed for gender differences.

Relatedly, another concern in research on African American children, which was a concern in the Newborn Study as well, is the over-reliance on quantitative measurement. As mentioned previously, we obtained several measurements of the children and their mothers using standard developmental assessment instruments. We quickly learned that our training and understanding of the research technology, as then developed, limited our ability to capture the childrearing and child development experiences of the sample. The use of quantitative assessments and the focus on outcomes rather than processes made us miss the other rich, qualitative data that we had the opportunity to capture. We observed mothers and infants in the newborn nursery, the mother's hospital room, the home on repeated occasions, our laboratory setting, and our child development clinic. The longitudinal, transactional approach we took and the use of multiple measures and multiple settings enhanced our view of the families' lives. However, our measurement techniques limited our ability to more fully understand how the child development context contributed to development.

Richard Lerner's comment in Chapter 14 of this volume concerning the lack of attention given to qualitative assessment loomed very large in our minds. However, we were trapped by sticking to the methods for administration and scoring of standard protocols. For example, we had the opportunity to present our attachment data at one of the empirical research conferences on black psychology. We focused on the quantitative aspects of the strange situation, with only infant attachment to mother; that is, we counted interactive behaviors, classified infant attachment, and documented rates. However, the strange situation could have also provided a rich opportunity to answer questions such as: What is going on in the mother-child system that is protective, nurturing, facilitative? What is happening that is disturbing? Is this their usual way of interacting? Are there consistencies in how African American mothers respond to their children in this situation? Is this paradigm a valid one for African American mothers? What about the notion of multiple caregivers in African American families? Is this the person who takes care of this child? Any yet, we simply review the tapes for presence or absence of certain interactive behaviors and use them to classify and quantify. I present this experience to point out that even as a black researcher, I miss these things. I fall prey to the usual ways of knowing African American children. Because black psychologists and other developmentalists (i. e., people interested in child development from other fields, primarily non-medical fields) represent only about two percent of all those who are out there doing research, I do not view this as only the responsibility of black researchers. Others will also have to bring this non-deficit perspective to bear on this research.

In terms of contributions, the reviews of research on black children indicate that black infants actually provide a lot of information about normative development that has been valuable in studying developmental issues. For instance, the preliminary work for development of the Ainsworth Strange Situation was done with children of African descent. The study of black children has also increased our knowledge about children "at risk" for various developmental problems because black children are disproportionately represented in the "at risk" population. We also know a lot in terms of both intervention and prevention with respect to low birth weight and prematurely born infants, infants born to teenagers, and related areas. Problems like teen parenthood, two-earner families, single-parent families, latchkey children, divorce, multiple caregivers, prenatal drug exposure, are all problems that are disproportionately represented among black families. Those problems are also now growing problems for society at large. "So goes the black infant, so goes other infants, and so goes America." That is, problems among black infants and their families can be used as a barometer for the problems in the larger

American society. Research on infant developmental outcomes associated with new problems or new morbidities such as HIV/AIDS, hopelessness, and unemployment and temporary poverty, is also aided by the study of black families. More than ever, we need to take a closer look at children in poverty and try to understand the "outliers," the resilient children. What is it about children's development in poor African American families? How is it that some actually thrive? I grew up in a neighborhood that, by all standards, even 25 years ago in New Orleans, would be considered low income. My father's business was and still is in a neighborhood in New Orleans that is considered among the lowest income, where pockets of poverty jump out at you. And yet, there are everyday examples of infants and children surviving and thriving in these communities. My interest in developmental psychology had to do with the fact that I wanted to challenge the perception that African American children somehow were not surviving in these environments. There are certain things within families, family units, neighborhoods, and individuals that make people resilient. What are these strengths? We have not yet adequately answered that question because we have been missing a lot of these things by not intentionally studying them.

Head Start gave us the opportunity to look at environment and context in child development research, although not particularly with infants. However, it is widely acknowledged that the first two years of the child's life has important implications for understanding developmental outcomes. In African American families in poverty we have the challenge of understanding the cultural basis for parent-child interactions, parenting style, and child outcomes as well as the impact of stressors due to poverty and institutional racism. The Centers for Disease Control and Prevention has just recently recognized the potential influence of racism as a stressor during pregnancy and has funded several sites to study the possible association between racism and premature delivery among *middle class* African American women. Such an initiative suggests that poverty (lack of income) alone may not adequately explain the disproportionate rates of poor pregnancy outcomes and related poor infant developmental outcomes among African Americans.

Therefore, we must continue to expand our ways of knowing about the development of African American infants.

A cursory inspection of *Child Development Abstracts* from 1980 to the present, indicates that ways of referring to black or African American children have changed. For example, as the focus has shifted toward looking at black child samples in more normative ways, researchers seem to have also shifted toward no longer referring to black infants or children as disadvantaged or low income. In fact, they are not necessarily referred to as black or African American either. Thus, what seems to have occurred is that no descriptors are being used (i.e., children are neither referred to by race/ethnicity nor by traditional descriptors that implied their race or ethnicity such as "disadvantaged" or "urban"). So now the problem seems to have become one of black child samples being used even more so as convenience samples. While this situation addresses the need for normative studies of black infants and children, because they are convenience samples, children are studied where they are conveniently found (clinics, hospitals, service agencies, etc.), and rarely are they studied in their homes and neighborhoods (i.e., the contexts in which the variables under study would naturally occur). Then, to what extent are we really studying normative behavior if we do not also study context? To what extent do we really know that the way a particular sample of black infants performs can be generalized to any other situation or group of children?

Another continuing problem in research on black infants is the use of race-comparative models (McLoyd & Randolph, 1984); that is, the use of research designs that compare the performance of black infants to that of white infants or a standard based on white normative samples. In comparing outcomes of one group to those of another, we are missing the interactive processes and underlying dynamics of behavior that may be shaping developmental outcomes. For example, in studying children using a comparative framework, what does a mean difference tell us? Behavioral differences cannot be simply explained by race. That is to say, even if one finds racial differences, one cannot change the race of children, so what might be underlying these racial differences? A more valuable finding would be an explication of the factors within a particular group that shape the observed behavior or variations in behavior even within the same group. More recent investigations have referred to this line of inquiry as examining "resilience." At a minimum our goal should be to try to understand in one cultural, racial, or ethnic group, what is going on and try to untangle or unravel, what has sometimes been referred to as, "the cultural matrix of development."

Relatedly, in examining the ecology of poverty, we have often over-emphasized the *culture* of poverty which is a "victim blame" perspective, and have less often discussed or examined factors associated with the structure of poverty. That is, a discussion of the culture of poverty would focus on individual or person level variables that may account for behavioral outcomes. A discussion focused on the structure of poverty would examine neighborhood, community, or societal level variables that may influence outcomes. Much more research is needed that focuses on cultural beliefs and norms that shape behavior, analysis of policies that impact child outcomes, and economic and social forces that influence child outcomes. For example, infant outcomes may be associated with intergenerational childrearing practices that influence parent-child interaction, feeding practices, and discipline techniques. Such associations might be found across socioeconomic levels for a particular cultural/ethnic group, but we are now limited in our understanding of such relationships because we have not focused our investigations at that level.

Very little research has been directed toward examining black infants' cognitive development, with the exception, again, of using criteria such as performance on standard assessment instruments. Instead of simply reporting the outcomes on these standard instruments, we need to move toward research that explores the underlying bases for such cognitive development. Children display intelligent behavior in various ways. For instance, I remember on a site visit to a public housing community, the Robert Taylor Homes in Chicago, that the child development program people there said, "These kids are really bright. They really know how to negotiate this environment ." That negotiation was viewed by program staff as a type of intelligence. The children's behaviors may not be what we consider intelligence, but we need to begin to view this and other behavior as reflective of optimal development in impoverished environments.

Finally, I think we have to more fully understand the structural aspects of poverty, like institutional racism. It is not enough to say that children are "at risk" because their neighborhoods are ten percent black or impoverished; it is not enough to explain that the affluent are moving out to the suburbs because the jobs have been redistributed. I agree with those structural explanations for the socioeconomic decline in communities, but we also have to look at the infrastructure that goes with the affluent when they go: the neighborhood centers, the recreational centers, the quality of the schools, the quality of the community centers, the grocery stores, and the neighborhood health clinics. Also, services that remain or are newly introduced are accessible, available, and affordable, and yet people do not utilize them. Could there be some other explanation for this non-utilization other than cost or lack of transportation? Understanding the cultural bases for seeking or not seeking support from formal agencies will perhaps help us understand this situation as well as how developmental outcomes for children of poverty may be facilitated or impeded by such cultural beliefs and norms.

REFERENCES

Boyd-Franklin, N. (1989). *Black families in therapy: A multisystems approach*. New York: Guilford Press.

García-Coll, C., Lamberty, G., McAdoo, H. P., Jenkins, J. M., Crnic, K. A., Wasik, B. H. (1993). An integrative theoretical framework for the study of minority families and the developmental outcome of their children. Symposium presented at the Second National Head Start Research Conference, "Translating research into practice: Implications for serving families with young children." Washington, DC, USDHHS/Administration on Children, Youth, and Families, November.

McLoyd, V. C., & Randolph, S. M. (1984). The conduct and publication of research on Afro-American children: A content analysis. *Human Development, 27,* 65–75.

———. (1986). Secular trends in the study of Afro-American children: *Child Development,* 1936-1980. *The Monographs of the Society for Research in Child Development,* Serial No. 211, *50,* 78–92.

Rosser, P. L., & Randolph, S. M. (1989). Black American infants: The Howard University Normative Study. In K. Nugent, B. M. Lester, & T. B. Brazelton (Eds.). *The cultural context of infancy* (pp. 133–165). Norwood, NJ: Ablex.

Winborne, D. G., & Randolph. S. M. (1992). Developmental expectations and outcomes for African American infants: An ethno-methodological approach. *Journal of Social and Behavioral Sciences, 37,* 29–42.

* * *

Round Table Discussion

Zuckerman. To go back to the qualitative notion, as you've looked at your tapes, and outside of looking at your data, what have you seen? What are some hypotheses about some of the processes that you've seen, that we should start thinking about.

Randolph. You know, there's one notion that Nancy Boyd-Franklin points out in her book, *Black Families in Therapy,* that has to do with us sometimes asking the wrong questions. A real simple illustration is that when the mothers and infants come in, we ask for the mother's name, father's name, and then we get a contact person because we want to follow them up. And it turns out that that contact person may actually be the person who's taking care of the child, so maybe we need to ask a question, "Who takes care of this child?" and try to understand that. Why is that person the main caregiver? Is it because the parent has to work? Or is it because the parent feels less competent, etc.? And one thing we found in our study, particularly when we were doing the attachment study, was that we were getting pictures of children in the laboratory situation, which was really a mother-infant interaction in a strange situation. When we debriefed the mothers while we rewound the videotape, they saw a little bit of it and would say, "Oh, but she'd be much better with her Daddy." We started to get richer information from them in that more informal setting. We gave the Brazelton at 28-days at home, and we also administered a developmental expectation scale that assessed parental expectations about infant development, such as when they expected their infants to sit up, walk, and crawl. But we also asked parents when they expected children to cook their own breakfast and cross the street. We wanted to try to understand that, if we did see differences in the Brazelton at 28 days, some of which would be expected to be maturational, were there really any that could lend themselves to cultural or child-rearing practices. And the one we found was the hand to mouth behavior. These infants were really good at self regulation and self-quieting, at two days. At one month, they fell off, and significantly so. But in our developmental expectation scale we asked, "At what age do you expect to discourage the child from sucking their fingers?" Well, in Black families, you have the childrearing attitude that you're not going to suck your fingers because we don't want you to have buck teeth. So they're pulling that hand down right from the start. And they said, "from birth." And then when we went into the homes, what we observed was the use of little terry-cloth covers on the infant's hands and the infant trying to tear through the terry-cloth in order to self-quiet. And the mothers say they like to put hot sauce on them, vinegar, and all that stuff because they're trying to discourage what is considered a very negative or less optimal behavior. So, some of that was qualitative for us.

When Berry Brazelton looked at our attachment tapes, he observed that the mothers use a lot of verbal disciplining and restriction—it wasn't physical restriction, because these kids were very mobile. They were literally walking, running, jumping, and crawling because of the motor precocity of Black children, I'm sure. Or a mother would use non-verbal cues, such as that stare that Black mothers can sometimes give you—mine did, anyway—where you're doing something and they give that look. So there were kinds of things that might be interaction regulators, that are not in the interactive scales. So there is that kind of qualitative behavior.

Ramey. I'd like to make a comment to underscore the importance of something that you've already said is important, but I think it's important not only for this meeting, but it is important for child and family research in general. I believe that, as a research community, we are guilty of using some of the worst sampling techniques of any subfields that I've seen. We frequently rely on samples of convenience. We have done comparisons within samples of convenience that frequently are invidious and scientifically non-supportable. I think the time has come when we can no longer, as a matter of routine, accept samples that are alleged to relate to policy-relevant issues that are not up to the scientific standards used in other fields. And that's going to mean extra work to get out and draw truly representative samples so that some of these comparisons can be made with confidence. It's going to mean, I believe, we have to do things on a larger scale. But if developmental psychology and cultural anthropology and sociology tend to be directly relevant to the shape of the agenda, and particularly as it applies to poverty, I don't think we have any choice but to do it.

Randolph. Well, I would think it's going to require both. You see, I would move to the other direction and say that, in our attempt to try to select samples using the scientific standard, we have gone the route of the NLSY trying to get nationally representative samples, but then we can only administer three items of the Bayley Scales.

Ramey. No, what I'm suggesting is that it's just not right, and we have to fight that issue. If we were here having a conference on cancer, we wouldn't be saying, you can only use three items from the temperament scale. We'd be saying, what should we be measuring, how should we be packaging it, what represents a scientifically useful insight? So, this is a conference about politics as well as about poverty. I think we have to bite the bullet and say that we must tell people that if you want serious answers for what I believe is the most serious problem in the United States today, we have to make serious investments. And we, as scientists, must find the right forums to stand up and say, we must scale up this effort. And it doesn't mean a choice between scale up vs. qualitative, ethnographic, or in-depth. Both of those approaches, I believe, have to move forward.

Randolph. I think the NICHD, NIMH attempts to do normative studies of minority children, and the adolescent health initiatives, were all attempts at that, but the piddling little money that was put behind those efforts, as you say, needs to be addressed. I agree.

CHAPTER 3

Hispanic Children and Their Families: On a Different Track from the Very Beginning

Cynthia García-Coll and
Heidie A. Vázquez García

Hispanics are soon to be the largest minority group in the United States. By the year 2030, it is estimated that the Hispanic youth population will reach 9.6 million, double what it was in 1980 (Children's Defense Fund, 1990). In other words, approximately one in every five youths in the year 2030 will be Hispanic. Yet these youths will be at more educational and economic risk than any other segment of the population.

The experience of growing up in poverty is a significant part of the lives of many Hispanic children in the United States. The poverty rate in 1991 was 40% for children of Hispanic origin compared to 17% for Caucasian children (U.S. Bureau of the Census, 1991). Furthermore, for the children of single mothers, Hispanic children have a poverty rate of 48% compared to 31% for Caucasians (Pérez & Martínez, 1990). So even when family constellation remains the same, Hispanic families tend to be poorer that Caucasian families. Other statistics suggest that in addition to experiencing higher poverty rates, there may be other important differences in the experience of poverty for Hispanic children. Analysis of the data obtained through the Survey of Income and Program Participation, a longitudinal income survey conducted by the Census Bureau, suggests that Hispanic children might experience extreme poverty more frequently and for more extended periods of time. Poor persons who were White were significantly more likely than their Hispanic-origin counterparts to exit poverty between 1987 and 1988: 30% of Whites who were poor in 1987 were able to exit poverty by 1988 compared to only 18% of Hispanics (U.S. Bureau of Census, 1991). Moreover, Whites who became poor were less likely than their Hispanic counterparts to fall below the 75% of the poverty level. While only 35% percent of White poverty entrants in 1988 experienced such severe poverty, 62% of Hispanic entrants did so (U.S. Bureau of the Census, 1991). In addition, according to a 1993 Census Bureau report presenting income data, Hispanics are falling behind in median family income compared to their non-Hispanic counterparts. While non-Hispanics' median family income increased about 10% from 1983 to 1991 ($34,381 to $37,013), Hispanics' median family income remained virtually the same from $23,151 in 1983 to $23,895 in 1991 (del Pinal & García, 1993). Thus, Hispanic children and their families are not only experiencing higher poverty rates, but their experience is also more extreme and pervasive.

In order to assess the impact of poverty on Hispanic children and their families, we cannot assume that the conceptualization, operationalization and measurement of the phenomenon is the same as in any other population. It can be postulated that the impact of poverty on Hispanic children and their families will be a function of the unique contextual circumstances under which they live. Thus, the unique characteristics of these families and their environments need to be taken into account when we study the effects of poverty in the development of Hispanic children. In other words, while poverty is a phenomenon that is experienced by many groups, the experience of poverty might not only be different for Hispanic children and their families (more frequent, more long lasting and more extreme) but the effects of poverty on developmental outcome might be mediated or moderated by other factors present in the Hispanic population that might exacerbate, ameliorate, or change altogether the effects of poverty. In this paper, we will consider the following factors: childrearing beliefs and practices, family structure and characteristics, migration patterns and acculturation levels, health status and health care practices, and internalized and externalized forms of oppression.

In addition, when research is conducted with Hispanic populations, several methodological factors need to be taken into account. From the conceptualization of the study to the choice of measures, the unique characteristics of Hispanic children and their families, and their context, will bring about important methodological considerations. Among these, the following will be discussed: the definition of competence, the validity of existent measures, the characteristics of the standardization samples, and the limitations of the translation and adaptation of most measures.

Before proceeding, several caveats need to be made about the use of the word Hispanic. Most studies to date use the term Hispanic/Latino, inclusive of all persons who identify themselves as of Hispanic heritage. However, important differences among Hispanic sub-groups are observed. For example, notable differences in the percentages of families living below the poverty line can be observed among different sub-groups. They range from 17% for Cuban Americans, 25% for Central and South Americans, 28% for Mexican Americans to 41% for Puerto Ricans (Pérez & Martínez, 1993). However, most of the research findings reported in this paper refer to Hispanics as a homogeneous group without taking into consideration national origin and other within-group differences. Therefore, we have to recognize that the research findings to be presented and the conclusions to be reached will not be representative or generalizable to all Hispanic sub-groups and individuals. Whenever possible, an attempt will be made to note within-group as well as between-group differences.

Childrearing Beliefs and Practices

When studying the impact of poverty on Hispanic children and their families we need to take into consideration how cultural variables interact with socioeconomic variables. Parental attitudes, values and behaviors are seen as greatly influenced by traditional cultural values and traditions. Studies have shown that Hispanic parents differ from Caucasian and African American parents in attitudes and perceptions toward their children's development, in their behavior as caregivers and in their developmental goals or what they value about their children's behavior, emotions, and cognitions. These attitudes, perceptions, and behaviors will be further influenced by poverty and will create a unique context for the child to develop.

Studies have compared Caucasian, African American, and Mexican American families in reports of child-rearing attitudes and behaviors in general. Durret, O'Bryant, and Pennebaker (1975) found that Mexican American parents of low socioeconomic status reported being less authoritarian, less achievement oriented, more protective, and as emphasizing less individual responsibility than African American and Caucasian parents of the same socioeconomic status. Zeskind (1983) observed differences in parental attitudes among Anglo, African American, and Cuban American mothers. He found that Anglo American mothers found infant cries more distressing, urgent, arousing, and "sick sounding" than did African Americans, while Cubans shared similarities of both groups, depending on the scale item. Cultural variations also occurred in the caregiving responses to the cries: Anglo Americans chose to wait and see and gave a pacifier less often than the other groups; they also chose to pick up and cuddle the infants more. On the other hand, African American mothers generally chose to cuddle infants the least, and Cubans chose to cuddle and give a pacifier more often than the other two groups. In other words, the differences in maternal perceptions, responses, and behavior towards the infants were guided by cultural differences.

Studies of mother-infant interaction patterns with Hispanic or Latino mothers in the United States have found differences in the mode of interaction (less verbal vs. more tactile) not only in play or face to face interactions, but also in teaching interactions. In a study of the maternal teaching strategies of Chicana and Anglo mothers, Laosa (1980) found that there is a clear difference between the maternal behavior of the two cultures. Chicana mothers tend to use modeling, visual cues, directives, and negative physical control. Anglo mothers rely more on inquiry and praise.

Not only are there observed differences among groups regarding childrearing beliefs, practices, and parental attitudes and behavior, but there are also within group differences. Socio-economic variables explain in part the observed differences. Wolf (1952) was one of the first to report the differences among Puerto Rican subcultures. She found that the patterns of parental behavior differed across subcultures based on the goals for that particular group. For a group of farmers, she found that parents encouraged their children to identify with their prescribed roles in the family as well as the neighborhood repressing goals for individual gain, needs, and self determination. In the group that was made up of sugar workers, she found the child training to center around a strong work group identification, minimizing competition and maximizing mutual aid. Unlike the farmers, individual autonomy was accepted to some extent among the people in the sugar workers group. The middle class group's childrearing behaviors differed greatly from the other two groups in that parents did not emphasize group identity or group identification in their childrearing strategies. More recently, Laosa (1978) has reported that Chicana mothers of varied educational and socioeconomic levels differ in their teaching strategies. He found that mothers who had less that an eleventh-grade education used modeling, visual cues, and directives to teach their children, whereas mothers who had completed at least an eleventh grade education taught for the most part through a combination of praise, visual cues, and inquiry, and less through directives and modeling. What these studies suggest is that not only are Hispanic children exposed to different patterns of affective and social interactions, but that their learning experiences might result in different communication and exploration strategies as well as developmental outcome.

Thus, the effects of poverty need to be assessed, taking into consideration different cultural contexts with unique systems of beliefs and practices that overlap but differ in some respects from other groups. These attitudes and behaviors might be guided by the competencies that adults are expected to have in traditional environments probably modified by the immediate demands and experiences acquired through migration and acculturation. In fact, all we know is that differences exist, the degree to which they influence outcome has not yet been studied: how they come about, what the consequences for developmental outcome are, and how they change over time as a function of acculturation are largely unknown. Moreover, the notion that these practices can get modified by poverty or can exacerbate or ameliorate the impact of poverty on these children deserves systematic investigation.

Family Structures and Characteristics

Not only are the attitudes, goals, and care-giving behavior different in Hispanic families, but these families are characterized by different structures and characteristics from those observed in other groups. Since the family is seen as the primary socialization agent for the child, these characteristics and their interaction with poverty as well as their influence on children's development deserve attention. Unlike their Caucasian counterparts, a high prevalence of adolescent childbearing is observed among Hispanic families: 16% of Hispanic mothers compared to 10 % among Caucasian, non-Hispanic mothers in 1988 were 19 years of age or younger. Of all of the Hispanic groups, Puerto Ricans have the highest rate of adolescent pregnancy. In 1990, 22% of Puerto Rican mothers were teenagers, compared to 17% Mexican teenage mothers, 8% Cuban teenage mothers and 10% Anglo teenage mothers (Ventura, 1994).

For the most part, adolescent childbearing is considered to be associated with increased adverse medical and social complications. Infants born to teenage mothers are more likely to be of low birth weight, and are placed at higher risk for mortality during the first year which lessens the optimal growth and development during childhood (Ventura, 1994). In general, because most teenage mothers do come from impoverished families, early childbearing does not only increase developmental risks for the infant but also increases the continuation of economic disadvantage to the mother as well as her children. Yet some studies have shown that there are other variables which can affect the outcome of the child as well as the competency of the adolescent mother. In a series of studies conducted with adolescent mothers in Florida, Rhode Island and Puerto Rico, García Coll and colleagues (Lester, García Coll, & Sepkoski, 1983; García Coll, Sepkoski, & Lester 1982; García Coll, 1988) have found that marriage and childbearing were seen and accepted more often as part of normal adolescent growth and development among Puerto Ricans. Therefore, the social contexts and support systems available to the adolescent mothers from the Puerto Rico sample differed from those of the Florida and Rhode Island samples. While all samples were from lower socioeconomic levels, the impact of teenage pregnancy was different for the mothers as well as the infants of the Puerto Rico sample in that expectations and adherence to family values played considerable roles in the support networks available to them. Therefore, there must be other considerations in addition to poverty, such as cultural norms and family structure and characteristics. What might be acceptable to one group, might not be to other groups.

Yet the incidence of childbearing in unmarried adolescent mothers is increasing. In 1990, 60% of all Hispanic teenage mothers, with the highest percentage being Puerto Rican (75%), were unmarried compared to 32% of women over the age of 20 (Ventura, 1994). These numbers are contributing to the high number of single heads of households among Hispanics. A Census report released in June 1992, states that over the past decade the incidence of unmarried childbearing among Latinos increased from 16% to 27%. In addition, 60% of Hispanic teenage births were out-of-wedlock (Bachu, 1993). However, single head of household does not necessarily imply the absence of family support.

As in African American culture, Hispanic culture's traditional conceptualizations of the family involve other members, especially females, in important aspects of caretaking (García Preto, 1982). The notion of extended family in addition to the nuclear family is one that is very important in Hispanic culture. Grandparents, godparents, aunts, uncles, cousins, etc.

are integral parts of the child's care giving environment in general and even more so in so called single head of households and when the mother is an adolescent. The institution of *compadrazgo*, or co-parenthood is commonly utilized across Hispanic groups as a network of blood and fictive kin, usually providing emotional, financial, and psychological support to other family members. Puerto Ricans for example rely heavily on personal relationships and family ties which in turn strengthen the deep sense of obligation, commitment and responsibility to family. Yet at the same time this network provides a sense of security and guarantees a certain level of protection for family members. Contrary to Anglo families where family is defined on the basis of the nuclear family membership, and where individualism is emphasized, the sense of collectivism in Hispanic families is very important and is the basis for many familial interactions.

Finally, Hispanic families do not only include a large number of adults but also a larger number of children than Caucasian families. While the overall fertility rate in the U.S. has been declining over the past decade, the fertility rate for Hispanic women has increased (Stroup-Benham & Treviño, 1991). Furthermore, it has been indicated that the fertility rates for different Hispanic subgroups vary: the fertility rate in 1981 for Mexican American women was 53% higher than the fertility rate for Puerto Rican women and double that for Cuban American women (Ventura, 1981). In addition, Hispanic women not only have a higher fertility rate than the non-Hispanic population but also a higher birthrate (Ventura, 1987).

In sum, the family characteristics of Hispanic families are very unique and might represent a unique context of poverty. In studying the impact of poverty on Hispanic children and families, these different family constellations need to be taken into account.

Migration Patterns and Acculturation

Within the Hispanic population in the United States, there is considerable variability in migration patterns and acculturation. Among Mexican Americans, we find families who have been residing in the same region for eight generations and are American citizens by virtue of historical processes. In contrast, among this same ethnic group, we have recent illegal immigrants or migrant workers who spend half of the year in one location versus another. Among Puerto Ricans, similarly, we have second and third generations whose main language is English versus those who have just arrived from the Island with no knowledge of English or those who come back and forth and contribute to the so-called revolving door phenomena describing one pattern of Puerto Rican migration. It is clear that the families' desire for assimilation or for rejection of the host culture, or their inability to access important resources because of their unfamiliarity with this culture, in addition to the disparity between the children's acculturation level and that of their parents, will permeate the effects of poverty on these children.

Acculturation refers to the changes in behavior and values made by any member of one culture as a result of contact with another culture. The process of acculturation is important not only for immigrants, but for any individual that by historic, economic, political, linguistic, and or religious reasons are exposed or demanded to adapt to a new cultural environment. The early literature on acculturation assumed that higher acculturation levels would be predictive of better behavioral and psychological outcome. However, recent research examining health outcome has reported an interesting relationship between degree of acculturation and negative outcomes for both Mexican Americans and Puerto Ricans. In several studies, higher acculturation and higher levels of acculturative stress have been related to more negative health and mental health outcomes for women and children (Taylor et al., 1986; Dressler & Bernal, 1982; Rogler et al., 1991). It seems that the process of acculturation for these more recent groups results in a marginalization from the traditional culture and its supportive and healthy lifestyles.

In addition, for the majority of Hispanic groups, the process of acculturation is into urban, chronic poverty and some of its associated destructive life styles. The Childrens' Defense Fund (1990) reported that more than half of all poor Hispanic children live in metropolitan areas, approximately one-third live in the suburbs and only a small fraction live in rural areas. A recent chartbook released by the Census Bureau in June 1993 states that the metropolitan areas of Los Angeles, New York and Miami-Fort Lauderdale each contain over one million Hispanics (del Pinal & García, 1993). In other words, the highest concentration of poor Hispanic children and their families is in the inner cities of the Mainland United States, usually sharing the area with African Americans. The impact of urban poverty and its associated lifestyles on Hispanic children deserves careful consideration.

In a study comparing the childrearing practices of Dominican, Puerto Rican, and African American adolescent mothers, Wasserman et al. (1990) found that length of residence in the United States Mainland was significantly related to the childrearing practices of adolescent mothers. The longer the time of Mainland residence, the more similar their attitudes, values and beliefs were to the local culture. Puerto Ricans with longer residence were found to resemble African Americans more closely than Dominicans who had just arrived.

Again, these findings suggest that not only is there an acculturation to the U.S. mainstream culture but specifically an acculturation to poverty. Because a large percentage of Hispanics on the Mainland live in poverty, new waves of immigrants that settle in areas with a high concentration of Hispanics become acculturated to the lifestyles associated with urban poverty. Therefore, this acculturation to poverty not only complicates the migration process but contributes to the negative childrearing attitudes and poor developmental outcome of Hispanic children.

Health Care Status and Practices

Another source of influence on developmental outcome of Hispanic children is their health status and health care practices. There is a striking difference in health status between many Hispanic children and the Caucasian population in the United States. This poorer health status is not necessarily an absolute predictor of poor developmental outcome but places the infant and child at risk for medical and neurodevelopmental problems and behavioral deficits.

While the growth of the Hispanic population has received considerable attention, the health status for Hispanics has not been widely documented. Overall, studies have shown that Hispanics in the United States are more likely to die from heart disease, stroke, cirrhosis, and diabetes than their Anglo non-Hispanic counterparts (U.S. Department of Health and Human Services, 1985). The incidence of diabetes among Hispanic women from low socioeconomic backgrounds is four times that of the total Hispanic population, which suffers from diabetes three times more than the non-Hispanic population (Stern, 1984). According to a report from the Centers for Disease Control (1991), Hispanic preschool children are seven times more likely to contract measles than their White non-Hispanic counterparts.

In addition, among pregnant Latino women, we see a higher incidence of lack of adequate prenatal care, three times the risk for diabetes, a higher prevalence of hypertension and substance abuse and HIV infection (Mendoza et al., 1991; Lederman & Sierra; Zorrilla, Díaz, Romaguera, & Martin, 1994). Needless to say, these maternal risk factors contribute to the health status of the infant. Among Puerto Ricans, for example, we see higher rates of prematurity, low birth weight and chronic diseases like asthma, all throughout childhood (Mendoza, Takata, & Martorell, 1994.).

However, when looking at health care status and outcomes of Hispanics, special attention needs to be placed not only on utilization of services, especially preventive services, but also on availability, access and delivery of care. Studies have shown that the utilization of physician care by Hispanics is influenced by economic, socio-demographic, and cultural factors (Markides, Levin, & Ray, 1985). There is extensive documentation on the under-utilization of health services, especially preventive, regular care among Hispanics. According to the HHANES , the 1984 National Health Interview Health Survey and the 1986 National Access Survey, Mainland Puerto Ricans were reported to have the lowest rate of health care utilization as compared to other Hispanic groups (Mendoza, Takata, & Martorell, 1994).

For many Hispanics, the availability of health care is weighted by economic as well as demographic variables. Lack of health insurance among Hispanics is prevalent. Even though Puerto Ricans have a higher rate of uninsured children (18.1%), Mexican Americans have a higher overall rate of uninsurance (35%) (Treviño et al., 1991). However, Mendoza et al. (1991) state that while Mexican-Americans' poverty rate is similar to that of Mainland Puerto Ricans, the rate of low birth weight is half as prevalent. In addition, while Mexican Americans have twice the poverty rate of Cuban Americans, their low birthweights are similar. There are therefore, other factors that play into the health outcome of Hispanics that deserve careful consideration.

The fact that the majority of Hispanics live in urban areas is also important when considering their health status as well as availability and access to quality of health care. According to Wernette and Nieves (1991), Hispanics are three times more likely to live in areas that do not meet EPA lead-air-pollutant standards. Eleven percent of 4–5 year old Puerto Rican children and 5% of 4–5-year-old Mexican American children have elevated blood lead levels compared to 3% of their non-Hispanic White counterparts (Carter-Pokras et al., 1990). It is important to consider availability and access to health care as a function of various demographic, socio-economic and geographic variables. Lack of health insurance and lack of geographic proximity to health services also contribute to the underutilization of health care services by Hispanics.

It is also important to note that availability of health care is not necessarily equated with better health status. Mendoza et al. (1994) report that while Mainland Puerto Ricans have the highest access to health care, they have the worst health status among Mexican Americans and Cuban Americans. This, however, has been attributed to the increased levels of poverty of Puerto Ricans compared to the other two Hispanic groups. The Hispanic population is not homogeneous in its access to quality health care nor their poverty levels.

In addition to the economic and socio-demographic variables that contribute to the unavailability and under utilization of health care by Hispanics there are some cultural variables. Some of these cultural variables include: family cohesiveness and enmeshment, cultural differences in perceived health needs, and the use of folk medicine (Marín et al., 1983). For example, Delgado (1979) suggests that Puerto Ricans' health seeking patterns are dependent upon their attitudes towards health and illness as being caused by metaphysical as well as biological factors. Such attitudes he suggests are also influenced by age, sex, level of education, socio-economic status and length of residence in the United States In addition, he suggests that because of the extended family network of Puerto Ricans, in most cases the healer is usually a family member, quite often the grandmother or mother. In other words, not only are there differing beliefs about what constitutes an illness but also who is qualified to cure the illness. This may explain the reluctance of many Puerto Ricans to seek modern medical services, because of their unfamiliarity with the terminology and/or procedures and also because of the lack of faith in the caregiver. In this case, it is also important to note that in addition to cultural reasons for not seeking conventional medical attention, language barriers also contribute to Puerto Rican's underutilization of health care services.

In sum, Hispanic children and their families have a different health status that is both influenced by poverty and also becomes a mediator of the effects of poverty on Hispanic children. More research needs to be done in the specific health risk factors that are overrepresented in the Hispanic population and the impact of accessibility and use of health care services on both health and developmental outcome.

Internalized and Externalized Forms of Oppression

The experience of the Hispanic population with poverty and other expressions of oppression is quite pervasive. If we examine the historical legacy of most Hispanics in this country, most of us are here escaping some sort of systemic oppression: poverty, sexism, colonialism or political or cultural persecution. In Puerto Rico, 500 years of colonialism have resulted in a collective dependency on outside forces, which might be contributing in part to the fact that 50% of the population depends on the welfare system for its subsistence. The world-views that are part of centuries of oppression are so entrenched in our culture, myths, symbols, and ways of interacting and behaving, that it might take generations to change.

Fatalism is a good example of a cultural tradition that makes sense as an adaptive response to a legacy and history of oppression but that might exacerbate or interact with the effects of poverty on Hispanic children. The concept of fatalism can be defined as the acceptance of one's lot or fate (Steward et al., 1956; García Preto, 1982). For Hispanics, fatalism is a characteristic which is embedded in religion. While the religious composition of Hispanic groups has been changing, for the most part, a tradition of Roman Catholicism is pervasive, although other alternative religious sects such as Pentecostal, Seventh Day Adventist, and Jehovah's Witnesses have become popular (Delgado & Humm Delgado, 1982). Hispanics' belief in the supernatural, either through magic and/or religion, is a crucial part of their support system. Used as a coping mechanism, this belief helps them to deal with or escape from life crises, insecurities, stress or physical impediments, channeling aggression and frustration in ways that would not be manifested or resolved otherwise. Therefore, while there are very strong emotions involved, adverse situations are passively accepted because they are "God's will and God's will is not questioned" (Steward et al., 1956). The belief that cultural patterns, norms, events, and hierarchies are predetermined contributes to the promotion of passive acceptance. The notion of doing the best under the circumstances and leaving the rest up to fate is very prevalent.

While fatalism does have its roots in religion, the concept and the attitudes involved have carried over into other aspects of the lives of Hispanics. For example, fatalism can be examined in a political sense. Five hundred years of colonialism for Puerto Ricans has instituted a system of external hierarchical control which discourages active resistance and makes political and cultural self determination for Puerto Ricans virtually impossible. In a similar manner, the institution of the Hispanic family can be analyzed. The patriarchal design of the family, the prevalence of *machismo*, and the strict gender roles for women as passive and subordinate to men, are not questioned but rather accepted as part of the system. In this sense the concept of fatalism can be applied to any situation wherein there is a force, whether it be religious, social, cultural, political, or economic which goes unquestioned, not only because it is considered intangible due to its institutional and cultural nature, but also because the consequences of questioning are considered to be predetermined.

For now, we need to take into consideration these factors when we study the effects of poverty on Hispanic children and families. The acceptance of oppressive conditions of living in poverty, the passivity or belief that nothing can be done to improve these conditions, and the inability to even perceive that there are opportunities for change can exacerbate the effects of poverty on these populations. This is especially important, since in the United States, Hispanics, like the other members of so-called minority groups, are subjected to prejudice, discrimination, racism, segregation, and others forms of oppression, along with poverty. These forms of overt oppression can interact with the internalized ones and create an almost impossible barrier to break.

One such form of externalized oppression comes in the segregation of the educational system. Stratification for Hispanics in education is very pervasive. Segregation, inadequate schools, the lack of culturally sensitive educational programs, the use or misuse of bilingual programs to keep students back, the low expectations by the administrators and teachers, are all factors that contribute to the high dropout rates among Hispanics. In 1988 the Hispanic dropout rate was 35.8% for youth between the ages of 16–24 compared to 14.9% for African Americans and 12.7% for Anglos (U.S. Department of Commerce, 1990). Coleman (1990) states that African Americans are 40% more likely to dropout than their Anglo counterparts while Hispanics are 250% more likely to do so. While some researchers estimate the overall dropout rates around 35% for Hispanics, others suggest that it is much higher ranging from 50–70% (Cavazos, 1989). In addition, there are differences among Hispanic subgroups in dropout rates. While the national dropout rate for Puerto Ricans and Mexican Americans is 40%, in some cities the dropout rate for Puerto Ricans is as high as 80% (Barreto et al., 1986).

Moreover, the repercussions of low quality education affect employment availability which in turn affects economic security and advancement. For example, according to a study by the Children's Defense Fund which examined the annual earnings of high school dropouts in 1973 and 1984, and their ability to maintain a family of three, less than 30% of the Hispanic male dropouts in 1984 had earnings that were above the poverty line compared to 40% of their Anglo counterparts ("Research and Reports," 1987). Even at the same educational levels, Hispanic individuals are poorer than Anglos. Therefore, what we see happening is the regeneration of the "cycle of poverty" by the existence of institutional and systematic segregation and discrimination which insures that Hispanics will be kept at the bottom.

Methodological Issues

So far we have discussed factors that are relevant to the study of poverty and its effects on Hispanic children and their families. There are also important methodological considerations that need to be addressed.

One of the most basic issues is the definition of competence. Inherent to most of our definitions of competence is a belief that there are absolute or universal indices of competence. As human developmentalists, our dominant theories are based on notions that there is an ultimate developmental outcome that we all should strive for. However, there is a growing body of work which points to the notion of context as a very powerful factor in the definition of competence. For example organizational views of development suggest that development includes a variety of variables—genetic, constitutional, neurobiological, biochemical environmental, sociological, psychological and behavioral—which form a series of qualitative reorganizations which are in dynamic transaction with one another. However, it is the organization and not the duration of behavior that is most important in development, since the meaning of behavior is derived from the context in which it occurs (Cicchetti & Schneider Rosen, 1986). From this perspective, development is perceived as the integration of social, emotional and cognitive competencies, which allow the individual to adapt to his/her present environment. Within these frameworks, behavior that is considered an expression of competence in one setting might not be in another. Non-verbal, passive modes of mother-infant interaction might be thought of as non-adaptive and as mediators of poor developmental outcome when displayed by a poor teenage mother, but the same behavior might be considered culturally appropriate when displayed by a middle-class Japanese mother. Moreover, alternative expressions of competence can be developed, as John Ogbu (1981) has argued, that make ecological sense in spite of how non-adaptive or destructive their results are in a different setting. Human competencies—cognitive, linguistic, social-emotional, and practical—as functions of culturally defined tasks, differ across cultures. Therefore, child-rearing beliefs and practices in any specific culture are shaped to meet the demands of that culture and eventually develop into adaptive adult competencies within the greater population (Ogbu, 1981). For example, non-verbal, passive modes of interactions can be very adaptive in an environment where assertiveness and challenge might get you into trouble. The basic question is how should we measure competence among Hispanic children and their families? Are our standard measures capturing all the expressions of competence displayed by Hispanic children? Are the mainstream definitions of competence embraced by the childrearing values and practices of traditional Hispanic culture?

Not only conceptually, but methodologically, the issue of measurement is an important one to consider. Very little is known about the validity and reliability of most standard measures of developmental outcome among Hispanics. Several studies have shown that translation of such widely used measures as the WISC and the PPVT have poorer reliability scores in Spanish than in the original versions (Henggeler & Tavormina, 1979). Others have shown different distributions of results when applied in Puerto Rico and in the United States, forcing the researchers to choose different cut-off scores (Bird,

Canino, & Shrout, 1985). Even back-translation methods do not guarantee full equivalence. For example, translators who are bilingual but not bicultural may be capable of translating an instrument, but might be more apt to miss the nuances of a language. In addition, grammatical differences in Spanish and English and literal translations are also factors that cause problems with the back-translation method. Finally, if the translator is good, he/she can usually make sense of a badly translated version even if the target language translation is of poor quality (Marín & Marín, 1991).

Other sources of measurement error are a function of culture specific response patterns. Less acculturated Hispanics prefer to make more extreme choices (e.g., definitely agree or disagree) in greater proportion and are more likely to agree with a statement or to answer yes to a question than the more acculturated Hispanics or non-Hispanic Whites (Marín & Marín, 1991). Others have suggested that Hispanics exhibit less self-disclosure than do non-Hispanic Whites (Dimand & Hellkamp, 1969; Gomez, 1987; LeVine & Franco, 1981). Therefore, cultural factors will play an important role in the assessment of the effects of poverty on Hispanic children and their families.

In sum, due to a combination of a more extreme and pervasive experience of poverty and other unique factors present in Hispanic children and their families, the developmental pathways for these populations might be following different tracks from the very beginning. Given the youthfulness of this population and the high fertility rate, more attention needs to be given to the underlying processes. It is interesting to see several reports in the literature that use existent theoretical frameworks and measurements failing to predict developmental outcome among Hispanics, when the same variables account for significant portions of the variance among Blacks and Euro-Americans (Beckwith & Cohen, 1984; Bradley et al., 1989). Perhaps more attention needs to be given to culturally relevant predictors as well as outcomes.

REFERENCES

Bachu, A. (June 1993). *Fertility of American women: June 1992.* National Center for Health Statistics. Washington DC: U.S. Government Printing Office, 1993.

Barreto, J., et al. (1986). *Puerto Ricans: Growing problems for a growing population.* A First Friday report. Washington, DC: Full Employment Action Council.

Beckwith, L., & Cohen, S. E. (1984). Home environment and cognitive competence in preterm children during the first five years. In A. Gottfried (Ed.), *Home environment and early cognitive development* (pp. 235– 269). New York: Academic Press.

Bird, H. R., Canino, G. J., & Shrout, P. E. (1985). Consideration on the use of the mini-mental state examination within the Spanish Diagnostic Interview Schedule. Paper presented at the meeting of the American Psychiatric Association, Dallas, TX.

Bradley, R. H., Caldwell, B. M., Rock, S. L., Barnard, K. E., Gray, C., Hammond, M. A., Mitchell, S., Siegel, L., Ramey, C. T., Gottfried, A. W., & Johnson, D. L. (1989). Home environment and cognitive development in the first three years of life: A collaborative study involving six sites and three ethnic groups in North America. *Developmental Psychology, 25,* 217–235.

Carter-Pokras, O., Pirkle, J., & Chavez, G. (1990). Blood levels of 4–11 Year old Mexican American, Puerto Rican, and Cuban Children. *Public Health Reports, 105*(4), 388–393.

Cavazos, L. F. (1989). Intervention is necessary at every level: Building bridges for at-risk children. *Education Digest, 55*(3), 16–19.

Centers for Disease Control, National Center for Prevention Services, Division of Immunization, October 8, 1991.

Children's Defense Fund. (Jan./Mar. 1990). *Latino youths at a crossroads.* CDF Publications, Washington DC.

Cicchetti, D., & Schneider-Rosen, K. (1986). An Organizational Approach to Childhood Depression. In M. Rutter, C. E. Izard, & P. B. Read (Eds.), *Depression in Young People: Developmental and Clinical Perspectives.* New York: Guilford Press.

Coleman, J. G. (1990). Characteristics of at-risk youth and the library's role in dropout prevention. *Tech Trends, 35*(4), 46–47.

del Pinal, J., & García, J. (1993). *Hispanic Americans today*. U.S. Bureau of the Census, June 1993.

Delgado, M. (1979). Herbal medicine in the Puerto Rican community, *Health and Social Work*, 4(2), 25–40.

Delgado, M. & Humm Delgado, D. (1982). Natural support systems: source of strength in Hispanic communities. *Social Work*, January.

Dimond, R. E., & Hellkamp, D. T. (1969). Race, sex, ordinal position of birth and self-disclosure in high school students. *Psychological Reports, 25*, 235–238.

Dressler, W. W., & Bernal, H. (1982). Acculturation and Stress in a Low-Income Puerto Rican Community. *Journal of Human Stress*, 32–38.

Durrett, M. E., O'Bryant, S., & Pennebaker, J. W. (1975). Childrearing report of white, black and Mexican-American families. *Developmental Psychology, 2*, 871.

García Preto, N. (1982). Puerto Rican Families. In M. McGoldrick, J. K. Pearce, & J. Giordano (Eds.), *Ethnicity and family therapy*. New York: Guilford.

García Coll, C. T. (1988). The consequences of teenage childbearing in traditional Puerto Rican culture. In J. K. Nugent, B. M. Lester, & T. B. Brazelton (Eds.), *The cultural context of infancy*, vol. 1 (pp. 111–132). Norwood, NJ: Ablex.

García Coll, C., Sepkoski, C., & Lester, B. M. (1982). Effects of teenage childbearing on neonatal and infant behavior in Puerto Rico. *Infant Behavior and Development, 5*, 227–236.

Gomez, E. A. (1987). Hispanic Americans: Ethnic shared values and traditional treatment. *American Journal of Social Psychiatry, 7*, 215–219.

Henggeler, S. W., & Tavormina, J. B. (1979). Stability of psychological assessment measures for children of Mexican American migrant workers. *Hispanic Journal of Behavioral Sciences, 1*, 263–270.

Laosa, L. M. (1978). Maternal Teaching Strategies in Chicano families of varied education and socioeconomic levels. *Child Development, 49*, 1129–1135.

———. (1980). Maternal teaching strategies in Chicano and Anglo-American Families: The influence of culture and education on maternal behavior. *Child Development, 51*, 759–765.

Lederman, S., & Sierra, D. (1994). Characteristics of Childbearing Hispanic Women in New York City. In G. Lamberty & C. García Coll (Eds.), *Puerto Rican women & children: Issues in health, growth and development* (pp. 85–102). New York: Plenum.

Lester, B. M., García Coll, C.T., & Sepkoski, C. (1983). A cross-cultural study of teenage pregnancy and neonatal behavior. In T. Field & A. Sostek (Eds.) *Infants born at risk: Physiological, perceptual, and cognitive processes.* Grune & Stratton.

LeVine, E., & Franco, J. N. (1981). A reassessment of self-disclosure patterns among Anglo Americans and Hispanics. *Journal of Counseling Psychology, 28,* 522–524.

Marín, B. V., Marín, G., Padilla, A. M. & de la Rocha, C. (1983). Utilization of traditional and non-traditional sources of health care among Hispanics. *Hispanic Journal of Behavioral Sciences, 5*(1), 65–80.

Marín, G., & Marín, B. V. (1991). *Research with Hispanic populations.* Newbury Park, CA: Sage.

Markides, K. S., Levin, J. S., & Ray, L. A. (1985). Determinants of physician utilization among Mexican-Americans. *Medical Care, 23*(3).

Mendoza, F., Takata, G. S., & Martorell, R. (1994). Health status and health care access for mainland Puerto Rican children: Results from the Hispanic Health and Nutrition Examination Survey (HHANES): 1981–1984. In G. Lamberty & C. García Coll *Puerto Rican Women & Children: Issues in Health, Growth and Development* (pp. 211–227). New York: Plenum.

Mendoza, F. S., Ventura, S. J., Valdez, B., Castillo, R. O., Saldivar, L. E., Baisden, K., & Martorell, R. (1991). Selected measures of health status for Mexican-American, mainland Puerto Rican, and Cuban-American children. *JAMA, 265*(2), 227–232.

Ogbu, J. (1981). Origins of human competence: A cultural-ecological perspective. *Child Development, 52,* 413–429.

Pérez, S. M., & Martínez, D. (1993). State of Hispanic America 1993: Toward a Latino anti-poverty agenda. *National Council of La Raza.*

Research and Reports: Earnings drop sharply for young adult males. (1987). *Education Week, 6*(39), 3.

Rogler, L. H., Cortes, D. E., Malgady, R. G. (1991) Acculturation and mental health status among Hispanics. *American Psychologist, 46*(6), 585–597.

Stern, M. (1984). Factors relating to increased prevalence of diabetes in Hispanic Americans. In U.S, Department of Health and Human Services, *Report of the Secretary's Task Force on Black and Minority Health. Volume VII. Chemical dependency and diabetes* (pp. 359–372)

DHHS Publication No. 85–487. Washington, DC: U.S. Government Printing Office.

Steward, J. H., Manners, R. A., Wolf, E. R., Padilla Seda, E., Mintz, S. W. & Scheele, R. L. (1956). *The people of Puerto Rico.* Champaign: University of Illinois Press.

Stroup-Benham, C. A. & Treviño, F. M. (1991). Reproductive characteristics of Mexican-American, mainland Puerto Rican, and Cuban-American women: Data from the Hispanic Health and Nutrition Examination Survey. *JAMA, 265*(2), 222–226.

Taylor, V. L., Jurley, E. C., Riley, M. T. (1986). The influence of acculturation upon the adjustment of pre-school Mexican-American children of single-parent families. *Family Therapy,* 13(3), 249–256.

Treviño, F. M., Moyer, E., Valdez, B., Stroup-Benham, C. A. (1991). *JAMA,* 265(2), 233–237.

U.S. Bureau of the Census. (1991). *Poverty in the U.S.: 1991.* Washington, DC: U.S. Government Printing Office.

U.S. Department of Commerce, Bureau of the Census. (1990). *Current population reports,* Series P-20, No. 443, School Enrollment-Social and Economic Characteristics of Students: October 1988 and 1987.

U.S. Department of Health and Human Services. (1985). *Report of the Secretary's task force on black and minority health* (DHHS Publication No. 85–487). Washington, DC: U.S. Government Printing Office.

Ventura, S. J. (1994). Demographic and health charactertistics of Puerto Rican mothers and their babies. In G. Lamberty & C. García Coll *Puerto Rican women & children: Issues in health, growth and development* (pp. 71–84). New York: Plenum.

——. (1981). Births of Hispanic parentage. *Monthly health statistics report, 33*(8). Hyattsville, Md: Department of Health and Human Services; December 1984. Publication PHS 85–1120.

——. (1987). Births of Hispanic parentage, 1983 and 1984. *Monthly Health Statistics Report, 36,* 1–19

Wasserman, G. A., Rauh, V. A., Brunelli, S. A., García Castro, M., & Necos, B. (1990) Psychosocial attributes and life experiences of disadvantaged minority mothers: Age and ethnic variations. *Child Development,* 61(2), 566–580.

Wernette, B., & Nieves. M. T. (1991). Minorities and air pollution: A preliminary geographic-demographic analysis. Presented at Socioeconomic Research Analysis Conference II, June 27–8, 1991.

Cited in *Environmental equity: Reducing risk for all communities.* Report to the Administrator from the EPA Environmental Equity Workgroup. Draft. December 6, 1991.

Wolf, K. L. (1952). Growing up and its price in three Puerto Rican subcultures. *Psychiatry, 15,*401–433.

Zeskind, P. S. (1983). Cross-cultural differences in maternal perceptions of cries of low-and high-risk infants. *Child Development, 54,* 1119–1128.

Zorrilla, C., Díaz, C., Romaguera, J., & Martin, M. (1994). Acquired Immune Deficiency Syndrome (AIDS) in women and children in Puerto Rico. In G. Lamberty & C. García Coll *Puerto Rican Women & Children: Issues in Health, Growth and Development* (pp. 55–70). New York: Plenum.

*   *   *

Round Table Discussion

Huston. Among Puerto Ricans, certainly, and within some other Hispanic communities, there are racial/ethnic differences. Puerto Ricans range from those who are almost entirely of African descent to those who are of European descent, with mixtures in between. Valoria Lovelace, associated with the Children's Television Workshop, has been doing research on children's understanding of ethnic and racial identities. Her research with Puerto Rican children is very interesting, because they respond to skin color in defining themselves and in forming their attitudes about themselves. So I wonder if you might want to comment on the role of that component within Hispanic groups, particularly Puerto Ricans.

García-Coll. Puerto Ricans use a variety of names to differentiate people by skin color; there are about ten or fifteen different descriptors based on coloration. However, it is not only skin color, but hair texture and other physical characteristics. We've been working in a study group composed of African Americans, Puerto Ricans, and others who have done research in this area, grappling with the notion of how we can measure things like skin color. Thus we are interested not only in identifying the racial features, but also the perception within the immediate family, within the immediate community, within the community at large, within the school system, and how all of these perceptions and beliefs are negotiated.

Huston. I guess what I'm thinking in this whole discussion is that poverty is a thing that runs through as a common element for a lot of different groups, but beyond that, groups are different in so many ways. Craig was talking about sampling. I'm not even sure we know on what criteria we ought to be sampling, in order to understand poverty within many different kinds of cultural frameworks.

García-Coll. One of the things that we're thinking, related to framework, is the notion of really trying to sample all neighborhoods. For example, Jamaica Plains, in Boston, has an incredible range of social classes and ethnic groups. I mean, that would be a great place to do this kind of research. And then really not only look at families, but look at the neighborhood. And again, the notion is not only racial and class distribution, but the processes of neighborhood life—following children around for a day and getting a sense of what their world is really like. It requires a mixed methodology. We're going to have to move out and do both our standard measures and more qualitative measurement as well.

Brooks-Gunn. I'd like to switch gears here, is that all right? I was really struck by your comments about different conceptions of families. It relates to measures of competence and how we consider competence. I'm thinking of the ethnographic work that's been done, some with Mexican Americans in Arizona showing that notions of family are different, and community and communal values are in tension with mainstream independence values. Some families want their children to succeed, but they don't want them going off to medical school or law school because that means they will leave the community. So when you have this high-achieving child, you may channel the child into something so he/she still goes to college, but you may work very hard for him/her to do something that would make it more likely that he/she would stay in the community. And I think you're right that our models really don't take into account how important the family or the community is, or how, as a mother, you teach your children bridging strategies, which are bridging to mainstream, saying you should go off—wherever a job is, you go—versus other values and strategies that you use. I do think what you're talking about addresses the tension and we need to consider the tension of these different values.

García-Coll. Let me just give you a very specific example. When Minuchin was developing the concept of enmeshment, he was working with Puerto Rican families—they were one of the main samples. And now we have people talking about the notion of normal enmeshment, the notion that for Puerto Rican families, moving to the next block represents a major change for the family. And so that notion really has to be taken into account.

Zuckerman. It is important to consider psychological factors separately from cultural and socioeconomic factors. Mothers' interactions with children that are described as passive and nonverbal may be a reflection of depression. Certainly among families I see at Boston City Hospital, the stresses of racism, finances, and isolation can result in depression. It is important that research identifies this specific factor and understands its relationship to other factors. Depression is an important proximal factor affecting children's development and is unlikely to be a normal healthy aspect of any culture or social class.

García-Coll. From a methodological point of view, I feel very comfortable in that we have to both measure such things as acculturation at the same time that we're measuring depression. We need to start moving into not only saying, "It could be cultural," to actually starting to measure culture. I just want to mention that a former student of mine is looking at acculturation levels among Hispanics here in the United States. What she is finding is that less acculturated mothers here looked like the Puerto Rican mothers that we have in Puerto Rico. So even though this is a low SES, less acculturated group of mothers, there are individual differences that relate to a pattern that we're finding in the traditional culture. So we just have to start moving in that direction: measuring acculturation, measuring attitudes about, "Do I want my child to become American and not talk any Spanish, because I don't want to have to deal with anything like that?" These are very fluid variables we need to study.

Lester. Why don't you talk about the methodological issue? This story of trying to get information about depression from these families, and the difference between questionnaires and interviews.

García-Coll. We get very little information from questionnaires. We talk with these families and everything looks fine. And then we go and sit and all sorts of information comes out—it's as Suzanne was saying, when you're rewinding the videotape, then these mothers start giving us the real information. So again, we need to have multi-method, multi-measure approaches to these issues.

Lester. Yes, the standard measures will tell you that they're not depressed and that everything is fine. Then you sit down and have a cup of coffee with them and they'll tell you they're miserable.

Barnard. So then why do you use the standard measures?

García-Coll. Well, I feel like I need to educate the community. The basic thing is that if I don't use the standard measures, then I'm left defending why I didn't use them. But, when I use the standard measure and nothing comes out, I can say, look at this other measure, this is really tapping it. So, in a way, it's really saying to the scientific community that we must have alternative measures.

Lamberty. You still have to use different measures, anyway. An instrument's convergent validity hinges on that.

García-Coll. I feel that the main thing here is the value judgment and using science to support a value judgment. Part of what happens is that because we are human beings we bring values to our scientific activities. Our objective is to know the truth. So, to a certain extent, what I am saying about the notion of looking at these populations with a deficit model is that we really believe that there is a fissure. Dan Quayle is right in this instance in that he is represented by a lot of people in the United States and a lot of people around the world. Part of one's task as a member of society is to become acculturated and to believe that there is a right way of doing things. But, what we are saying is when we look at the human population, there is so much diversity that we have to go one step further. We are saying that there is one way for me but there might be a different way for you. So, it is a completely different issue.

CHAPTER 4

Literacy and Poverty: Intergenerational Issues within African American Families

Vivian L. Gadsden

The intergenerational effects of low literacy and poverty constitute a growing segment of research on children, parents, and families. Children who live in poor families experience the effects of poverty not only in their cognitive and physical development but also in their behavioral and social growth—i.e., in the way they see the world and negotiate their lives (Chase-Lansdale & Brooks-Gunn, 1991; Kelly & Ramsey, 1991). Adults who are low-literate are unable to help their children develop literate abilities, engage in many literate activities, or access resources requiring literate competence (Van Fossen & Sticht, 1991; Wigfield & Asher, 1984). In discussions about the consequences of low literacy and poverty, literacy is seen as a contributor to conditions such as unemployment which, unless transitory, leads often to long-term poverty. Policy efforts at the federal level reflect this concern for the deleterious effects of chronic poverty and the relationship between poverty and literacy. Other discussions point to poverty as the source of the problem with negative effects ranging from limited literacy to poor schools and schooling (Hill and Duncan, 1987). Those who support this position suggest that if children were in homes with sufficient income to support the family, with adequate child-care resources, and effective schools, the children and families might be better equipped to develop life-plans in which literacy is seen as achievable and linked to positive social and economic outcomes.

Despite research that links the two, a causal relationship between literacy and poverty is difficult to establish; both poverty and low literacy are mediated by several other conditions, such as race and joblessness. What we do know is that disproportionate numbers of low-literate people live in poverty and that poverty limits both the nature and quality of educational access and literacy resources, of which many poor children and their families may simply not be aware. When considered as separate circumstances, each—low literacy and chronic poverty—reduces possibilities for children and other family members to reach their full developmental and cognitive potential. Together, both may create obstacles, such as limited job opportunities, health-related problems, and stress, that children and adults find difficult to surmount. These environmental events associated with low literacy and poverty in early childhood are "key determinants of later development" reaching into adulthood and parenthood (Baydar, Brooks-Gunn, & Furstenberg, 1994, p. 2).

The consequences of poverty and low literacy are often described in research on families and literacy, particularly the effect of parents' literacy and parent-child literacy interactions on children's school performance (e.g., Snow, Barnes, Chandler, Goodman, & Hemphill, 1991). Although not exclusive to children in poverty, research studies in this area provide findings that link children's performance in school to parents' (usually mothers') educational attainment. In literacy studies on parent-child reading, findings suggest that children whose parents engage with them in literacy activities, such as book reading, perform better than their peers whose parents do not participate in these activities or who are unable to do so (Pellegrini, Brody, & Sigel, 1985; Sulzby & Edwards, in press). Much of the current effort in family literacy is developed out of these studies.

An equally compelling body of research, however, notes that many of the shared literacy activities in these studies fit a narrow definition of literacy and parent-child interactions and do not explain the sometimes strong school performance of children whose parents have never read to them (Heath, 1983; Schieffelin & Cochran-Smith, 1984; Taylor & Dorsey-Gaines,

1988). Pointing to the variety of cultural and social differences in parent-child interactions in general, these studies state that, just as family structure is dominated by a Western perception, the definition of literacy and literacy interactions is constrained by a Western standard which falls outside the traditions of many families.

Discussions emanating from this work suggest that research examine more intensively how literate acts (e.g., problem-solving and orality) are practiced in some of the homes and how children use literacy from basic home encounters to negotiate life activities within and outside of school. These studies and other research tracing family development and literacy education also note that in many families children's persistence in literacy learning, particularly when parents have low literacy, may be a function of the stated value of literacy and the transmission of coping strategies in the face of economic hardship (Gadsden, 1993). In such cases, the intergenerational impact of low literacy and poverty may be reduced. This paper reviews issues in literacy and poverty and their impact on intergenerational development within African American families.

The discussion in this paper is not limited to adults *or* children in families but utilizes a life-span perspective on family development to examine critical issues facing parents and children as family members and learners. The paper is divided into four parts. The first examines the relationship between literacy and poverty, e.g., the significance of declining literacy rates and increasing poverty rates, and the implications of changing family formation patterns. The second part reviews literacy and poverty issues within African American families. The third focuses on intergenerational factors described in a case study of two low-income, low-literate African American families participating in a Head Start-based literacy study. The fourth part provides conclusions and implications.

Literacy, Poverty, and Families:
Cross-cutting Issues

The Significance of Literacy

Research on the consequences of low literacy for children and families has increased dramatically over the past decade (Powell, 1991). Several characteristics distinguish the current work from earlier discussions. First, it is strongly linked to a sense of urgency in which practitioners and policymakers assert a strong presence in the conceptualization and development of agendas (Gadsden & Edwards, 1993). Second, the definition of literacy focuses on more than discrete reading and writing abilities; rather literacy is seen as encompassing a wide range of problem-solving abilities, work skills, and life-course competencies (Reder, Wikelund, & Hart-Landsberg, 1992). Third, literacy engages a broader discussion than learning within school contexts and is studied as a significant part of the discourse across domains such as child care, medicine, and social work (Palmer, Smeeding, & Torrey, 1988). For example, with increasing frequency, findings from interdisciplinary intervention studies with young mothers and their children demonstrate that low literacy may exact a high price when a young mother is unable to read well enough to provide her child with appropriate health care (Ramey, Bryant, Sparling, & Wasik, 1985). Fourth, literacy is linked to a variety of intergenerational outcomes: i.e., behaviors, experiences, and practices within families which enable or inhibit children and their parents to overcome difficult life circumstances (Smith, 1983; Snow et al., 1991). Like previous efforts, however, current literacy campaigns are developed around the view that improved educational experiences will result in better life circumstances, from improved life chances for children to declining poverty within families (Brizius & Foster, 1993).

There is little doubt that literacy is essential for participation in the larger society. However, millions of adults in the United States are considered low-literate with inadequate reading and writing ability to achieve their goals or to obtain and sustain employment (Ferguson, 1992). The United States ranks 49th among 159 members in the United Nations in its average level of literacy. Recent estimates from the U. S. Department of Education indicate that 90 million adults—about 47 percent of the U.S. adult population— demonstrate low levels of functional literacy.

The most recent report to describe the problem of literacy in the United States is the National Adult Literacy Survey (NALS), reported by the Office of Educational Research and Improvement's National Center for Education Statistics. Adult literacy is described at five levels within three types of literacy necessary for a person to use printed and written information effectively: (1) prose literacy, requiring the ability to understand and use information from texts, including editorials, news stories, poems, and fiction, (2) document literacy, requiring the ability to locate and use information contained in forms and other materials such as job applications, transportation schedules, maps, and tables, and (3) quantitative literacy, requiring the ability to apply arithmetic operations, either alone or sequentially, using numbers embedded in printed materials, e.g., restaurant checks, order forms, and loan advertisements. Based on interviews with more than 26,000 adults aged 16 and older, the report suggests that 40 to 44 million of the 191 million adults in the United States possess literacy skills in the lowest of five survey assessment levels and 50 million in the next to lowest level; 34 to 40 million perform in the highest two levels. The assessment scores of survey participants 21 to 25 years-old were 11 to 14 points lower than the scores of a comparable age cohort that was assessed in 1985. Other data from the study indicate that between 41 and 44 percent of all adults in the lowest level on each literacy scale were living in poverty compared with only 4 to 8 percent of those in the highest proficiency levels.

Low literacy in several other reports has been linked to low productivity, high unemployment, low earnings, and high rates of welfare dependency (Berlin & Sum, 1988; Sum & Fogg, 1990). As Baydar, Brooks-Gunn, & Furstenberg (1994) suggest, to the degree that a society's well-being is judged by the literacy levels of its members, the well-being of the United States and its members is in jeopardy. However, the jeopardy is much more intensive than the data may suggest. The potential impact of the literacy problem for young adult parents and children living in poverty is severe. Children whose parents are poor are also poor, and unless there is support in the form of educational assistance and income, a disproportionate number of these children may grow up to be poor adults, living in conditions worse than those of their parents (McLoyd, 1990; Wilson, 1988). When parents have adequate literate abilities, have access to intensive literacy support, and are able to sustain a belief in the value of literacy, their children may flourish in spite of obstacles. When parents do not have functional literate abilities, are isolated from support systems, and have lost faith in the value of literacy and education as a means out of their situation, they convey the strain of life through subtle and direct messages. The intergenerational costs of low literacy are high for all children and their parents. These costs significantly increase for children and families who are living in poverty (Chase-Lansdale, 1993). In families of color these costs are mediated by racial and cultural discrimination and the absence of programs, models, and policies that consider the cultural experiences of these populations.

The Distribution of Poverty in Families: The Impact on Children

Poverty has been linked to low literacy by suggestion, innuendo, and statistics. The urgency of focusing on poverty among children captures two concerns. First, children are dependent upon others for their economic security. When this security is unavailable in their homes, both children and the adults upon whom they rely are adversely affected. Second, there is a growing body of evidence that links outcomes such as completed schooling and career attainments to the economic resources available during childhood (Hill & Duncan, 1987). The intergenerational nature of poverty may be attenuated by intergenerational low literacy, including cultural expectations and beliefs, attitudes, behaviors, and strategies for survival from one generation to another.

The distribution and intensity of poverty have shifted significantly over the past twenty years. One out of every five children lives in a family with an income below the federal poverty line. Of the 13 million children living in poverty, five million are desperately poor, living in families that have an income that is less than one-half the federal poverty level (National Commission on Children, 1991). While there are differing opinions about how to categorize these families, little dispute exists about the fact that the poor are increasing, that disproportionate numbers are young and parents, and that African Americans and other people of color are over-represented in the numbers. Particularly alarming is that the poor are increasingly young, male, minority, and relatively unskilled, facing the simultaneous and interactive effects of racial discrimination and steadily deteriorating urban labor markets to which they have limited access.

As Kelly and Ramsey (1991) note, there is a mismatch between population traits and needs and labor market opportunities, decreasing the abilities of young families to sustain themselves through male participation in the labor force and increasing the attractiveness of informal economies, such as hustling and drug sales or other criminal activities (Anderson, 1990). Despite the high price such economies may exact in physical harm and incarceration, the short-term economic reward provides long-term incentives for participation. However, the effects of participation in these economies often contribute to the permanence of father absence for many children in the form of long-term incarceration or loss of life.

Poverty as a short-term experience is riddled with stress. When families and children are exposed to chronic poverty, they are confronted with a panoply of stressful conditions and events (Masten, Morison, Pellegrini, & Tellegen, 1991). More than economic loss—especially transitory economic loss—chronic poverty limits choices in all domains of life, from choice of school to choice of neighborhood; subjects individuals to control of others, such as social workers; increases the probability that the child will be viewed negatively and receive less positive attention and more criticism from teachers; and results in the child often shouldering responsibility for younger siblings or the family's survival (McLoyd, 1990).

During recent times, almost three-fourths of the children under the age of six living in poverty were in single-parent families (U.S. Bureau of the Census, 1991). In the 1980s the percentage of all children under the age of six living in poverty was 24%. Fifty-one percent of all African American children live in poverty, 44.3 percent of all Latino children, and 18.6 percent of all white children (U.S. Bureau of the Census, 1991). The effects of poverty on African American and Latino children, not unlike many other children, influence all other segments of their lives, from self-esteem to educational persistence. While some children demonstrate high levels of perseverance and resilience (Garmezy & Rutter, 1983), they have the difficult, and decreasingly revered, task of "beating the odds" or prevailing in spite of the system.

The expectation that children or their families will be able to rise above all the odds, particularly African American children living in poverty, is both unrealistic and beyond the normal expectation for most children or families in American society. African American families in poverty are among the most studied groups in educational and psychological research, not necessarily because they represent an interesting cohort but primarily because of the persistence of poverty and its effects on children's socioemotional development and academic performance. Problems in school performance, in children's educational and literacy persistence, and in their self-perceptions regarding learning have been linked to poverty, much of it resulting from the inability of their fathers to support them in both one- and two-parent homes (Vosler & Proctor, 1991). There are several instances when it is difficult to tease out the effects of poverty from those of limited social support for children, e.g., developmental, personality, and emotional growth; however, the implications of poverty and changing family forms are far-reaching for discussions about the intergenerational nature of literacy within families.

The Importance of Changing Family Constellations

Poverty research has focused heavily on changing family formation patterns in the United States over the past twenty years. A significant portion of this work, for example, examines the impact of poverty on children and adults in single-parent, female-headed households. The discussion of changing family forms is rarely a part of the discourse in literacy, although several studies, particularly those on Head Start and other low-income populations, often examine problems of children in mother-headed households. With the exception of a few studies (e.g., Lamb & Elster, 1985), research on family literacy and parent-child interactions focus almost exclusively on mother-child interactions around literacy. Changing family constellations are implied in some research on families and literacy. Research in developmental psychology and sociology does examine the impact of changing family forms in greater depth but has focused primarily on changes resulting from marital disruption.

The change in family patterns is important because it represents a change in both the relationships that might exist within families in regard to literacy and the ways in which interventions are planned and implemented. Changing patterns of family formation are not simply applicable to low-income, single mothers in African American or other minority families. Within the past twenty years family formation patterns have changed across cultural communities. The incidence of poverty resulting from lost wages in divorce is itself an issue of much concern in literature from multiple disciplines.

In traditional intact family models up to the 1960s, the role of the father was defined by a decidedly western interpretation of family functioning in which fathers provided for the economic well-being of their children and mothers ensured their children's developmental progress (Miller, 1993). Much of family research through the 1970s focused on the degree to which ethnically diverse families, particularly African American families, adhered to this model (see Coleman et al., 1966; Moynihan, 1965, Katz, 1993). Current policy is still developed around a unilinear view of families that equates effective family structure with the nuclear family model (Kelly & Ramsey, 1991). Not until the recent resurgence of interest in family studies has research or policy highlighted the diversity of functioning, interactions, and expectations embedded in the cultural and ethnic histories of families and communities in the United States (Anderson, 1989; Katz, 1993); neither addresses fully the insidious role of discrimination in reducing the strength of family development, particularly within many families of color (Miller, 1993; Trotter, 1993).

Recent studies on families and children of color (e.g., Gadsden, 1993; LaFromboise & Low, 1989) point to the variations in the nature of family patterns, child-parent relations, male-female relationships, and responsibilities for childrearing as communal work. For example, Gadsden (1993) in a recent study builds on the role of community effort within African American families. Here the notion of extended families is broadened to include what are called "family communities"—a collection of biologically and non-biologically connected individuals who assume responsibility for the development of children. A reciprocal relationship exists between the children and the community requiring children to assume responsibility for achieving in school, avoiding criminal activities, and treating others with respect. Similarly, LaFromboise and Low (1989) describe how childrearing practices within American Indian communities are centered on the development of children's sense of self with nature and the joint responsibility of the community and family in childrearing. While some of the work over the past ten years focuses on economic disparities between blacks and other groups (e.g., Wilson, 1988), increasingly studies examine the cultural richness and contextual variety within families—characteristics that might be harnessed to support children (Billingsley, 1993; Heath, 1983; Hill, 1972; McAdoo, 1991; Spencer, Brookins, & Allen, 1985).

Family research over the past ten years also has examined closely changes in role definitions and expectations of fathers and mothers. For example, as one result of the changing status of women in the home and labor market, significant changes have occurred in fathers' participation in their children's development, often expanding to include responsibilities for nurturing and providing daily care. In fields such as developmental psychology, once characterized by a singular focus on mother-child relationships, the significance of fathers in the daily routines of child support and nurturance is widely discussed (see Lamb, 1987; Furstenberg, Brooks-Gunn, & Morgan, 1987; Furstenberg & Harris, 1993). Thus, researchers have moved beyond the boundaries of mother-child attachment and bonding (e.g., Ainsworth & Bell, 1969) to investigate the involvement of fathers as caregivers (e.g., Cervera, 1991; Lamb, 1987) and the impact of father involvement into adolescence and over the lifespan of children. The implications of this work are that the role of fathers and the family itself contributes to the affective development of children, to the shaping of personality, and eventually to a sense of belonging, meaning, and socioemotional stability.

Little research exists that cuts across the three areas of literacy, poverty, and families; however, the interrelatedness of these three issues is highlighted in statistics on poor families and children. The deleterious effects of poverty on the cognitive and psychosocial well-being of children and families and, more recently, on their literacy development have been chronicled in a growing body of research (e.g., Chase-Lansdale, 1993; Sulzby & Edwards, in press). The implications of long-term, multi-generational, sustained poverty is widely discussed in current analyses of family support policy and educational research and practice (Cherlin, in press). The growing number of family support efforts, the revival of parent education programs, and the expansion of family literacy from Head Start to traditional adult literacy programs are but a few examples of the responses to the problems (Powell, 1991; RMC Corporation, 1992).

Much of the work that has been done on poor families thus far continues to investigate poverty as a pathological condition, located between the undeserving poor and the culture of poverty. Other research focuses on the relationship among poverty, stress, and family organization over time. Relatively little work examines what it is about poverty that results in worse outcomes. As Katz (1993) notes, questions about how some families survive obstacles, strategies that they develop, family processes that govern daily interactions, and the meaning and behaviors attached to "success" in families represent much needed foci in research on poverty.

In research on families and literacy, issues of family development, family interactions, race, and poverty are assumed in references to "breaking the cycle of poverty," but rarely are stated as a critical domain in the field. A variety of questions persist: how poverty is experienced by different children and parents within a family or across families; what the relationships are between poverty and other home, community, and family variables; why families "surmount, as well as succumb," to the stressors of poverty and discrimination; and how families use personal and social resources. Research typically examines the effects of poverty *or* family development. What is needed is a more intensive focus on the intersection of poverty and family organization and discussions about how this intersection varies in different family forms and across different cultures (Gadsden & Philadelphia Children's Network, 1993).

Literacy and Poverty within African American Families

African American children and their families are among the most studied groups in both literacy and poverty research. African American families have been at the center of policy discussions for almost half a century (Wilson, 1988). Research on literacy focuses on the performance of children in schools and the obstacles that low-literacy creates in seeking and obtaining employment; relatively fewer studies exist that examine intergenerational effects of low literacy or the impact of poor school performance on adult life.

Poverty persists as a major problem facing disproportionate numbers of African American children and families. Recent estimates show that among all African American children and their families, 45.6% live below the poverty line, and over 50% of children six years-old and younger live in families experiencing chronic economic hardship (U.S. Bureau of the Census, 1992). Although white children and their families constitute the majority of poor in absolute numbers, African American families are associated with poverty in both popular impressions and growing over-representations within statistical data (Katz, 1993). Real or perceived, the problems of poverty and the attendant conditions of limited economic access, inadequate schools and schooling, poor health care, and reduced educational opportunities threaten the development of African American children and families (Children's Defense Fund, 1991). For many of these families, the valuing of literacy and hope for children that Anderson (1988) and Holt (1990) describe as legacies within the African American community appear to have been replaced, in part, by an intergenerational legacy of despair. In such cases, the viability of literacy and learning as a way out of poverty is questionable, messages about the importance of literacy and of persistence may be muted, and knowledge of cultural strengths may be constrained. Yet, in other difficult situations, African American families in poverty convey strong messages about the importance of literacy and learning and construct strategies that assist them and their children to persist in the face of hardship (Billingsley, 1993)

Despite some similarities in the experiences of all families living in poverty, significant differences often exist in the way that children and families negotiate their experiences, view their ability to sustain or improve their social condition, and construct survival strategies. Some of these differences are attributable to the historical problems associated with racism and discriminatory practices; others center on cultural factors within different communities and the interpretation of western practices to accommodate cultural beliefs, for example, about the relationship between children and their parents. African American families living in poverty differ significantly in the historical and political roots of their problems from other ethnic groups and from other people within the collective called African Americans, e.g., people of varied African ancestry, from the Caribbean to the African continent. It is little wonder that monolithic intervention efforts to multifaceted educational and social problems have had limited success for the group as a whole.

Issues of educational achievement, persistence, and poverty are central to discussions about African American families with children. These discussions increasingly examine cultural, environmental, and historical factors that may debilitate African American families in poverty as well as cause discontinuities between family and children's school life (e.g., Hess & Holloway, 1984). Comparatively little research examines these cultural differences in context or attempts to explore what meanings are attached to literacy and how relationships between cultural beliefs and practices of groups are constructed, particularly for African American and other groups of color. The absence of critical analyses about the structural strengths of these families in forestalling the effects of poverty and disadvantagement often result in global statements about the group, with little or no attention to differences among mini-cultures that constitute the group and the unique circumstances that guide their development.

Much of the data from literacy studies and poverty research on poor African American families rely on snapshots of the problem within a single time frame. One exception is a recent study by Baydar, Brooks-Gunn, and Furstenberg (1994) which identified early predictors of adulthood literacy levels to define high-risk groups. Based on a 20-year longitudinal study from a sample of black children of teenaged mothers from the Baltimore metropolitan area, the study found as other studies suggest that family environmental factors such as maternal education, family size in early childhood, maternal marital status, and income in middle childhood and early adolescence are predictive of literacy. Another longitudinal study that provides information on intergenerational effects is the Panel Study of Income Dynamics (PSID), a longitudinal study of over 5,000 families conducted by the Survey Research Center at the University of Michigan (1984). Focusing on motivational factors within families, including those headed by women who were never married and who were divorced, separated, or widowed, the study has charted the economic well-being of a nationally representative sample of American families each year since 1968, testing several causal models. Findings from the study suggest that differences between individuals on psychological dimensions are the result of changes in past economic status, not the cause of future improvement or deterioration (see Duncan & Rogers, 1988; McLoyd, 1990).

An emerging body of research on intergenerational learning within low-income homes examines the nature and construct of the family as an active, changing context—affected significantly by cultural and community beliefs and traditions (e.g., Taylor & Dorsey-Gaines, 1988; Taylor & Strickland, 1986). The relationship between culture and family as contexts for learning is seen as central to the formation and development of African American children's beliefs about educational access and their ability to persist in the face of poverty and the social barriers of discrimination and racism.

Literacy and poverty are particularly important issues to examine in reference to African American children and families. Both issues revolve around access to educational, social, and economic institutions, e.g., good schools, instruction, literacy assistance, and employment. Data from the NALS show that Black Americans, along with American Indian/Alaskan Native, Hispanic, and Asian/Pacific Islander adults, were more likely than white adults to perform in the lowest two literacy levels.

Perhaps the issue that contributes most to the problems facing African American families is the increasing numbers of single-parent, female-headed households and the decreasing participation of African American males in the labor force. Although there is suggestion that African American males experience serious literacy problems, there is little empirical evidence in this area. What adds to the perplexity of the situation is that despite decreases in high school dropouts, increases in high school graduation rates, and increases in college attendance and graduation rates for African American males, perceptions of a literacy problem and the reality of high unemployment rates persist for black men (Sum & Fogg, 1990). Much of the confusion around this issue may be found in problems facing African American families and schooling. Children in poor African American families ask questions that cannot be explained simply or easily by their parents—e.g., will literacy provide them with opportunity? The question may likely receive a negative response when we consider that black men 20 to 29 years of age with twelve or more years of schooling made less money comparatively than they did in 1973 as did men with twelve years of schooling (Sum & Fogg, 1990).

Intergenerational Issues about Literacy, Poverty, and Persistence: Two Parents' Stories

The discussion in this part is developed out of findings from a study with 25 low-income Head Start parents participating in literacy development activities. The project, called the Parent-Child Learning Project (PCLP), was based in a Head Start program in a large urban area. The project focused specifically on two generations of learners and examined parents' perceptions of the role of literacy in their children's development, barriers to literacy and educational access, and the value of literacy in negotiating life demands and children's school performance. The aim of the project was to understand better the range of needs that parents experience in attempting to improve their own life chances and enhance the academic performance of their children. The study followed African American and Puerto Rican parents (23 mothers and 2 fathers) aged 21 to 45 over two years. The participants in the study participated in workshops and were interviewed for a total of three hours per week for 48 weeks over two years. Participants had completed an average of nine years of schooling and had an average of three children.

Possible limitations of the study's design could restrict the generalizability of the conclusions, over and above the fact that the findings focus on a small cohort of African Americans recruited for the study; the participants in the studies were not selected at random. Participants in both studies participated voluntarily. Parents' reasons for not participating included competing demands for their time, the relative unimportance of literacy amidst more crucial family problems, and fear of disclosing their literacy needs. Many other parents reported a high level of confidence in their literate abilities, but records and Head Start staff assessments of parents' literacy suggested that parents' literacy rates were lower than they had reported. In a survey of 100 parents in the Head Start program, over 60% stated that they felt their literacy was "good." The parents identified the need for a better life, out of poverty, as a key issue for them and their children. These data are consistent with reports from the NALS in which 66 to 75 percent of the adults in the lowest level and 93 to 97 percent in the second lowest level described themselves as being able to read or write English "well" or "very well."

Eight (all mothers) of the 25 participating parents in PCLP were interviewed in depth and observed over two years. Of these eight mothers, four are African American and four are Puerto Rican. Two of the four African American mothers are single heads of household and one Puerto Rican mother. Seven of the eight range from 23 to 30 in age; one mother is 40. Six of the eight mothers (all of the African American mothers and two of the Puerto Rican mothers) have worked outside the home for more than one year (but not consecutive months).

The discussion that follows is based on responses from in-depth interviews with two of the four African American families, representative of other African American mothers in the program. Informant 1 is married and is in her mid-20s. She has three children, ranging from two to eight years in age. She was a teenage mother and has 11 years of schooling. She was raised in a low-income home with two parents. Informant 2 is the single head of her household. Currently in her mid-20s also, she was a teenage mother. She has two children, five and ten, and receives little social support from her family. She was raised in a female-headed household which she describes as "poor." Informant 2 has 10 years of schooling.

This section discusses issues related to two themes on poverty and literacy: (1) the human costs of poverty, i.e., what are the specific experiences of poverty that make literacy difficult to achieve and (2) importance and accessibility of literacy. Parents in this study were asked to describe their current experiences as parents, the contributions they feel they will make to their children's success, indicators of success, and the types of opportunities that will be available for their children. A third issue, persistence, that emanated from a study I am conducting with four generations of African Americans originally from the rural South also is discussed.

The Human Costs of Poverty

What is the price of poverty? The price of poverty may be measured in a variety of ways: children's academic performance, feelings of self-esteem, emotional stability, personal aspirations, expectations and goals for children and adults, persistence, or resiliency. Parents in PCLP described the price of poverty in several of these terms. However, the immediacy of financial need, low self-esteem, and limited aspirations dominated the responses. What was striking was the differences in the reports of the two young mothers and the reports from older adults in other communities and from historical reports (e.g., Anderson, 1988). These young parents, although they held expectations for themselves and their children, did not seem to believe that current circumstances would allow their children to achieve high goals. The young mothers appear to base their assessments on what they described as increasingly "worse conditions and problems that [no generation] prior to their own ha[d] experienced—nothing except slavery and [post-slavery]":

> I don't really think I am poor; I just don't have enough money to do the things I think I need to do, like get nice things for my children, live in a decent neighborhood, get a car so I don't have to catch those buses—that don't run on time anyway. You know when you don't have enough money, other people know it. They can look at you and tell, and maybe that's the worst part of being poor—feeling that you and your children are not good enough to be treated with respect. You just don't feel good about yourself and your children don't either. . . .and there's nothin' you can do to change it!

Not only does Informant 1 have feelings of low self-esteem for herself, but she also describes the problem as outside of her control, "and there's nothin' you can do to change it!" When asked who has the power to change things, she implies that there is a systemic problem and refers to her family's poverty throughout her childhood:

Who can change it? I sure can't. My husband and I do the best we can. He's laid off again, but even when he was working, there wasn't enough money and he could never count on the job. . . . You know, as a black man, he never knew when he would be laid off. If I could change this system, I'd make it so my children would have a chance, have a father who could get a decent job, live in a nice neighborhood, and get a good education—go to college and become a doctor or somethin'—who knows? It would be good to have a chance. I don't want welfare; I don't like the way they [the social workers] treat you. . . like you're lazy. Do they know what it feels like to be poor all of your life and to know unless something changes your children will be poor too?

Suddenly, the informant refers to herself as poor, as she speaks of the embarrassment experienced in collecting welfare. She then describes her own history, her future, and the future of her children in bleak terms, tempered with a sense of strained hope:

When I was growing up, things were hard in our house. There was never enough money, no matter how hard my father worked. But things didn't seem quite as bad then— maybe because you didn't see so many people with so much. That's the problem with the children now. They see how other people have so much and it doesn't seem like they worked hard for it or anything, and. . . well the kids now want it too and are willing to do anything to get things—to look like everybody else. . . . But you know, I think back to how hard things were for me growing up, and I don't really see that things are better for me. To tell the truth, I don't know what will happen to my children. Growing up in this neighborhood with crime and seeing a lot of other people just makin' it, I just don't know. I think maybe, though, if I can kind of get things together, you know, before they become teenagers, they might be able to make it.

Most importantly, many families in poverty, as this informant suggests, feel that poverty equals isolation, despite familial support systems. The husband of the informant noted:

> If you're poor and if you don't have much education—and if you are poor you probably don't have much education—you sometimes don't know where to get help. Rich people have all kinds of loopholes and act as though it is something when a poor person just wants one. For example, I was applying for this job and was trying to fill out the application]. They [personnel staff] could tell I needed the job. Nobody would help me. If you are poor, you are out here on your own, especially up here [in the North]. Down South, at least somebody made sure you and your children ate. Even when there is help for poor people, it's not good help. . . you know the kind of help that you would get if you were in a better part of town, if you weren't black, and if you had more money. To be black and poor, . . . man, people give you so little respect! If you're black with a little money, things may not be too bad, or if you're white and poor, at least if you can pull yourself up a little, you have the race thing going for you. But black and poor, forget it! What am I going to tell my children, work hard and you can make it? They would look at me like I am out of my mind! Let's say they did believe that they could make it. Who's goin' show them how?

As these commentaries suggest, poverty is expensive in the loss of human capital available in two generations within this family of five. Perhaps what makes the outcome of poverty so much worse for children and adults living in poverty is the sense of alienation and isolation in the midst of problems, inability to identify and use resources effectively, and feelings of hopelessness resulting from more than one or two generations of poverty. Poverty creates inertia around achievement, and when the issue of race is added, children and families may feel that the risks required to move out of poverty, given their culture, may very well result in a situation that is no better, just different. With few opportunities to see how people "make it" as Ogbu (1987) might call it, these children and their parents proceed through life with a restricted knowledge of the possibilities and about how different African Americans and others whom they might want to emulate negotiate the complex experiences of learning, schooling, survival, success, and racism. Informant 2 makes this point:

Poor children just don't see anybody doing any better than they are. My daughter used to say she wanted to be a teacher. That's when she liked her teacher. Since then, she has been having problems in school, and I can't help her. I don't even feel comfortable [confronting] the teacher. She [daughter] has no idea how she can become a teacher. I don't know what I would have to do for her to become a teacher. But, you know, her teacher doesn't live around here. The people she sees are hard-working without much to show for it or not working at all. If she becomes a teacher or makes it out of this neighborhood, it will be because she knew how to dream. My only reason for wanting to improve my reading is to help her. I mean not just with her schoolwork but help myself so I can help her. I think maybe I can get a good job, you know with my GED or somethin' and expose her to some things. . . because I would have the money and know a little more about things. I don't want my daughter to end up with nothin', dropping out of school, getting into trouble.

Research on poverty points to a variety of negative effects for children and adults in poor families. For children the impact may range from difficulties in cognitive development to behavioral problems resulting in crime, poor school performance, and school dropout (Krein & Beller, 1988; Hare & Castenell, 1985). Adults in poor families do not fare much better. In two-parent families in poverty, fathers in the family experience problems in not being able to provide adequately for the family. This problem is exacerbated for African American men who find it more difficult to obtain jobs and to keep them. In addition to an unbalanced economy, many potential employers of African American men and others do not reside in or near urban areas where poverty is most obvious. To reach the job, people with little income must manipulate travel and funds to reach jobs that may be paying minimum wage.

Research suggests that for mothers who are heads of their households, the picture is much the same as that of the fathers— both feeling incapacitated by inadequate income (McLoyd, 1990). Poor women who are the sole providers for their households experience greater stress, feelings of inferiority, emotional problems, and difficulties with parenting. The lack of income and the absence of a second person to participate in decisionmaking for children together present single mothers with apparently insurmountable obstacles that may affect parenting. Informant 2 states:

> I am sometimes so impatient with my daughter. . . and my son. Maybe if there was someone to help me, I wouldn't be so mean. I could be a better parent. If I could get a good job and have somebody to help me with them [the two children], I know I would try to be involved with them different. The truth is when I don't have any money, I don't even want to see them. I hate seeing them without, you know, and knowing that I don't have the skills to help give them a way out. I hate feeling like I can't help them.

Through direct reference or inference, both informants identified education and literacy as important. Both suggested that people who are educated are not poor or as poor as they. However, neither typically has the opportunity to be in the presence of well-educated people and when one has, she is not positioned to learn about the experiences of the people. Thus, the parents have little knowledge of what an alternative lifestyle to poverty might involve, or what the range of possibilities is with adequate literacy. Although both referred to a cousin or other family member who had "made it," neither seemed to analyze what made the difference for this person, i.e., why this family member surmounted economic hardship or how literacy is needed or used. Literacy and education are seen as contributing to economic stability but not the primary motivator for success. The next section asks what role the parents feel literacy plays in poverty and in their children's ability to find a way out of their current circumstances.

Importance and Accessibility of Literacy

Many in society assign intrinsic value to literacy and education; yet, others see literacy and education in their purely utilitarian functions. In this second case, the concept, "Get a good job, get a good education," is dominant as a basis for trying, a motivator for many. It helps to answer questions about the importance of literacy. In other instances, parents and children may well ask what Informant 1 asked: "[What value does literacy hold] when even the most well educated African Americans have been discriminated against?" How if at all does a young, second-generation poor mother reconcile the admonitions to get a good education and the perceptions of the importance of literacy with the realities of daily poverty?

The relationship between poverty and low literacy is a part of the discourse of the two informants. Their comments reflect the same inconsistencies found in research and popular discussions, some of which attribute low literacy to poverty while others attribute poverty to low literacy. Both informants agreed that literacy should be functional, e.g., help people get jobs. Both described their literacy as low; neither can read a book for children up to seven with ease. Informant 2 has sought assistance from a formal literacy program. Each attended the literacy workshop regularly, stating in Informant 2's words, "maybe [the parents] could help themselves and their children."

Literacy is described as something that separates the world into those who will make it and those who won't. Informant 1 stated:

> If I had been a better student, I wouldn't be poor, at least not as poor, I don't think. But, you know, my husband finished school, and he has been laid off, laid off, more than once, and he is poor. I do think that if you have reading and writing you have a better chance, but if you are poor, no one seems to take you seriously. In school, the way teachers teach make you not want to learn, make reading seem hard. Then [the stories] weren't even interesting. It would have been nice to read that a girl like me made it out of the ghetto and be able to understand what I had read. I am going to go and take some classes to improve my reading—as soon as my baby goes to Head Start. Maybe if they [her children] see me reading, they will want to read, too, and make it out of this neighborhood. But education gives you one way out, and some people do it.

Beside the fact that the last two sentences in Informant 1's commentary could well be a commercial for literacy, the poignant nature of her experience in school appears to have dictated the course of her life experience. In other meetings, she demonstrated some shame about her inability to read. For this parent, an intensive program of assistance would be needed to provide her and her family with strategies for learning and "making it." The informant not only recognizes the potential seriousness of intergenerational low literacy but also expresses a degree of self-determination about her ability to be a model of literacy for her children. In subsequent interviews, the informant discloses that her desire to seek literacy is not matched by knowledge about how to gain access to programs that are responsive to her needs as a young low-literate, caring, African American mother and wife. The association between low literacy and poverty is echoed by Informant 2:

> When you are poor, you don't feel that you can achieve anything. So, even if you go to school, you have no reason to pay attention to the teacher or take reading and writing seriously. Your friends from the neighborhood are telling you to do something other than learn to read. That's because they aren't doing [well] in school either. But then, there are some kids who do listen to their parents who tell them to study, and they do okay. Some of them make it, but some of them have other family who help them. For example, there was this girl in my block who was good in school. She would go down South every summer and come back telling us about her important cousins and stuff. I think going down South helped her. She finished school and went to college, I think. To make it, you had to think you were better than anybody else in the neighborhood . . . being good with books was one thing that made you different. But what child can see that far into the future?

Although literacy's utility is alluded to throughout the interviews, the significance of literacy as a contributing factor out of poverty was highlighted particularly by Informant 1, after she was asked to respond to what was a frequently referenced statement in African American communities, "An education is somethin' no one can take away from you; it is your possession":

> You know, that's right. What I would like my children to understand is that they don't have to be poor—that literacy is theirs for the tryin'. The problem isn't that I don't know what to say to them; it's that I don't know

how to back up what I'm saying. Old people use to tell us to work hard in school, but [in truth], some of us weren't taught much reading in school. People who are literate and well educated, they run the world, but how many of them started off poor. I don't mean their white grandparents, I mean them. What I am going to tell my children is that they have to do good work in school, and I need to be able to help them. If you are [literate], I think you just know better where to find the things you need. You don't have to be as embarrassed as if you are poor and illiterate.

The parameters of literacy are also confusing. What makes a person literate? How do you know when you are literate enough or how literacy can shape goals? It is not clear that the informants have responded to these questions in any meaningful way. When asked about the aspirations for their children, one informant responded that she hopes her son will make it in the military. The other wanted her son to be a doctor, and the other wants her daughter to be a teacher. The problem for these two families may lie in the fact that neither has any notion of what is required for the children to achieve those goals, and unless there is support, they will be unable to guide their children. Equally alarming is that the parents feel unable to help their children navigate their lives out of poverty. This is not surprising, since neither informant has had role models or resources with whom to discuss this issue.

Both informants have siblings who have high school diplomas. Parents of both informants have no more than eight years of schooling and what appears to be limited literacy skills. One informant stated that her father had grown up in a small, southern, rural town, where there were 50 children in a class, and that "nobody learned to read too well." Thus, the issue of intergenerational literacy for this informant may center on intergenerational access, i.e., availability of resources, that does not reside simply in the literacy of parents and children but also in the response of schools and society to issues of poverty and limited opportunity.

Persistence, Intergenerational Poverty, and Literacy

In a series of interviews conducted in a separate study with 25 African American adults, 78–90, and their children, persistence has emerged as a primary theme of the families. Several features of persistence as described by the informants in the study make it worth pursuing and make it applicable as a context for the present discussion. First, the informants have conceptualized persistence as culture-embedded, unique to African Americans. Second, persistence is a planful program of preparation, in which coping, intrinsic motivation, and resiliency are subsets. Third, persistence encompasses a form of metacognition in which the individual charts his or her future in light of racism, regulates his or her activity, and monitors his or her ability to surmount obstacles.

While much of the literature on families and on black families specifically focus on resilience within the unit and on the resilience demonstrated by children and adults in poverty and other stressful home situations, relatively little work speaks to the issue of persistence outside of motivation within school contexts—within communities and with learning. For the 25 older informants in the study, persistence refers to emotional and human stamina—to insist on education for their children, to insist on learning to read, to continue with a belief in schools and the people in them, and to seek alternatives to human and educational plight when faced with it. Persistence also refers to the immutability of aspirations associated with literacy beliefs, practices, and strategies and their transformation within families over time, as a result of migration and a variety of life events. In this work, the need for persistence is described as inherent to the African American experience.

What was absent from much of the discussion with the PCLP informants was the notion of persistence. This may be true just as a result of urban life and the poverty that is associated with it. It may be true, in part, because of isolation—what Informant 2 described about the girl in her block whose family ensured that she maintained a relationship with the larger family network through visits to the South annually. Yet another explanation may be found in the nature of communities and the resources within those communities that can reinforce the importance of literacy and guide young parents and their children to ways out of poverty.

This sense of community and the function of neighborhoods has only been counterproductive for African Americans in the past decade or so. Throughout history the value of literacy was attached to the community and the products of learning were shared there, as evident in the commentary of the son of an 83 year-old informant:

> If there was one thing that my parents taught me, it was to think about what and who I wanted to be: how do you make it, well you begin by reading. What made a difference in our little country community was that we knew everybody— you know the principal could just as soon come to your house as your kin. The other thing was that our parents expected us to demonstrate that we were learning something and what we were learning. Educated or not, many parents wanted to hear children read and made them read; they trusted schools in a way that their children find it hard. The encouragement they gave us said that we had to persist in the face of difficulty and that persistence was tied to the struggle of . . . not black people in general but to the values of our small community. Don't get me wrong, not everything was pleasant, not everyone cared equally. But, I think people who were not successful saw their failures as individual, not family, and kind of kept hope for their sisters and brothers and their own children.

These and other views of what I have called the message of persistence are embedded in the meanings that many African Americans attach to literacy, particularly within poverty. So whether educated or successful, "you had a plan," sometimes an intuitive sense of the journey of learning and living, not necessarily a part of the experiences of many young, poor African American families.

Conclusion

The problems facing children, parents, and families in
poverty are not limited to problems in literacy. However, there is
some indication that poverty mediates literacy and vice versa.
There is evidence to suggest, from interdisciplinary domains of
study, that education and improved literacy result in greater
access to jobs for some African Americans (e.g., Mikulecky,
1982). There is also ample evidence to suggest that where low
literacy is a problem, access to higher level jobs is limited (e.g.,
Ferguson, 1992). There is anecdotal evidence, at least, to indicate
that African American children from low-income homes are
acutely aware of the limitations of literacy and their ability to
move out of their neighborhoods and out of poverty. Here lies
much of the problem, to move out of low literacy and poverty,
children and families may need to move out of neighborhoods.
As the commentaries of the informants suggest, the likelihood
that this could happen and the possibility that their economic
well-being or literacy can be improved substantially within the
next generation seem slim.

There is cross-disciplinary evidence that holds that
traditions in African American families and culture, despite the
experiences of the group, encourage education, literacy, and
persistence as a means to personal access, community respect,
and social mobility. Then, sometimes there is the resonating
claim that the goals for reducing poverty and increasing the
levels of literacy for children and adults may be unrealistic.
Gordon (1970), in referring to the expectations of Head Start
children, cautioned that it is a mistake to say to children, "The
school is your hope because it is there you will learn the skills
and competencies that will help you get out of poverty;" it may
not be so. Yet, there is the almost uncanny reality that in the face
of poverty, poor schools, limited literacy within families, and
social barriers such as discrimination, disproportionate numbers
of African American children and parents persist in their
educational and literacy development. In fact, these children and
their families appear to survive in spite of the system, not
because of it. The reasons are unfolding but require research that

examines the multiple sides of poverty and low literacy and the nature of family organization and the intergenerational effect.

Research efforts need to be directed at understanding more about families and learning more about the specific features of poverty that impede or encourage literacy development intergenerationally. This requires that families be studied as they live, not as they oppose traditional or mainstream family patterns. A critical question that might be asked is how do culture and family functions provide for educational assistance. A second might focus on the impact of existing practices and concepts within the African American community, e.g., kinship and family communities. Embedded in these questions are factors in family development that contribute to persistence in literacy learning that may hold promise for reducing literacy as a major mediating effect of poverty.

Despite thirty years of programs to improve the lives of African American children and families, children in poverty, and low-literate adults, we are faced in the United States with persistently high poverty rates and low literacy rates. What has been standard across the years is that social policy for minorities, the disenfranchised, and dispossessed has been defined within a poverty-centered rather than family or culture-centered perspective. Thus, the strengths of families are unavailable and the cultural traditions of families lie outside the development of policies. Literacy and policies cannot be limited to poverty or literacy or to short-term responses to the problem. What is needed is a commitment to developmental approaches to assist families in need and in crisis, approaches that provide parents and families with intensive learning assistance and give parents opportunities to develop the necessary literacy skills to move out of poverty and support their children in meaningful ways. Such policies would build on parents' desires to improve their own lives and secure the future for their children. Most important, such policies may begin to mitigate against the negative effects of low literacy, poverty, and isolation, using African American cultural legacies of community and supporting community institutions as a means to sustaining growth.

Acknowledgment

This work was supported by funding from the National Center on Adult Literacy at the University of Pennsylvania, which is part of the Educational Research and Development Center Program (Grant No. R117Q00003) as administered by the Office of Educational Research and Improvement, U.S. Department of Education, in cooperation with the Departments of Labor and Health and Human Services. The opinions expressed here do not necessarily reflect the position or policies of the National Center on Adult Literacy, the Office of Educational Research and Improvement, or the U.S. Department of Education. Portions of this paper were presented in an invited Roundtable, "Children of Poverty," at the Biennial Meeting of the Society for Research in Child Development, New Orleans, LA, April, 1991, and at a social policy Roundtable, "African-American Male Labor Force Participation and Family Formation, co-sponsored by the Center for the Study of Social Policy and the Philadelphia Children's Network, Washington, DC, November, 1993.

REFERENCES

Ainsworth, M. D., & Bell, S. M . (1969). Some contemporary patterns of mother-infant interaction in the feeding situation. In A. Ambrose (Ed.), *Stimulation in early infancy*. New York: Academic Press.

Anderson, E. (1990). *Streetwise: Race, class, and change in an urban community*. Chicago: University of Chicago Press.

Anderson, J. (1988). *The education of blacks in the South*. Chapel Hill: University of North Carolina Press.

Auerbach, E. R. (1989). Toward a socio-context approach to family literacy. *Harvard Educational Review*, 59, 165–187.

Baydar, N., Brooks- Gunn, J., & Furstenberg, F. F. (1994). Early warning signs of functional illiteracy: Predictors in childhood and adolescence. *Child Development, 64*, 815–829.

Berlin, G., & Sum, A. (1988). *Toward a more perfect union: basic skills, poor families, and our economic future* (Occasional paper No. 3). New York: Ford Foundation, Project on Social We;fare and the American Future.

Billingsley, A. (1993). *Research on the African-American family: A holistic perspective.* Westport, CT: Auburn House.

Brizidus, J.A., & Foster, S. E. (1993). *Generation to generation. Realizing the promise of family literacy.* Sponsored by the National Center on Family Literacy. Ypsilanti, MI: High/Scope Press.

Cervera, N. (1991). Unwed teenage pregnancy: Family relationships with the father of the baby. *Family in Society, 72*, 29–37.

Chase-Lansdale, P. L. (1993). The impact of poverty on family process. *The Child, Youth, and Family Services Quarterly, 16* Washington, DC: Division 37, American Psychological Association.

Chase-Lansdale, P. L., Brooks-Gunn, J., & Paikoff, R. (1991). Research and programs for adolescent mothers: Missing links and future promises. *Family Relations, 40*, 396–404.

Cherlin, A. J. (in press). Child care and the Family Support Act: Policy issues. In P. L. Chase-Lansdale & J. Brooks-Gunn (Eds.), *Escape from poverty: What makes a difference for poor children?* New York: Cambridge University Press.

Children's Defense Fund (1991). *Child poverty in America.* Washington, DC: Children's Defense Fund.

Coleman, J. S., Campbell, E. Q., Hobson, C. J., McPartland, J. M., Mood, A., Weinfeld, F. D., & York, R. L. (1966). *Equality of educational opportunity.* Washington, DC: U.S. Government Printing Office.

Duncan, G. J., & Rogers, W. L. (1988). Longtudinal aspects of poverty. *Journal of Marriage and Family, 50*, 1007–1021.

Ferguson, R. (1992). Social and economic prospects of African American males: Why reading, math, and social development should be leadership priorities. In B. W. Austin (Ed). *What a piece of work is man: A discussion of issues affecting African American men and boys* (pp. 81–114). Battle Creek, MI: W. K. Kellogg Foundation.

Furstenberg, F., Brooks-Gunn, J., & Morgan, S. P. (1987). *Adolescent mothers in later life.* New York: Cambridge University Press.

Furstenberg, F., & Harris, L. (1993). When fathers matter/why fathers matter: The impact of paternal involvement on the offspring of adolescent mothers. In A. Lawson & B. L.. Rhodes (Eds.). *The politics of pregnancy: Adolescent sexuality and public policy* (pp. 189–215). New Haven, CT: Yale University Press.

Gadsden, V. L. (1993). Literacy, education, and identity of African Americans: The communal nature of learning. *Urban Education, 27,* 352–369.

Gadsden, V. L., & Edwards, P. A. (1993). Defining literacy. In A. Purves (Ed.), *Encyclopedia of English studies and language arts.*

Gadsden, V. L., & Philadelphia Children's Network (1993). The absence of father: Effects on children's development and family functioning. Paper presented at the Policy Roundtable on "Labor force participation and family formation." Sponsored by the Center of the Study of Social Policy and the Philadelphia Children's Network.

Garmezy, N., & Rutter, M. (Eds.). (1983). *Stress, coping and development in children.* New York: McGraw-Hill.

Gordon, E. (1970). Theoretical and practical problems in compensatory education as an antidote to poverty. In V. L. Allen (Ed.). *Psychological factors of poverty.* Chicago: Markham Publications.

Hare, B. R., & Castelnell, L. A. (1985). No place to run, no place to hide: Comparative status and future prospects of black boys. In M. B. Spencer, G. K. Brookins, & W. R. Allen (Eds.), *Beginnings: The social and affective development of black children* (pp. 185–200). Hillsdale, NJ: Erlbaum.

Heath, S. B. (1983). *Ways with words.* Cambridge: Cambridge University Press.

Hess, R. D., & Holloway, S. D. (1984). Family and school as educational institutions. In R. D. Parke (Ed.), *Review of Child Development Research: The Family*, vol. 77 (pp. 179–222). Chicago, IL: University of Chicago Press.

Hill, M. S., & Duncan, G. J. (1987). Parental family income and the socio-economic attainment of children. *Social Science Research, 16,* 39–73.

Hill, R. (1972). *The strengths of black families.* New York: Emerson-Hall.

Holt, T. (1990). Knowledge is power: The black struggle for literacy. In A. A. Lunsford, H. Moglan, & J. Slevin (Eds.), *The right to literacy.* New York: Modern Language Association.

Katz, M. B. (Ed.). (1993). *The "Underclass" debate: Views from history.* Princeton, NJ: Princeton University.

Kelly, R. F., & Ramsey, S. H. (1991). Poverty, children, and public policies. *Journal of Family Issues, 12,* 388–403.

Krein, S. F., & Beller, A. H. (1988). Educational attainment of children from single-parent families: Differences by exposure, gender, and race. *Demography*, *25*, 221–234.

La Fromboise, T. D., & Low, K. G. (1989). American Indian children and adolescents. In J. T. Gibbs & L. N. Huang (Eds.), *Children of color* (pp. 114–147). San Francisco, CA: Jossey-Bass.

Lamb, M. E. (1987). *The father's role: Cross-cultural perspectives*. New York: John Wiley.

Lamb, M. E., & Elster, A. B. (1985). Adolescent mother-infant-father relationships. *Developmental Psychology*, *21*, 768–773.

Matsen, A., Morison, P., Pellegrini, D., & Tellegen, A. (1991). Competence under stress: Risk and protective factors. In J. Rolf, A. Masten, D. Cichetti, K. Nuechterlein, & S. Weintraub (Eds.), *Risk and protective factors in the development of psychopathology*. Cambridge: Cambridge University Press.

McAdoo, H. P. (1991). *Black families*. Newbury Park, CA: Sage.

McLoyd, V. C. (1990). The impact of economic hardship on Black families and children. *Child Development*, *61* 311–346.

Milulecky, L. J. (1982). Job literacy: The relationship between school preparation and workplace actuality. *Reading Research Quarterly*, *17*, 400–419.

Miller, A. T. (1993). Social science, social policy, and the heritage of African-American families. In M.B. Katz (Ed.), *The "Underclass" debate: Views from history*. Princeton, NJ: Princeton University.

Moynihan, D. P. (1965). *The Negro family: The case for national action*. Washington, DC: U.S. Department of Labor, Office of Policy, Planning, and Research.

National Commission on Children. (1991). *Beyond rhetoric: A new American agenda for children and families*. Washington, DC: U.S. Government Printing Office.

Ogbu, J. (1987). Variability in minority school performance: A problem in search of an explanation. *Anthropology and Education Quarterly*, *18*, 312–334.

Palmer, J. L., Smeeding, T., & Torrey, B. B. (Eds.). (1988). *The vulnerable*. Washington, DC: Urban Institute Press.

Pelligrini, A. D., Brody, G. H., & Sigel, I. (1985). Parents' book-reading habits with their children. *Journal of Educational Psychology*, *77*, 332–340.

Powell, D. (1991). *Strengthening parental contributions to school readiness and early school learning: Expanding theories of adult literacy participation*. Technical Report 92-1, National Center on Adult Literacy, University of Pennsylvania, Philadelphia, PA.

Ramey, C. T., Bryant, D. M., Sparling, J. J., & Wasik, B. H. (1985). Project CARE: A comparison of two early intervention strategies to prevent retarded development. *Topics in Early Childhood Special Education, 5,* 12–25.

Reder, S., Wikelund, K. R., & Hart-Landsburg, S. (1992). *Expanding theories of adult literacy participation* (Technical report No. 92-1). University of Pennsylvania, National Center on Adult Literacy.

RMC Corporation. (1992). *Literacy, families, and programs.* Workshop draft. Portsmouth, NH: RMC Corporation.

Schieffelin, B. B., & Cochran-Smith, M. (1984). Learning to read culturally: Literacy before schooling. In H. Goelman, A. Oberg, & F. Smith (Eds.), *Awakening to literacy* (pp. 3–23). Portsmouth, NH: Heinemann.

Smith, M. S. (1983). Training poverty mothers in communication skills. In D. Taylor (Ed.), *Family literacy* (pp. 360–367). Portsmouth, NH: Heinemann.

Snow, C. E., Barnes, W. S., Chanler, J., Goodman, I. F., & Hemphill, L. (1991). *Unfulfilled expectations: Home and school influences on literacy.* Cambridge, MA: Harvard University Press.

Spencer, M. B., Brookins, G. K., & Allen, W. R. (Eds.). (1985). *Beginnings: The social and affective development of children.* Hillsdale, NJ: Erlbaum.

Sulzby, E., & Edwards, P. A. (in press). The role of parents in supporting literacy development of young children. In B. Spodek & O. N. Saracho (Eds.), *Yearbook in early childhood education: Volume 4, Early childhood language and literacy.* New York: Teachers College Press.

Sum, A., & Fogg, N. (1990). The changing economic features of young black men in America. *Black Scholar,* January–March, 47–53.

Survey Research Center (1984). *User guide to the Panel Study of Income Dynamics.* Ann Arbor: Inter-University Consortium for Political and Social Research, University of Michigan.

Taylor, D., & Dorsey-Gaines, C. (1988). *Growing up literate: Learning from inner city families.* Portsmouth, NH: Heinemann.

Taylor, D., & Strickland, D. S., (1986). Family literacy: Myths and magic. In M. Sampson (Ed.), *The pursuit of literacy: Early reading and writing.* Dubuque, IA: Kendall/Hunt.

Trotter, J. W. (1993). Blacks in the urban North: The "Underclass Question" in historical perspective. In M. B. Katz (Ed.), *The "Underclass" debate: Views from history.* Princeton, NJ: Princeton University.

U.S. Bureau of the Census. (1991). Poverty in the United States: 1990. *Current population reports. Series P-60.* Washington, DC: U.S. Government Printing Office.

————. (1992). Marriage status and living arrangements. *Current population studies. Series P-20.* Washington, DC: U.S. Government Printing Office.

Van Fossen, S., & Sticht, T. G. (1991). *Teach the mother and reach the child: Results of the Intergenerational Literacy Action Research Project.* Washington, DC: Wider Opportunities for Women.

Vosler, N. R., & Proctor, E. K. (1991). Family structure and stressors in a child guidance clinic population. *Families in Society, 72,* 164–173.

Wigfield, A., & Asher, S. R. (1984). Home, school, and reading achievement: A social motivational analysis. In P. D. Pearson, R. Barr, M. L. Kamil, and P. Mosenthal (Eds.), *Handbook of reading research* (pp. 423–452). New York: Longman.

Wilson, W. J. (1988). American social policy and the ghetto underclass. *Dissent, 35,* 57–64.

*   *   *

Round Table Discussion

Randolph. We have had very little discussion about gender effects and given the issue of problems facing young Black males in this society, particularly in education. There are now more Black males in prison than in college. Is it anecdotal evidence or is there now research evidence to support that there is some differential experience for Black males in the educational process?

Gadsden. There is evidence to suggest that Black boys are treated differently. Depending on the slant, the findings may be surprising. The most recent evidence that I read actually is coming out soon. It speaks quite specifically about the differences in treatment of young Black boys and the fact that there is a fear; that is, some may fear Black boys. There are negative expectations, even when the Black boy is clearly academically successful. In a study by Slaughter-Defoe and Richards, particular study, the young boy is in first grade. So, the response is not even a function of his physical appearance, his strength or his physical prowess. It's simply that he is black and the projection is for him to be an older Black male who is potentially dangerous. But we also had that same discussion in a study that I am doing that looks at issues, looks at social distance, and the impact of geographic distance also on relationships across generations, particularly the messages that are conveyed across generations about persistence and self-valuing and about community. Much of this is based on Glen Elder's work. We are attempting to look at the messages that mothers convey to daughters and mothers convey to sons and fathers to daughters and to sons. And, in this study, we find that the messages that fathers claim they are trying to convey to their sons is actually quite different from what they convey to their daughters—it is just the reverse of what you might expect in some cases—fathers telling their sons, preparing their sons for the fact that they are going to be feared. We don't know any culture that wants to encourage their sons to think of themselves as feared individuals. You see the impact of that as the kids move into general society. There's a growing body of evidence about relationships.

Brooks Gunn. Are mothers also talking to their sons? About fear? It's not just the fathers, right?

Randolph. Mothers, however, at least in the study we are looking at, are also conveying freedom messages about the children's ability to overcome some of the obstacles, both the boys and the girls. But, there is what I call, "boot camp" in some cases for the boys, in preparing them for rejection and for humiliation once they get into society. Not so much in the experiences in schools because in general, experiences in schools are not getting fixed. So, the expectation is that they are going to have problems in society but it is not translated as an expectation of what will happen when the kids get in school.

Ramey. It seems to me that we have a very difficult task for a field and that we are trying to do two different things that, I think, sometimes tend to confuse. One is we need to do a better job of understanding within group values, mores, styles, whether you lump these groups as ethnic groups, or lump them as cultural groups. It's clear that there are substantial differences. At the same time, I believe, that we need to focus on the differences within these groups, particularly in reference to this round table with respect to varying levels of resources available to members within each group or to the different modes of behavior that will be encouraged. So, whether it is crosscut by gender or crosscut by any of the structural characteristics, there's still this issue that a lack of resources, be they economic or what frequently translates into inadequate educational experiences, tends to be associated with not doing well even within a particular ethnic or cultural subgroup. I am struck when I look at all the evidence from around the world and at our own crosscultural work that there is almost no society where I can find a clear example of people who have very limited resources doing substantially better as a group than people who have a lot of resources. There's almost a universal there and somehow when we have these conversations, I think we have to bring these two things constantly into focus. The point made earlier about classifying African American children as disadvantaged is just wanton linguistic use and bad research.

Gadsden. Could you call that racism and discrimination?

Ramey. I think that there is no question that there is substantial racism in this and many other cultures. I don't think the United States is at all unique in this. But, even on top of the issues of racism and sexism, there are the issues of resource differences and I think we have to understand whether the forms of the relationships between having low or high levels of resources turn out to be the same or different as we go across different cultural subgroups or different ethnic groups and my reading of the literature at this point would make a sweeping generalization that I hope would become a lightning rod statement would lead to me to put many qualifiers on it. I find in almost every circumstance that people who have had more resources economically do better.

Gadsden. On what?

Ramey. They do better with respect to health status, with respect to performance, and whatever the educational system is that they're in. They tend to be more physically fit, they're taller. What the challenge is, I think, is to find the exceptions to what I'm proposing as a near universal rule and then to understand how that could be the case.

García-Coll. Craig, I agree with you that it is almost universal, the notion that if you have less resources, you do less well. The problem that I have is with stopping there and saying therefore we should get more resources to people. I think that one of the problems is the notion that when there are limited resources, the solution to the problem is in the resources. Then, what happens is usually that people believe that everyone just needs more income, more resources. What that does is negate the notion that peoples' experience of poverty is so different that putting food in front of them is going to be a completely different experience for those who are expecting to have it for the rest of their lives, as compared to those who are just experiencing it for the first time.

What I am saying is that we need to put resources and racism together. We can't just stay with one of them. You can't just say it's only racism, and if racism is gone then everything is going to be fine. So, we'll just be nice to Black people and everything will be great. We need to emphasize that the two things really have to be integrally together all the time for everything, for research, for policy, and for services.

Lamberty. One of my central ideas is that the distribution of resources, the distribution of rewards in this country is based upon the system of social stratification that is in place. And, the social stratification system in place is based essentially on two ascriptive characteristics: racism and ethnicity. So, if you're Black, if you're Puerto Rican, the chances are that in the distribution of the rewards, leaving everything the same, you are going to get less. So, not only do you have to be considering more equity, more equity in the distribution of the work, you have to make fundamental changes in the social stratification system. The changes that we have to make, have to be changes that impact decisively on the way that racism is used.

Ramey. What you are saying is clear. I don't want to go away having confused. I am saying there are two things that need to be considered simultaneously. One is, and we'll put it in statistical terms for a moment, that there are mean differences in things like income, amount of education. Those mean differences go across different ethnic and cultural groups. That is likely indeed to be tied up very intimately with discrimination, with historical factors of nonequality, etc. That we must address. We also have to address the fact that within each of those groups there are people who have become very successful and people who are not successful at all, by any standard, whether you apply the standards that are particular to a given culture, whether you do it with a wonderful sensitive graphic research, whether by giving a bunch of tests. And, that variation within as well as across needs to be understood simultaneously if we are to come up with an understanding of the causal factors that operate, so that we can time and place various interventions, be they new laws or be they particular programs for children and families. So, that we can test whether these ideas we have for improving the quality of life really work out. I think that nothing less than that can allow us to have clear insights.

Lamberty. You forget the fact that racism is not only part of the United States structure. It is everywhere. The valuation that you are seeing in terms of resources might be a function of the same thing that is happening here. It is European in nature.

Gadsden. I think that the issue of quality of life is very important. One of the things that we have noticed in our own project is that whenever we talk about issues, whenever we report anything other than poverty-related measures, poverty related issues, there is resistance. When we talk about the problems that parents have in schools, the fear that they have that their children will not be able to make a living; when we talk about thinking about different family configurations and what that might mean, whether it involves the relationship between schools and parents, there was total resistance. That's because we do have to deal with the institutional forces that work against as well as for these children. We do have to talk about racism! We do have to talk about racist attitudes in people in the schools. I think we must be looking at two things. One, is that the family needs to be looked at historically, the children need to looked at within the family, and the families need to be looked at within an historical context. The second thing is that there is a major need for systemic change not just for African American children but for all children in poverty. People cannot really expect poor families to do more than any family is able to do. Poor families have fewer resources. We expect them, if they want to make their lives better, to figure out how to do many more things than we can. A fine example is that I put everything in my American Express which I often forget to mail in on time. But my American Express card is never taken from me. I am not punished when I don't adhere to the system. Poor families are punished. And, behaviors of poor families are seen in many ways that simply are not the same if you have more money. So, there is an issue of the availability of resources but there is another issue about perceptions, about cultures and context, within which these families develop.

CHAPTER 5

Socioeconomic Status and Alcoholism: The Contextual Structure of Developmental Pathways to Addiction

Hiram E. Fitzgerald and Robert A. Zucker

> *The evils resulting from the abuse of alcohol were never so prevalent as at present, and are now traceable in the diseases of youth, as well as in those of adult existence. Amongst the results of the killing pace at which the race of life is too generally run, from its start to its finish, one of the most serious is, that the period of childhood has become so abridged, in many instances, by the necessity of entering on the struggle for existence before the sufficient development of the moral, mental, and physical powers, that a premature break-down in any of these is no longer exceptional.* (Madden, 1884, p. 358).

The societal consequences of alcohol abuse and alcoholism are very great, and beyond those imaginable even by Madden (1884). In 1994, economic costs related to alcohol abuse and dependence are estimated to exceed 100 billion dollars annually (Rice, Kellman, & Miller, 1991; Parker & Harford, 1992). Human costs of the effects of alcohol abuse and alcoholism are even greater. Of the more than 16 million Americans who meet DSM-III-R diagnostic criteria for alcohol abuse or dependence, approximately 100,000 die annually from alcohol related causes (Grant, Harford, Chou, et al., 1991). Estimates of the number of children of alcoholics (COAs) in the United States range as high as 28 million (Russell, Henderson, & Blume, 1985), with COAs six to ten times more likely to develop drinking problems than are nonCOAs (Cotton, 1979). Alcohol abuse and alcoholism are linked to a wide variety of health problems including liver cirrhosis, pancreatitis, various neurological, cardiovascular, and endocrine disorders, cancer, disorders involving the reproductive system, and gross as well as subtle teratogenic damage to the fetus (Day, 1992). In addition, there is evidence indicating that alcohol nonspecific factors may be as important as alcohol-specific factors in setting COAs on a developmental pathway leading to maladaptive functioning (Zucker & Fitzgerald, 1991a). COAs are more likely than nonCOAs to live in households characterized by high rates of family violence as well as other forms of antisocial behavior (Martin, 1992). Data from the National Institute of Mental Health (NIMH) Epidemiologic Catchment Area study of the United States adult population indicated that comorbidities, excluding drug disorders, occur in 37 percent of the alcohol abuse/dependent population (Regier et al., 1990). Such comorbidities include antisocial personality disorder, bipolar disorder, schizophrenia, panic disorder, obsessive-compulsive disorder, affective disorder, and anxiety disorder. Clearly, being reared by an alcoholic parent exposes the child to a host of factors that may induce, facilitate, or maintain developmental pathways (Gottlieb, 1991) to substance abuse and related psychopathological behavior.

The Michigan State University–University of Michigan Longitudinal Study

Our purpose in this chapter is to illustrate how socioeconomic status variables, particularly as indexed by family income, may help to structure the developmental pathways to which COAs are exposed. Since our illustrations involve some of the data from the Michigan State University–University of Michigan (MSU–UM) Longitudinal Study (Zucker, Noll, & Fitzgerald, 1986; Zucker & Fitzgerald, 1991b) a brief overview of this ongoing study is in order. Three groups of families are participating: (a) court-recruited alcoholics, (b) community-recruited alcoholics, and (c) community comparison families. The court-recruited alcoholic families were systematically recruited via a net of administrative arrangements with six local district courts in a four-county area covering all male drunk driving convictions. Men needed to have a blood alcohol concentration (BAC) of 0.15% (i.e., 150 mg/100 ml) or higher at the time of arrest, or a BAC of 0.12% and at least one prior alcohol related driving arrest. Eighty percent of the fathers in the alcoholic sample met a definite alcoholism diagnosis, and the remaining met a probable diagnosis on the basis of the Feighner criteria (Feighner et al., 1972). Subsequent to obtaining each alcoholic family, a matched community control family from the same census tract as the alcoholic family was located in a door-to-door canvass that began one block away from the alcoholic family. To the extent that it was possible, the control family was also selected to match the sibling composition and birth order of the alcoholic family. In the course of our work, 18,989 families were contacted. Of the 509 families with an age-appropriate male child, 475 of these were contacted and 441 agreed to participate; 215 families were ineligible due to ethnicity, socioeconomic status (SES), or parentage (i.e., non-biological); 105 were ineligible due to alcohol/drug involvement, 39 were not contacted due to successful recruitment of a comparison family. Ninety-one of these families were successfully recruited. To restrict ethnic variation that we were not able to oversample because of study locale, all subjects are nonHispanic Caucasian. The same screening procedures were used to ensure that neither the father nor the mother in a control family met either an alcoholism or drug abuse or drug dependence diagnosis. Any community control family whose father met either a probable or definite alcoholism diagnosis, was reclassified as a Community Alcoholic Family. Of the 105 families so classified, 60 were successfully recruited. Of the residual 45, all families had either moved away or separated by the time we attempted to recruit them, so acceptance rates here were actually 100 percent of the families that were available.

In accord with study exclusion criteria, no child manifested characteristics of fetal alcohol syndrome (Fitzgerald, Sullivan, Ham, et al., 1993). Specific characteristics are required for a diagnosis of FAS in three areas: (1) prenatal and/or postnatal growth retardation, (2) central nervous system involvement, and (3) characteristic facial dysmorphology. Although fetal alcohol effects (FAE: Barr, Streissguth, Darby, & Sampson, 1990) may be characteristic of these children, there are doubts as to whether such effects can be reliably documented (see Plant & Plant, 1987), and whether FAE should be used in scientific publications due to the difficulty of operationally defining such effects (Sokol & Clarren, 1989).

Although all Wave 1 data has been collected, not all of it has yet been intensively analyzed. Moreover, at the time of this report, only about 40% of Wave 2 data has been collected. Nevertheless, cross sectional Wave 1 analyses have already provided valuable information about these families. For example, a variety of analyses have documented an overall increased incidence of behavior problems (Fitzgerald, et al., 1993), hyperactivity and attention deficit (Ham, Fitzgerald, & Zucker, 1993), difficult temperament (Jansen, Fitzgerald, Ham, & Zucker, 1993) and impulsivity (Fitzgerald et al., 1993)—among the high risk 3- to 5-year olds than among the comparison children. Among these children's fathers, higher levels of drug involvement are related to higher rates of antisocial behavior, and are inversely related to level of mental health, adaptive functioning, and socioeconomic status (Gonzalez, Zucker, & Fitzgerald, under review). In addition, differences along a dimension of antisociality provide strong evidence for different developmental pathways for two types of alcoholics (Zucker, 1987), which have been labeled antisocial alcoholics (AALs) and nonantisocial alcoholics (NAALs; Zucker, Ellis & Fitzgerald, 1994). Specifically, AALs have an earlier age of onset for first alcohol problems, more alcohol related difficulties, co-occurring psychopathology, and lower achieved socioeconomic status than NAALs (Zucker et al., 1994).

Approximately 45% of wives of alcoholics also make a DSM-III-R diagnosis for alcohol abuse or dependence, and in a number of analyses involving maternal variables—particularly antisocial behavior, lifetime alcohol problems, and depression— maternal variables were more predictive of their son's behavior problems than were paternal variables. For both mothers and fathers, lifetime alcohol problems predicted child maltreatment (Muller, Fitzgerald, Sullivan, & Zucker, 1994). For fathers, social support and stress contributed independently to child maltreatment, whereas, for mothers social support seems to moderate the effects of stress on child maltreatment. Although father's lifetime alcohol problems predicted child behavior problems, the effect was moderated by a composite family psychopathology index consisting of mothers' alcohol problems, and measures of mother and father antisocial behavior, depression, and drug use (Moses, Gonzalez, Zucker, & Fitzgerald, 1993). Note that in a number of instances, socioeconomic status appears as a significant contributor to findings related either to individual or family functioning.

Socioeconomic Status and Alcohol Problems

At the point of entry into the longitudinal study, high risk families can be characterized as mid-level lower class, as indexed by family income, and as mid-range to lower level blue collar by way of occupation. Recently, Humphreys and Rappaport (1993) have argued that social science research on substance abuse is guided by researchers who accept the premise that the causes of substance abuse are to be found within the individual, not in ecological variables such as poverty or environmental stress. Their scan of PSYCHLIT for the years 1981 through 1992 yielded 170 citations pertaining to personality factors and drug addiction, but only 3 citations for drug addiction and poverty. Irrespective of Humphreys and Rappaport's position, it does not automatically follow that poverty or environmental stress cause substance abuse. That poverty or other ecological factors may contribute etiologically to substance abuse may be sufficient reason for rejecting single cause, internal models of causality, but, alternatively, such causal patterning is not sufficient proof for the exclusive action of external, or victim models. Developmental systems theory provides an bridge between internal and external causal models. From this perspective, it is as legitimate to hypothesize a linkage between personality characteristics and substance abuse, as it is to hypothesize a linkage between poverty and substance abuse. Moreover, the personality-poverty-substance abuse triad is an even more plausible, multicausal interactive hypothesis to consider.

Within such a systems framework it is reasonable to ask how variables such as socioeconomic status contribute to the etiology of substance abuse as well as of family functioning. Commenting on the dangers of using "labeled environments" to group proximal variables, Richters and Weintraub (1990) note that one such label, social class, ". . . conveys no information about specific *proximal* experiences to which children within a given level of social class are exposed" (Richters & Weintraub, 1990). To be sure, spousal violence, child abuse, depression, and drunk driving, occur within all socioeconomic classes. Indeed, as Adler et al. (1994) conclude, "There is evidence that the association of SES and health occurs at every level of the SES hierarchy, not simply below the threshold of poverty. Not only do those in poverty have poorer health than those in more favored circumstances, but those at the highest level enjoy better health than do those just below." (p. 15). Nevertheless, there is increasing evidence to suggest that at least one type of alcoholism, antisocial alcoholism (Zucker, Ellis, & Fitzgerald, 1994) is more likely to be linked to or to co-occur with low socioeconomic class than are other types of alcoholism. We have, on a number of occasions, found indices of socioeconomic status to enter into regression equations as mediator or moderator variables in models designed to test direct and indirect effects of parent characteristics on child outcomes. These analyses have involved cross-sectional data from Wave 1 of the longitudinal study.

Socioeconomic class typically is measured by one or a combination of the following factors: occupational status (Stevens & Featherman, 1981), individual or family income, or years of education. A number of investigators have reported that the rate of alcoholism increases as socioeconomic level, education, or income decreases (Calahan, 1974; Helzer, Burnam, & McEvoy, 1991). Helzer et al. (1991) reported correlations of −.80 for men and −.54 for women between income and rates of alcoholism. Mulford (1964) found that male problem drinkers most likely to have related spousal, health, employment, or legal problems were those most likely to have either the least or the most education, lowest occupational status, and lowest income. Using data from the 1990 census, Hilton and Clark (1991) found a U-shaped function between socioeconomic status and alcohol abuse/dependence. As indicated in Table 1, Midanik and Room's (1992) analysis of data from a representative sample of the adult household population of the 48 conterminous states of the United States, provide support for a U-shaped function when considering an index of average volume based on a mean intake level of two drinks per day (or 60 drinks per month). However, when an index of maximum consumption is used—namely one that evaluates the tendency to drink large amounts per occasions, then a different pattern emerged; drinking five or more drinks per occasion was more likely to be associated with lower income levels and the pattern is closer to linear. A parallel linear function also exists for the group that approximates binge drinking (that is, drinking eight or more drinks per occasion, at least weekly).

In her study of the geographic distribution of families participating in the MSU Longitudinal Study, Pallas (1991) compiled demographic information for each of the 67 census tracts over the five-county region from which our sample was recruited. She then used tract-level data as the unit of analysis to explore the relationship of appearance of alcoholism and a variety of indices of social dysfunction. Consistent with general trends in the literature, Pallas found the highest rates of alcoholic families (number of alcoholic families discovered per 1000 population) occurred near the central part of the largest urban city in the population area; correlations between total rates of appearance of alcoholic families and census tract level of urbanization were .34 for court-recruited alcoholics and .42 for community-recruited alcoholics (both ps <.01). Again at the tract level, both individual and family median incomes were inversely related to rates of recruitment of alcoholic families (−.51 and −.44, respectively; p <.001). As predicted, there were positive correlations between rates of alcoholic families and the percentage of families living below the poverty level (.64 for the

TABLE 1

Variation in Level of Alcohol Consumption Among Adults in the Contiguous 48
United States by Income Level During 1990 (Percentages)

Income Groups	Percent of Adult Population					
	60+ drinks/month		5+ drinks at least once/week		8+ drinks at least once/week	
	Men	Women	Men	Women	Men	Women
0–9,000	30	8	19	6	10	4
10,000–19,999	29	3	12	3	4	1
20,000–29,999	22	8	11	1	4	0
30,000–39,999	18	1	7	<.5	5	<.5
40,000–59,000	20	6	6	2	2	1
60,000+	26	8	6	3	3	1

Note: Data in the table were adapted from Midanik and Room (1992) and are in the public domain.

court-recruited alcoholism rate, and .67 for the community-recruited alcoholism rate). Pallas also found that elevated rates of alcoholism at the census tract level corresponded with elevated rates on other indices of family stress (separation, divorce, public assistance families, female heads of households, renter occupied households). Interestingly, there also was a positive correlation between tract level rate of drunk driver convicted families, and the individual father's blood alcohol concentration at the time of his arrest ($r = .30$, $p < .05$).

Income, Antisociality, and Lifetime Alcohol Problems

Pallas' analysis suggests that at the community context level, indices of status, including family income, operate in a meaningful way to enhance or maintain the vulnerable environments in which children of alcoholics are reared. In addition, at the individual level unit of analysis, such measures, including income, occupational prestige, and education, repeatedly account for 5 to 10% of the variance and/or emerge as significant moderators of outcome variables, in analysis after analysis of data from the first wave of the study.

It seemed reasonable, therefore, to look more closely at the relationship between one of these SES measures, family income, and a number of theoretically important variables (i.e., parental antisocial behavior and parental lifetime alcohol problems) that have been demonstrated to have direct effects on children's ongoing functioning. The Antisocial Behavior Checklist (ASB; Zucker & Noll, 1980) is a 46 item scale that asks the frequency of the respondent's participation in a variety of aggressive and antisocial activities. The total score is derived by summing across all items; a total score of 24 or greater is indicative of antisocial personality disorder based on DSM-III-R criteria (sensitivity = .85; specificity = .83; Zucker et al., under review). The ASB has adequate test-retest reliability of .91 (over 4 weeks) and internal consistency (coefficient alpha = .93) and differentiates among groups with varying histories of antisocial behavior including felons, alcoholics, misdemeanor offenders, and college students (Ham, Zucker, & Fitzgerald, 1993).

The Lifetime Alcohol Problems Score (LAPS; Zucker, 1991) assesses differences in the extent of drinking problems over the lifespan. It provides a composite score derived from three component subscores: (a) the primacy component, involving the squared inverse of the age at which the respondent reported first drinking enough to get drunk; (b) the variety component, involving the number of areas in which drinking problems are reported; and (c) the life percent component, involving a measure of interval between most recent and earliest drinking problems, corrected for current age. Scores are standardized separately for males and females within the longitudinal study sample. Thus, a female score identical to a male scores indicates fewer problems of the female relative to the male. This measure is unrelated to current drinking consumption in problem drinking samples and has been shown to be a valid indicator of differences in long-term severity of drinking difficulty (Zucker, 1991).

In order to examine the relationship of income level to ASB and LAPS, and to determine if either of these proximal variables would be more strongly connected among families with the lowest incomes, we divided each group at the modal income category for the sample ($18,000). Table 2, therefore, contains means and standard deviations for ASB and LAPS for individuals in families with incomes above and below $18,000. Because at the time of this analysis, available ns in the data base were so few for community alcoholic families reporting incomes of less than $18,000, statistical comparisons were only made between the Court Alcoholic and Community Comparison groups.

Analysis of variance on ASB scores revealed significant main effects for RISK [$F(1,360) = 68.31$, $p = .00$] and SEX [$F(1,360) = 36.05$, $p = .00$] as well as a RISK x SEX interaction [$F (1, 360) = 9.93$, $p = .002$]. These findings mirror those obtained in many prior studies involving data from Wave 1 of the longitudinal study. Specifically, ASB scores are higher in alcoholic families than in control families (17.74 vs. 9.28), and are higher in men

TABLE 2

Means and standard deviations for antisocial behavior (ASB) and lifetime alcohol problems LAPS) for court and community recruited alcoholic and community control families of higher and lower income level:

MSU Longitudinal Study

Groups	<$18,000 M	SD	N	>$18,000 M	SD	N
ASB						
Court Alcoholics	21.89	12.11	62	15.79	9.90	132
Men	26.19	13.05	31	21.08	10.34	65
Women	17.58	9.47	31	10.66	6.04	67
Community Alcoholics	14.33	9.20	6	12.00	8.17	92
Men	20.00	9.00	3	14.95	7.76	44
Women	8.67	5.86	3	9.29	5.38	48
Controls	11.69	6.52	26	8.88	5.71	148
Men	13.31	7.16	13	10.23	6.25	74
Women	10.08	5.38	13	7.53	4.80	74
LAPS						
Court Alcoholics	11.04	2.22	63	10.40	2.00	127
Men	11.38	1.92	32	10.53	1.75	65
Women	10.69	2.47	31	10.26	2.24	62
Community Alcoholics	10.33	2.46	4	9.61	1.38	32
Men	9.26	2.87	2	9.52	.98	16
Women	11.40	2.31	2	9.70	1.72	16
Controls	8.80	1.60	20	8.08	1.68	107
Men	8.41	1.64	10	7.16	1.61	53
Women	9.20	1.54	10	8.99	1.21	54

Note: Family income is based on father's report. Note also that all court and community alcoholic men meet Feighner alcoholism diagnostic criteria as do some of the wives in the court alcoholic group.

than in women (16.71 vs. 10.37), although low income high risk women score higher than control men in both the low and high income groups (see Table 2). There also was a significant main effect for INCOME [$F(1,360)$ =18.06, p = .000]; low income families had higher ASB scores than high income families. Moreover, there were no interactions involving income, indicating that it contributed independently to differences involving antisociality.

ANOVA of the lifetime alcohol problems index (LAPS) revealed main effects for RISK [$F(1,360)$ = 73.09, p = .000] and INCOME [$F(1,360)$ = 6.59, p = .01]. Individuals in alcoholic families had higher LAPS scores than did individuals in the community comparison families (10.61 vs. 8.20); whereas individuals in low income families had higher LAPS scores than individuals in high income families (10.40 vs. 9.45). Thus, income also contributes independently to LAPS. At the individual level, these analyses parallel findings from Pallas' study, as well as the extant literature linking income and other indices of socioeconomic status to alcohol abuse and dependence. Specifically, they suggest that investigators should consider entering SES indicators in their models as potential mediators or moderators of the relationships between parent and child variables. Of course, this presupposes that investigators view etiology as a dynamic process that changes in relation to changes in the stochastic relationships among system components external to the individual over the life course, as well as in relation to variation of internal factors.

Developmental Systems Theory and Models of Addiction

In recent years investigators have turned increasingly to developmental systems models of addiction in an effort to understand the complex biopsychosocial organizational dynamics that create pathways to and from alcohol abuse and dependence (Fitzgerald, Davies, Zucker, & Klinger, 1994; Zucker, 1994). Developmental systems theory views adaptive functioning as a set of dynamic organizational processes that involve change and transformation, and that views behavior as embedded within contexts. Thus, substance abuse is conceptualized as a life-span problem with origins that to some degree are manifestations of the social structure, well beyond the confines of the individual (e.g., living in a drinking culture, being of lower social status), that begin to play themselves out even at conception (Boyd, Howard, & Zucker, 1994). Returning to late 19th century London:

> *Dr. Barlow (London) . . . confessed it was quite a revelation to him to hear about little children of tender years coming out of public houses in a state of actual intoxication. But he had seen the evil results among the London poor of giving small doses of spirit; especially gin, to little babies, even at the breast, on account of flatulence. This was a very common habit. He had also found it to be customary to give to quite young children, among some of the poorer classes, a daily quantum of beer. He was quite certain that physicians should pay attention to this habit of giving small doses of alcohol to children over long periods.* (Madden, 1884, p. 359)

Clearly the behavioral outcome of substance misuse is also impacted by influencing structures operating at the individual organism, as well as the suborganismic levels (e.g., biological variation). The dilemma of modelling this multilevel structure is that there is reason to posit both across structure influences (i.e., interactions), as well as within structure semi-independence. Thus, social class variation may impact early developmental processes both by providing a climate of poverty, within which jobs are hard to come by, psychosocial stress is higher, and impulsivity and action and heavy drinking are highly valued for their escape and masking functions as well as by way of its impact upon child rearing processes, spousal abuse, and family instability. Similarly, alcohol specific variation may impact individual development by way of societal level structures regulating alcohol availability, costs, consequences of use, by way of its likely sustaining influences upon poverty and the adversity of life circumstances (cf. Brenner, 1973), by way of its impact upon family structures including spousal violence, and by way of its impact upon individual social achievement. If one is frequently drunk, job stability is impossible to sustain and downward occupational drift is one outcome.

In parallel fashion, the complexity of these processes is likewise illustrated at the biobehavioral end of the biopsychosocial continuum. For example, substantial evidence links difficult temperament to behavior problems in childhood and antisocial personality and alcohol abuse in adulthood (Tarter, 1988; Tarter, Moss, & Vanyukov, in press). Characteristics of difficult temperament include withdrawal from novel stimulation, low adaptability, high response intensity, negative mood, low distractibility, and have been identified early in infancy. The consensual view is that individual differences in temperament are heavily regulated by genetic mechanisms, but that environmental factors can moderate its expression. Young children with difficult temperaments who are reared in chaotic, antisocial, substance-abusing households are more likely to be on a developmental pathway that will reflect continuity for psychopathology from childhood to adulthood. Conversely, young children with difficult temperaments who are reared in stable, loving, and non-substance abusing households are likely to be on a developmental pathway that will reflect discontinuity for psychopathology. A relevant question, of course, is whether the diathesis for such biobehavioral organismic characteristics as difficult temperament interact with SES, such that the risk for difficult temperament increases as socioeconomic level decreases.

Elsewhere we proposed a multifactorial systems approach to the study of alcohol (Fitzgerald et al., 1994) that is theoretically and methodologically linked to developmental systems theory (Ford & Lerner, 1992; Lerner, 1991), dynamical systems modeling (Levine & Fitzgerald, 1992), and probabilistic contextualism (Zucker, 1987; 1994). Five levels of analysis related to the structure and function of the alcoholic family system are posited. The first level requires identification and description of the presenting state characteristics of individual members of the family, including genetic differences that may trigger different behavioral propensities or sensitivities. For example, one may want to assess parental antisociality given the strong link between antisocial behavior and alcohol abuse/dependence

(Zucker, 1994). The second level requires analysis of the structural and functional connections of subunits; that is, assessment of spousal, parent-child, and sibling relationships. For example, one may be interested in assessing how an increase in the rate of parental prosocial behavior will affect the rate of children's externalizing behavior (Maguin, Zucker, & Fitzgerald, 1994). The critical proximal influences on the developing child are to be found at these first two levels of organization.

Level three focuses on the analysis of the properties that emerge when system components couple and generate a specific dynamic structure. Functionally, this means assessing family traditions, values, beliefs, resources (including financial resources), and cohesiveness. It is from this level and the next that more distal variables, such as those that traditionally comprise socioeconomic status, may exert their mediating or moderating influences on proximal variables. The fourth level incorporates analysis of adjunctive systems and their direct and indirect effects on the family unit and/or individual members of the family. This level includes evaluation of cultural standards related to drinking, the availability of alcohol and other drugs, the economic status of the neighborhood, and the social-historical events (cohort effects) that contribute to cultural values. Finally, level five requires analysis of predictive models of individual, family, and ecosystem stability and change over time. Note that this level demands analysis of continuity as well as the bifurcations that disorganize systems and impel reorganization and change. At the most elementary level, this scheme provides a convenient way to categorize findings across diverse methodologies. At a more sophisticated level, however, it provides an organizing framework from which one can generate and test alternative etiologic models, or developmental pathways, to addiction (e.g., Zucker et al., 1994). Of course, to this point, most of our discussion has been based on assumptions of linearity. It is possible that the disorganization associated with alcohol abuse/dependence may better be represented by chaotic models; that is, by nonlinear dynamics rather than linear dynamics (Ehlers, 1992), further complicating the search for the critical determinants of alcoholism and alcohol related problem behavior.

Summary

Evidence that children reared in alcoholic environments are exposed to heightened levels of parental antisocial behavior, alcohol related problems, and other types of psychopathology seems incontrovertible. The data we presented here suggest that socioeconomic status variables may play a mediating or moderating role in regulating the effects of proximal influences on child outcome. However, we know little about where SES variables enter into the person-environment equation. While it is critical that investigators continue to identify the causal factors that lead to alcohol abuse and dependence, it is equally critical to identify the factors that exacerbate or buffer proximal causes. Perhaps we will find that substance abuse is one of the invisible threads woven through the fabric of poverty that, when identified, may help to unravel it.

Acknowledgment

Preparation of this chapter was supported by grant AA07065 from the National Institute on Alcohol Abuse and Alcoholism.

REFERENCES

Adler, N. E., Boyce, T., Chesney, M. A., Cohen, S., Folkman, S., Kahn, R. L., & Syme, S. L. (1994). Socioeconomic status and health. *American Psychologist*, *49*, 15–24.

Barr, H. M., Streissguth, A. P., Darby, B. L., & Sampson, P. D. (1990). Prenatal exposure to alcohol, caffeine, tobacco, and aspirin: Effects on fine and gross motor performance in 4-year-old children. *Developmental Psychology*, *26*, 339–348.

Boyd, G. M., & Howard, J., & Zucker, R. A. (1994). Alcohol involvement and the biopsychosocial panorama of risk: An introduction. In R. A. Zucker, J. Howard, & G. M. Boyd (Eds.). *The development of alcohol problems: Exploring the biopsychosocial matrix of risk. (Research Monograph No. 26).* pp. v–xx. National Institute on Alcohol Abuse and Alcoholism, Rockville, MD.

Brenner, M. H. (1973). *Mental illness and the economy.* Cambridge: Harvard University Press.

Calahan, D. (1970). *Problem drinkers.* San Francisco: Jossey-Bass.

Cotton, N. (1979). The familial incidence of alcoholism: A review. *Journal of Studies on Alcohol, 49,* 89–116.

Day, N. L. (1992). The effects of prenatal exposure to alcohol. *Alcohol Health & Research World, 16,* 238–244.

Ehlers, C.L. (1992). The new physics of chaos. *Alcohol Health & Research World, 16,* 267–272.

Feighner, J. P., Robins, E., Guze, S., Woodruff, R. A., Winokur, G., & Munoz, R. (1972). Diagnostic criteria for use in psychiatric research. *Archives of General Psychiatry, 26,* 57–63.

Fitzgerald, H. E., Davies, W. H., Zucker, R. A., & Klinger, M. T. (1994). Developmental systems theory and substance abuse: A conceptual and methodological framework for analyzing patterns of variation in families. In L. L'Abate (Ed.) *Handbook of developmental family psychology and psychopathology* (pp. 350–372). New York: Wiley.

Fitzgerald, H. E., Sullivan, L. A., Ham, H. P., Zucker, R. A., Bruckel, S., & Schneider, A. (1993). Predictors of behavior problems in three-year-old sons of alcoholics: Early evidence for the onset of risk. *Child Development, 64,* 110–123.

Ford, D. H., & Lerner, R. M. (1992). *Developmental systems theory.* Newbury Park, CA: Sage.

Gonzalez, F., Zucker, R. A., & Fitzgerald, H. E. (under review). Adaptation and psychopathology among drug-involved and nondrug-involved alcoholic men: Testing a developmental hypothesis.

Gottlieb, G. (1991). Experiential canalization of behavior development: Theory. *Developmental Psychology, 27,* 4–13.

Grant, B. R., Harford, T. C., Chou, P., Pickering, R., Dawson, D. A., Stinson, F. S., & Noble, B. A. (1991). Prevalence of DSM-III-R alcohol abuse and dependence. *Alcohol Health & Research World, 15,* 91–96.

Ham, H. P., Fitzgerald, H. E., & Zucker, R. A. (June, 1993). Recent evidence of behavior disregulation in sons of male alcoholics. Paper presented at the annual meeting of the Research Society on Alcoholism, San Antonio, TX.

Ham, H. P., Zucker, R. A., & Fitzgerald, H. E. (June 1993). Assessing antisocial behavior with the Antisocial Behavior Checklist: Reliability and validity studies. Paper presented at the annual meeting of the American Psychological Society, Chicago, IL.

Helzer, J. E., Burnam, A., & McEvoy, L. T. (1991). Alcohol abuse and dependence. In L. N. Robins, & D. A. Regier (Eds.), *Psychiatric disorders in America* (pp. 81–115). New York: The Free Press.

Hilton, M. E., & Clark, W. B. (1991). *Alcohol in America: Drinking practices and problems.* Albany: State University of New York Press.

Humphreys, K., & Rappaport, J. (1993). From the community mental health movement to the war on drugs. *American Psychologist, 48,* 892–901.

Jansen, R. E., Fitzgerald, H. E., Ham, H. P., & Zucker, R. A. (under review). Pathways into risk: The linkages of temperament and behavior problems in three- to six-year-old sons of alcoholics. Michigan State University, Department of Psychology, East Lansing.

Lerner, R. M. (1991). Changing organism-context relations as the basic process of development: A developmental contextual perspective. *Developmental Psychology, 27,* 27–32.

Levine, R. L., & Fitzgerald, H. E. (1992). Systems and systems analysis: Methods and applications. In R. L. Levine & H. E. Fitzgerald (Eds.), *Analysis of dynamic psychological systems: Methods and applications* (Vol. 2, pp. 1–16). New York: Plenum Press.

Madden, T. M. (1884). Alcoholism in childhood and youth. *British Medical Journal,* Aug. 23, 358–359.

Maguin, E., Zucker, R. A., & Fitzgerald, H. E. (1994). The path to alcohol problems through conduct problems: A family based approach to very early intervention with risk. *Journal of Research on Adolescence, 4,* 249–269.

Martin, S. E. (1992). The epidemiology of alcohol-related interpersonal violence. *Alcohol Health & Research World,* 16, 230–237.

Midanik, L. T., & Room, R. (1992). The epidemiology of alcohol consumption. *Alcohol Health & Research World,* 16, 183–190.

Moses, H. D., Gonzalez, F., Zucker, R. A., & Fitzgerald, H. E. (June, 1993). Predictors of behavior problems in children at risk for later alcohol abuse. Paper presented at the annual meeting of the Research Society on Alcoholism, San Antonio, TX.

Muller, R. T., Fitzgerald, H. E., Sullivan, L. A., & Zucker, R. A. (1994) Social support, child belligerence, and child maltreatment: A study of an alcoholic population. *Canadian Journal of Behavioural Science, 26,* 438–461.

Mulford, H. A. (1964). Drinking and deviant drinking U.S.A., 1963. *Quarterly Journal of Studies on Alcohol, 25,* 634–651.

Pallas, D. (1992). The ecological distribution of alcoholic families: A community study in mid-Michigan. Unpublished Master's Thesis, University of Wisconsin, Oshkosh.

Parker, D. A., & Harford, T. C. (1992). The epidemiology of alcohol consumption and dependence across occupations in the United States. *Alcohol Health & Research World, 16,* 1992.

Plant, M. L., & Plant, M. A. (1987). Family alcohol problems among pregnant women: Links with maternal substance use and birth abnormalities. *Drug and Alcohol Dependencies, 20,* 213–219.

Regier, D. A., Farmer, M. E., Rae, D. S., Locke, B. Z., Keith, S. J., Judd, L. L., & Goodwin, F. K. (1990). Comorbidity of mental disorders with alcohol and other drug abuse. *Journal of the American Medical Association, 264,* 2511–2518.

Rice, D. P., Kelman, S., & Miller, L. S. (1991). The economic cost of alcohol abuse. *Alcohol Health & Research World, 15,* 307–316.

Richters, J. & Weintraub, S. (1990). Beyond diathesis: Toward an understanding of high-risk environments. In J. Rolf, A. S. Masten, D. Cicchetti, K. H. Nuechterlein, & S. Weintraub (Eds.), *Risk and protective factors in the development of psychopathology* (pp. 67–96). New York: University of Cambridge Press.

Russell, M., Henderson, C., & Blume, S. B. (1985). *Children of alcoholics: A review of the literature.* New York: Children of Alcoholics Foundation.

Sokol, R. J., & Clarren, S. K. (1989). Guidelines for use of terminology describing the impact of prenatal alcohol on the offspring. *Alcoholism: Clinical and Experimental Research, 13,* 597–598.

Stevens, G., & Featherman, D. L. (1981). A revised socioeconomic index of occupational status. *Social Science Research, 10,* 364–395.

Tarter, R. E. (1988). Are there inherited behavioral traits that predispose to substance abuse? *Journal of Consulting and Clinical Psychology, 56,* 189–196.

Tarter, R. E., & Blackson, T. (1992). Objective measurement of behavioral activity in sons of substance abusers. In symposium, "Childhood and familial characteristics and alcohol and substance abuse: risk and etiology." (W. E. Pelham, chair). Annual meeting of the American Psychological Association, Washington, DC.

Tarter, R. E., Moss, H. A., & Vanyukov, M. M. (in press). Behavior genetic perspective of alcoholism etiology. In H. Begleiter & B. Kissin (Eds.). *Alcohol and alcoholism* (Vol. 1). New York: Oxford.

Zucker, R. A. (1987). The four alcoholisms: A developmental account of the etiologic process. In P. C. Rivers (Ed.), *Alcohol and addictive behavior: Nebraska Symposium on Motivation*, 1986. Lincoln: University of Nebraska Press.

———. (1991). Scaling the developmental momentum of alcoholic process via the Lifetime Alcohol Problems Scores. *Alcohol and Alcoholism* (Suppl. No. 1), 505–510.

———. (1994). Pathways to alcohol problems and alcoholisms: A developmental account of the evidence for multiple alcoholisms and for contextual contributions to risk. In R. A. Zucker, J. Howard, & G. M. Boyd (Eds.), *The development of alcohol problems: Exploring the biopsychosocial matrix of risk. (Research Monograph No. 26).* pp. 255–290. National Institute on Alcohol Abuse and Alcoholism, Rockville, MD.

Zucker, R. A., Ellis, D. A., & Fitzgerald, H. E. (1994). Developmental evidence for at least two alcoholisms: I. Biopsychosocial variation among pathways into symptomatic difficulty. *Annals of the New York Academy of Science, 708,* 134–146.

Zucker, R. A., Ellis, D. W., & Fitzgerald, H. E. (under review). Other evidence for at least two alcoholisms, II: The case for lifetime antisociality as a basis of differentiation.

Zucker, R. A., & Fitzgerald, H. E. (1991a). Early developmental factors and risk for alcohol problems. *Alcohol Health & Research World, 15,* 18–24.

Zucker, R. A., & Fitzgerald, H. E. (1991b). Risk and coping in children of alcoholics: Years 6 to 10 of the Michigan State University Longitudinal Study. NIAAA Grant Proposal.

Zucker, R. A., & Noll, R. B. (1980). *The Antisocial Behavior Checklist.* Unpublished instrument, Michigan State University, Department of Psychology, East Lansing.

Zucker, R. A., Noll, R. B., & Fitzgerald, H. E. (1986). Risk and coping in children of alcoholics. NIAAA Grant AA-07065, Department of Psychology, Michigan State University, East Lansing.

* * *

Round Table Commentary

Barnard. I found your paper to be very interesting. I guess the bottom line is that anything in and of itself is not the genesis of future functioning, rather that a complex of things (problems) are.

Fitzgerald & Zucker. Well, of course, but the scientific question is, what is the complex? In other words, systems have boundaries, even open systems, and we know relatively little about the way in which boundaries are constructed or how they are affected by exogenous and endogenous variables. For example, family systems theorists have described some alcoholic families as essentially closed systems with very rigid boundaries, boundaries that isolate the family and fuel internal processes that act to maintain alcoholism and other aspects of family pathology.

García-Coll. Several times you refer to the possibility of poverty being either a mediator or moderator between parent and child variables. Since mediators and moderators are so different conceptually can you elaborate which of these two concepts fits your multifactorial systems approach better ?

Fitzgerald & Zucker. This is an intriguing question and one that we wrestle with every time we test another model. At this point it seems that SES variables may be best conceptualized as moderators, if by moderator we mean variables that affect the duration or strength of the relationship between a predictor and an outcome variable. If SES was a mediator we would expect it to account for the relationship between predictors and outcomes. So, for example, for males there is increasing evidence to support a strong relationship between antisociality and alcoholism. Does SES account for this relationship (mediate), or does it affect the duration or intensity of the relationship. If antisocial behavior is a trait, we suppose that one might look for mediational effects. On the other hand, if antisocial behavior is a state, then it may be that SES enters the equation more as a moderator than a mediator. What is becoming clear is that the days of treating SES as something to control rather than something to explain are rapidly going. It is one of psychology's litanies, often recited with some disdain, that, "SES is a marker variable." Well, it may be, but it sure is one remarkably powerful marker!

García-Coll. The role of genetics in your systems approach is still confusing to me. How do you operationalize and assess the first level of analysis, including what you call "genetic differences that may trigger different behavioral propensities or sensitivities?" Are you implying that parental antisociality has a genetic component?

Fitzgerald & Zucker. Genetics enters into a systems perspective in much the same way that Environment enters; that is, there are sources of variance that can be tied to biological variables just as there are sources of variance attributable to psychological and social variables as well. Arnold Sameroff has described the relationships among genotypes, phenotypes and what he refers to as environtypes, quite eloquently. If one views the nature of nature systemically, then one must build all potential sources of variance into one's model at least at some level of analysis. Yes, it may be the case that antisociality has a genetic component, but we are not sure what such a statement means. One interesting line of work involves the study of amplitude differences in the P300 event-related brain potential. Although to date this work cannot support a strong genetic component for alcoholism, there is good evidence that P3 amplitude differences can be linked to individuals with an antisocial personality that is co-active with alcoholism. Methodologically there are a number of well known techniques for studying biological aspects of the biopsychosocial triad: pedigree studies, twin studies, biological marker studies via analysis of blood samples, MRI and CAT scans, and electrophysiological studies such as those that identified the P300 event-related brain potential.

Barnard. Do you foresee a time when childrearing by antisocial alcoholic parents will be discouraged? That is, that the children will be eligible for, or in foster care in order to reduce exposure to the affected parent(s).

Fitzgerald & Zucker. Remember some years ago Harriet Rheingold published a paper in the *American Psychologist* that discussed a variety of issues related to the "rights" of adults to bear children? She suggested that it may be beneficial to require adults to demonstrate parental competence before they were allowed to bear children. She cited licensing individuals to drive as an analogy. In a way we have made some progress, although not to the extent advocated by Rheingold. No, there is nothing on the horizon to suggest that such interventions are in the offing, despite the fact that alcoholism in general is one of the major health issues in contemporary society. Problems of substance abuse comprise the third largest health problem in the United States, right after cancer and heart disease. If we consider only mental health issues, substance abuse is right at the top; it is worse than problems of depression, anxiety, and delinquency. And alcoholism is the drug related to the biggest problems. It involves more people in traffic accidents, is closely linked to crime, delinquency, family violence, physical and sexual abuse, and leads to more deaths per year than any other drug. Just as we often excuse SES as a variable by controlling for it, so too we excuse gender by failing to note that all drugs of abuse are abused more by males than by females. Evidence that males are more aggressive than females is overwhelming. So, the combination of antisociality, alcoholism, and poverty in males, especially, is potentially explosive. Regardless of how powerfully we can predict risk at the population level, we are considerably less credible with respect to predicting individual outcome. For example, even though the sons of alcoholic fathers are four to eight times at greater risk for alcoholism than are sons of non-alcoholic fathers, nearly 70% of the sons of alcoholics do not become alcoholic! It seems we are stuck by the very probabilistic processes that we believe will eventually lead, paradoxically, to greater understanding of the dynamic forces that structure developmental pathways to substance abuse as well as other forms of psychopathology.

García-Coll. You note that social class variations may impact early developmental processes in a variety of ways. One possibility that you do not mention is whether there can be a biological predisposition to alcoholism by being exposed to alcohol in utero? Are there any data that suggest or disprove this hypothesis?

Fitzgerald & Zucker. A great deal of research attention has been directed toward specification of the defining features of Fetal Alcohol Syndrome and this effort has been quite successful. This research not only defined the characteristics of FAS, but it has had a direct impact on public health practice and public health policy with respect to drinking and pregnancy. Evidence for Fetal Alcohol Effects is less clear cut. To date, neither the FAS nor the FAE literature provides evidence to suggest a link between prenatal exposure to alcohol and increased susceptibility to alcohol abuse or dependence later in development.

PART TWO

Health Care Agenda

CHAPTER 6

Reducing Infant Mortality and Improving Birth Outcomes for Families of Poverty

Milton Kotelchuck

The field of child development has had relatively limited involvement in national efforts to reduce infant mortality and improve birth outcomes in the U.S. This was not historically predetermined since the field of child development and the beginnings of public health efforts to improve infant mortality both emerged at the same time in this country, around the beginning of this century. At that time, both fields were focused on postnatal mortality and maternal education and responsibility. These mutual interests occurred during the first of the two major eras of infant mortality reduction efforts in the U.S., at the turn of the century, when many of the public health models that we have today were developed. [The second major era is occurring now during the past ten years].

However, the two fields quickly split apart when the public health field's analysis of its improving of vital statistics data showed that the critical focus for infant mortality reduction needed to be more on neonatal than post-neonatal issues, and the public health field moved to address them. The public health field, after some struggle, adopted a basically medical model paradigm, a model that focused on pregnancy as a medical or even a pathologic medical event. Public health shifted to a model of infant mortality improvement in the United States based on offering prenatal medical care, hospital based obstetric care, health education for mothers, particularly encouraging mothers to get obstetric care, and infant hygiene. Public health had adopted a population-based health service delivery focus. By the late 1920s, the dominant public health infant mortality reduction efforts were separated from studies of the social context of child development and family functioning. The child development field, by contrast, went on its way to focus on a different area, individual growth. Moreover, for the longest period of time, the child development field also had very little to contribute to the understanding of the newborn. Public health, in turn, had virtually no developmental prospective; maternal risks were and are seen as fixed and unchangeable; life span approaches are rarely considered; and obstetricians are not well linked to pediatricians, the medical profession with the strongest ties to child development. By the 1930s, the two fields had diverged in quite different directions.

The particular orientation of the public health field in the United States needn't have followed this more medically oriented model to reduce infant mortality. Europe, by contrast, chose a very different model than the United States. There, improvement of birth outcomes is not only a medical issue, but a social issue. Europeans emphasized what can be called "maternity insurance," a program of initiatives to deal not just with medical care but with the financial and social issues around poverty and lack of employment, which are found disproportionately among women with poor birth outcomes. They developed a series of public health models that tried to directly provide social supports to women and their families, replace lost income during the course of the pregnancy and early infancy, as well as directly provide needed medical services. Such a non-medical approach in the United States might have helped prevent the split between public health and child development.

For seventy-five years, the United States has emphasized the provision of medically oriented prenatal care, hospital-based obstetrical deliveries and increasing neonatal intensive care services as its main routes to improve birth outcomes. These have been very effective and there has been tremendous improvements in birth outcomes in the United States. However, we may be coming to the end of the effectiveness of this medical model. There are many disquieting signs about infant mortality in the United States today. The United States' national infant mortality rate ranks poorly (21st) among the nations of the world and the racial and social class disparities are unacceptably large. There is much debate again in the United States about how we should make further improvements in our infant mortality rate, and there are lots of new initiatives and demonstration projects. [We are now in the second era of infant mortality reduction.]

This is an exciting period which offers the opportunity to **re-link** the child development field to the public health field and its national efforts to reduce infant mortality—a linkage which this conference can help further. And a linkage that I believe has great importance for both fields. If one reads the publications of the public health community, they repeatedly say that we need to pay more attention to psychosocial factors, that medical prenatal care visits alone are not sufficient. As a developmentalist, I always ask "what does psycho-social mean?" Right now for the public health field it is a kind of undifferentiated catch-all term for a host of non-medical services. The public health community is coming around to examine, for the first time in 75 years, some of the contextual topics that people in child development field have been working on for many years. And the field of child development has made major strides in the study of younger and younger infants and even premature infants. Both fields, public health and child development, are increasingly focused on some similar issues. The low birth weight babies that are born are both the public health "failures" and the "compromised" babies whose growth the child development field studies extensively. The prevention initiatives that the public health community is trying to develop are increasingly the same as those being developed in the child development field—home visitation, parental education, teen parenting programs, etc.

One can see the very beginnings of common synergistic efforts to deal with infant mortality in this era. But truthfully, we still remain quite discrete fields. I have come to several meetings of SRCD over the recent years where infant mortality just barely gets on the program; and unfortunately, I no longer expect to discuss this theme at these meetings. And, when it is discussed, the level of discourse is really quite inadequate. Developmentalists, in general, have too simple a model of infant mortality. Let me share with you a model of infant mortality that I use in public health forums.

DETERMINANTS OF INFANT MORTALITY AND
OTHER POOR BIRTH OUTCOMES
- MATERNAL RISK
- ACCESS TO INTERVENTIONS
- EFFECTIVE INTERVENTIONS

Infant mortality, or any poor birth outcome, is not a function of solely one factor, maternal risk. Yet that is what virtually everybody in SRCD appears to express. We talk as if infant mortality is solely a function of maternal drug usage, or some aspect of the mother, or poverty, etc. Maternal risk factors are causally and directly related to poor birth outcomes. We forget that in addition to the risks, our society offers ameliorating interventions. Some of them are efficacious, some are not. Birth outcomes are thus at least a function of *risk plus interventions to ameliorate those risks*. Social factors, such as poverty, impact not merely on maternal characteristics, but also on whether or not these interventions are effective and, on whether or not these interventions reach the women who have the specific risk factors. To do any analysis of infant mortality and only examine maternal risk factors without studying the interventions is ludicrous. And yet, too many developmentalists tend to do just that. The study of intervention effectiveness and access to interventions is where the public health field tends to differ from the child development field. Public Health is as interested in studying the intervention programs, as they are in studying maternal risks. In child development, it's not that we don't ever study program characteristics, we simply talk about these as "context" variables. We don't tend to think directly about the organizational functioning of an "intervention program", except occasionally for a few very specific interventions, such as IHDP and a few others. We talk about many contextual themes— education, the family, the community—that influence the child's development; whereas, public health broadly views many of these themes as intervention services, and attempts to organize these "contextual" variables into public health programs and then assess their effectiveness.

The social expression of infant mortality is thus more complex than simply looking at correlates of poor birth outcomes; and efforts to reduce infant mortality are more complex than simply "lessening" maternal risk. Intervention programs have multiple characteristics: efficacy, accessibility, etc. Each stage of the social expression of infant mortality—risk, services, access (from the earlier Model)—needs to be examined in detail. We in the child development community have much to offer to the analysis and ongoing discussions within each of the three domains of the model presented. I would like to briefly mention a couple of these ideas here today.

Maternal Risk

Most of us have been discussing maternal risk at this conference—especially ethnic and income influences. I would just note that for the last fifty years public health professionals and demographers have also studied the impact of these topics on birth outcomes. I can show you repeated studies demonstrating differences between blacks and whites or between social classes on a host of different health status measures. However, public health can only demonstrate that group differences exist, it can't explain the differences and neither can other fields at this moment. In fact, if you looked only at sociodemographic risk predictors, one could predict, at best, only fifty percent of poor birth outcomes, and even that's a high estimate. There remains significant amounts of unexplained poor birth outcomes. So there's plenty of room to look for other (maternal) risk issues.

To address the specific theme of this conference, we know that poverty does influence poor birth outcomes, but we don't understand how. One has to ask, how does the social phenomenon of poverty transform itself into the biological outcome of a poor birth outcome? That is, how do we explain the social transformation of a biological phenomenon? There are many possible psychosocial mechanisms. There's the directly physiologic stress theory; stress inhibits oxygen flow to the fetus. There are counter-productive maternal behavioral responses to alleviate stress that could produce a poor environments for their fetus's development, such as the use of cigarettes or drugs. And, there are maternal stress induced failures to obtain proper prenatal or other medical care. There are multiple pathways that could be examined in which psycho-social factors, including poverty, play themselves out to produce poor birth outcomes. The same kind of stress hypotheses also apply to other aspects of child development, besides birth outcomes.

There has been a tremendous amount of growth in the public health field of efforts to study how poverty manifests itself in poorer physical health status. The Centers for Disease Control, for example, has recently initiated a major effort to look at the influence of psycho-social factors in the initiation of prematurity in the African American community. They are putting a lot of money into developing new methodologies to measure psychosocial stress, including measuring racism. Interestingly, the same topics (maternal stress, sense of control, and competence) reappear as causal hypotheses about the continuous impact of poverty. The National Institute for Child Health and Human Development (NICHD) and the Center for Disease Control (CDC) are both also exploring the intergenerational persistence of poor birth outcomes. Inter-generational phenomena is currently a very popular topic. We have heard today about ways that a poor birth outcome could manifest or recreate itself across generations without having to have a genetic component. Intergenerational persistence needn't be an excuse to do nothing about poverty and racism.

There has been a tremendous effort to disentangle poverty from ethnicity in the study of poor birth outcomes. Birth outcome studies repeatedly show differences among income, education, and poverty. Yet, too many public health and child development professionals discuss SES as a simplistic unidimensional construct. There are major ethnic difference in birth outcomes within and between different ethnic communities of color in the United States. And, there have been major transformations within the same ethnic groups (Asian Americans) over a very short number of generations in the United States. Disentangling race, class, and ethnicity should help us better understand some of the causal factors in the high U.S. infant mortality rates.

The child development field, as a field, could make a substantial theoretical and practical contribution to the study and understanding of maternal risk. The public health community sees maternal risk as a yes-no phenomenon. Yes, you are a teenager; Yes, you're black; Yes, you smoke, etc. We need to help public health professionals develop a concept of *developmental risk*, an appreciation that risks change over a lifetime and that some risks are important in one stage of life and not another. We might be able to help them develop the concept of an age/stage risk measure. This might help them increase the accuracy of their risk predictions.

Effective Interventions

Birth outcomes are as much a social expression of the effectiveness of services, as they are of the underlying maternal risk. The goal of the public health field is to develop ameliorative interventions for identified risks. How effective are our interventions to reduce infant mortality? This is intervention efficacy research—a type of health service research. I think SRCD should be doing more of this type of research. There are a few people in our field, like David Olds and Craig Ramey, who have systematically conducted intervention research—both as an end in itself and as a means to improve developmental theory—but they are the exceptions. SRCD and most psychology departments have not been very friendly to what is derogatorily, and incorrectly, labeled applied research. Applied research is not "soft" research, it is the "hardest" research; finding causal relations in the real world, where one cannot control all the variables, is much more difficult than in an artificial laboratory with all but one randomized variable controlled for.

The Maternal and Child Health field, within Public Health, has the unique mission to develop, implement and assess ameliorative interventions for mothers, children, and families; including compensating for the ill health effects of poverty. To their credit the federal Maternal and Child Health Bureau is fully supportive of these intervention activities, as well as furthering the development of the MCH science knowledge base. MCHB is one of the few agencies of the federal government that is interested in applied or intervention research. The MCH field is actively assessing the effectiveness of a variety of psycho-social interventions that have been proposed in recent years to improve infant health status—such as home visiting, social supports, behavioral advice, etc. Psychosocial or psychoeducational support is one of the main new popular efforts to improve birth outcomes in the public health field, and in a parallel effort, as SRCD members know, to improve early childhood development.

Prenatal care utilization appears to have only a weak influence on birth outcomes. This is surprising and disappointing to many people. MCHB is encouraging an analysis of the components of prenatal care. Which components of prenatal advice make a difference? Are there effective psycho-social prenatal care interventions? The traditional obstetric medical world is remarkably open, at this moment, to new intervention efforts. They are as baffled by the persistence of poor outcomes as anyone. And Medicaid is now willing to pay for some non-medical interventions. But, can we, as developmentalists, come up with meaningful new prenatal interventions? Identifying maternal risks is not sufficient. One cannot simply assume that prenatal care, during nine months of a pregnancy, will cure a lifetime of ills for a woman. If one thinks self-efficacy, for example, is the critical maternal risk factor linking both poor birth outcomes and poor early development, then maybe our two fields can develop a common intervention. I don't mean to be simple-minded; but I think that for every maternal risk we identify, we should be able to come up with some kind of programmatic intervention. That's the way I and most other public health professionals think, and the way, I believe, that people in the child development field also need to begin to think.

SRCD could play an important role in the development and assessment of maternal services, particularly in the area of psycho-social interventions. While there are many biological and other risk factors that produce poor birth outcomes over which our field has little influence, the contribution of psychosocial factors—a theme strongly linked to child development—is being examined extensively at this moment. Child development's historical moment in the sun is right now. We need to move aggressively to develop our ability to assess the effectiveness of psychosocial interventions and to participate in making them more effective. Federal and state governments are debating what is going into comprehensive services today. SRCD should participate more strongly than we have in these debates.

The public health field, however, often has a limited concept of an "intervention." We need to broaden our concept of what are "maternal interventions." They are not just medical services; advice from your mother is another type of intervention. I believe that as a field, child developmentalists view intervention services, or the child's context, in a much more broad-minded manner than does the public health field. Again, I also think that we need to establish the concept of the developmental assessment of services. Being a teenager is not the only developmental marker in the world. Since there are very good services for teens, one could study such topics as whether segregated teens' services or integrated teens' services result in healthier babies and mothers. But there are other age groups besides teens. Pregnancy, at any age, is often a time of great learning and openness to new experiences. All services are not equally developmentally effective.

Access to Interventions

The overall effectiveness of an intervention is not only determined by the efficacy of the treatment, but by whether that efficacious intervention also reaches all the women who need it. There are many examples of known efficacious public health interventions which are simply not available to all needy persons. Access to interventions is, thus, a critical dimension in the analysis of infant mortality. While the examination of access or "health services research" may seem far removed from laboratory based child development, it is a critical component of any analysis of birth outcomes or other health status measures. It influences what is in the child's context. Public health professionals conduct lots of very interesting studies about barriers to perinatal care. They study access issues much more than do child developmentalists; who certainly also note barriers to public health programs, but are less systematic in their analysis of these barriers.

Public health has, however, a very limited repertoire of access barriers they consider—finances, personnel, transportation, language of providers, etc. Public health could do a much better job of understanding some of the psychological variables which internally inhibit a woman's access to care. Some of the contextual studies that child developmentalists conduct are very rich in describing these personal barriers. Repeatedly, follow-back studies of prenatal care barriers show that many women do not like their health care providers; they do not find their providers very sensitive to them. This is dyadic behavior interaction. It's a topic that the public health community flees from. The public health community is wonderful in studying financial barriers, systems barriers, lack of availability of providers, etc. But, in virtually every study, when you ask mothers why they don't come in for health care, the second reason (after finances) is that they are afraid of doctors, they didn't like their doctors, etc. We should be studying this. These are developmental and behavioral issues, and we, as the social scientists, should be studying them more effectively. Analysis of access to health care is an area which would benefit from the insights of the child development field, though this theme is generally far removed from most developmental research.

Birth Outcomes

In SRCD, we have a responsibility to help the public health community broaden their vision of birth outcomes, beyond infant mortality. Infant mortality is obviously very important, but other infant health status measures are also important. Low birth weight is important. Prematurity is important. But these are still markers about birth outcomes only. The developmental community has been successful at broadening our concepts of infant morbidity, and its measurement. The public health community has much to learn from us in this area. Both fields, however, could do a better job of assessing maternal morbidity and studying women's development over the life span, especially as it interrelates to the birth process.

In conclusion, I believe that the child development field could be much more active and effective in the national efforts to reduce infant mortality during this second historic period of attention to infant mortality in this century. In particular, there are interventions that bridge the gap between the work that is done in the prenatal prevention period (public health) and the postnatal period (child development)—home visitations, for example. There are many common themes that unite our separate disciplinary domains (such as early intervention studies). We should not let the earlier historical split between the public health and child development communities impede our mutual interests and activities today. We each have many skills, insights and concerns which would benefit each other's fields. I should not only be seeing my SRCD friends at special meetings like this, because we no longer attend the same meetings. The public health and child development fields should be at the same infant mortality reduction meetings. This symposium is an important contribution to restarting the dialogue and linkages between my two professional identities.

* * *

Round Table Discussion

Ramey. One of the changes that I experienced recently in the move to Birmingham was to move from being in the child development community to, among other things, being a professor of public health. Your comments about the two worlds prompt this comment. I think that the child and family development community has really done a remarkably good job of laying out the vertical foundations toward development, toward what I'll call a systems framework. When I look at these issues—getting at multi-factorial causation, getting that promotion of multiple risk— in principal, I think that we have demonstrated the utility of thinking about complex problems that way. What we haven't done, and now I put on my public health hat, is that we have not held our feet to the fire to make what we do directly relevant in the multiple service delivery systems that we acknowledge as being important co-determinants of the development. I mean simple things, like taking very complex scales and after we finish the work, translating them into the form to allow them to be useful in public health settings, in physicians' offices, in school systems. I think that we really have to find a way to have the child development community be systematically better informed about how the institutions that we acknowledge are important, how they are impacting on children, and how in turn we can give back to them some kind of partnership, fashion some tools that allow the sort of insights we now have to get translated into reality. Because increasingly, the child and family development community is perceived as irrelevant to the fundamental issues of child and families. We're seen as a luxury instead of a fundamental partner, a basic science partner, if you will, in addressing complex problems.

Barnard. I would speak in strong support of that and I think that one only has to look at the journal system of this society to realize that actually child development as this society describes it, is child development in the laboratory. We need to move to much more contextual child development. There are a lot of things that we can bring to it and that move toward what I am going to say is really what child development has to offer in terms of preventative health care strategies that we have not begun to define. We have been very elitist about our knowledge. We're in peril.

Kotelchuck. It is our ability to translate our understanding of risk, and even possibly ideas for programs, into actual services that we have really been neglecting. This is a topic worthy of study. Some interventions are more successful and some less successful. Take barriers to prenatal care. I have to say that people who work with maternal literacy have also been effective in work with prenatal care. People finally realized that many of these mothers without prenatal care didn't read or didn't read well. Somehow, once you can make a literacy campaign tie in with prenatal care, you get the benefits of both. You can study the relative efficacy of it. What I tell my students is that while I do lots of studies, and I have the data here if anybody wants to see it, that show how relatively ineffective prenatal care is; my goal is not to prove that prenatal care is not an effective intervention, but to figure how to make it more efficacious. It's primary care for women during pregnancy. It's not going to disappear because it's not that effective, but we could make it much more effective, maybe if we just go from a correlation of .2 to one of .24. That's a gain and we need to be thinking along lines of how to make it more efficacious. And, that's how I translate some of what you said.

Zuckerman. The relationship between literacy and health needs more emphasis in practice. The birth of a child can be a special opportunity to intervene because children can be an important stimulus for parents to change their behavior and grow and learn. I would like to give you an example from our own work. At Boston City Hospital we have trained our pediatricians in the importance of literacy and have been giving books to children and their parents at each pediatric visit starting at six months of age. When the pediatrician gives a child a book, its face lights up in delight which in turn puts a smile on the mother's face. Unlike advice, this intervention reinforces positive interactions between mother and child and is likely to continue if the parents have the book at home. Giving parents children's books is especially important because many of our families don't have money for books and/or have had difficult experiences in school regarding reading and it is not something they think about doing with their children. We explain to parents that at this young age they are not teaching their children decoding but rather that books contain information and children will see books as important because it is something that they do with their mother who is important to them. Thus, when children get ready to read, they will have a positive feeling about books because of its association with their parent. This has become one of my favorite interventions because of its simplicity and face value. Parents tell us that their children are collecting their libraries by coming to see the doctor. Linkages going beyond traditional health and educational settings makes sense and should be implemented.

Brooks-Gunn. I wanted to pick up on the question of the interventions that have been tried and what we might want to do for the next generation of interventions. I am worried that we aren't in a position to tell people where we ought to be in the basic intervention package given the results of most of the prenatal interventions today. I am thinking about a conference on maternal and child health that was NICHD funded, on the Cape, four years ago, where they brought together people who had been trying different types of interventions to reduce the incidence of low birth weight, keeping in mind that was only one outcome. Among those people that presented, there were randomized trials and they were done beautifully, on the social support stress-reductions, none of them showed a difference at all. After two days of listening to this, I got kind of depressed about the whole thing. David Olds would be a notable exception. So, I think, given that finding, we really do have to think about what models we want to use. Because it's my guess—actually it's my reading of David Olds' findings—that the way social support of stress reduction studies actually influences low birth weight was all due to smoking. That's actually my belief of how to interpret that data. For, if that really is the major pathway, that would suggest different kinds of interventions. The literacy things you were talking about is very interesting. What kind of ways might we expect those interventions to work? So, I don't know if you agree with my reading of all those interventions.

Kotelchuck. I actually do agree with your reading of those interventions. But I assume a different finding from all those studies, which is that they all work for teenagers only. In every study, all the home visitation programs are very well received by teenagers. Teens are at risk because of their age, that's how they get selected, by age. But, in fact, they're not all really high risk.

Some are not so high risk teens. Teens respond very well when you bring services to their home, and they are really open for a lot of insight. Olds' study was effective for teens. Otherwise, all the other ones have all been really quite poor. I think you do have to ask why the Europeans have had some success in their reduction of low birth weight relative to the United States. Here's what I tell people, if you have six home visits by some strange person who may or may not be in rapport with you, it's not going to change your entire life. I just think that prenatal home visits are a very unlikely intervention. And, it's also not that clearly focused on a specific aspect of poverty, the topic of this conference. Some say just a little support, that'll do it. I am dubious. The Europeans have a much fuller social support—maternity insurance programs—than we do despite what we were discussing before about not just giving money. The Europeans do have family leave that's paid. I can't believe that we didn't get more to discussing this. We in the U.S. are glad to get some family leave, but it's unpaid. Women who have to work are still going to have to work, whether their job is secured or not. We should be talking about maternity allowances. The French give $175/month to women who are pregnant if they come in for their first prenatal care before three months and have three visits before delivering. That's a lot of money, $175. And, not surprisingly, they have phenomenal early attendance at their prenatal care.

Lerner. The French don't have to pay for nuclear arsenals . . .

Kotelchuck. I won't disagree with you. If I go to a meeting and I say to people, tell me what you think is the cause of infant mortality, everybody says it's poverty. I then say, what are your interventions? They say more prenatal care. And I say somehow we haven't linked the interventions (prenatal care) with what we say women need. Prenatal care is not a poverty reduction intervention.

Randolph. That doesn't make any sense.

Kotelchuck. I am not that simple-minded, it's not only money. But I do think we should attend to women's economic issues. We may have to and that may be a much more profound thing in people's lives than a few social visits.

Randolph. I just want to comment that the Center for Disease Control and Prevention just funded several sites to study racism as stress, because the low birth weight infant mortality phenomenon is still high amongst middle class black women. So, they're getting away from the notion that it's not just educating them more, providing access, etc.

Kotelchuck. I give the MCHB credit for a lot of things, but I also give CDC credit. They are really taking the psychosocial stress hypothesis and trying to really see if it relates to prematurity in the African American community. They said, "What are the barriers to us moving forward with understanding of the process?" A lot of people think there is racism and that's the issue. But how does it, a social phenomenon, impact on a biological phenomenon, like infant mortality? I have to tell you a lot of people think that racism is really actually an unlikely mechanism to explain our poor birth outcomes. But CDC is developing new methodologies, is asking how can we get the necessary data to look at these hypotheses. I have one of their grants to look at this issue.

Zuckerman. Single factor studies, even if it is racism, are missing the boat unless they identify interrelated psychological factors, social and health behaviors and their independent relationship to outcome. Psychosocial phenomena such as racism or social class have an impact on psychological factors such as depression which can be modified by the presence or absence of social support. Depression can lead to drug use to self-medicate uncomfortable affective state. A biopsychosocial model needs to be understood to develop interventions.

CHAPTER 7

Preventive Health and Developmental Care for Children: Relationships as a Primary Factor in Service Delivery with At Risk Populations

Kathryn E. Barnard and Colleen E. Morisset

> *Poor children may learn early on to survive with lessened protection, support, and validation from caregivers and the broader environment. But the cost is in their trust of and beliefs about reciprocal relationships; and in their capacity to use these relationships as a foundation for their own development.*
> (Halpren, p. 84)

Traditionally we think about health care in an illness or disability framework. We promote services linked with dysfunction. Most health plans have not provided for health promotion visits; thus ruling out preventive care. For children whose families do not have health care coverage the provision of preventive health care is further limited because of the inadequate and unfriendly health care resources.

Developmental preventive health care for children must begin with preconceptual services and include prenatal, intrapartum and post partum follow-up in addition to child health services starting at birth. Our current system of care does not deliver adequate developmental preventive health care. There are many reasons. One is that as a society we do not value health, we value and pay for the absence or cure of disease. Society still lives on the cusp of life. We are interested in dealing with problems such as treating cancer, doing heart surgery,

167

institutionalizing criminals, but have basically not been interested in paying for strategies that would promote health.

Promoting health can be relatively inexpensive from the standpoint of the necessary services. On the other hand the effort and behavioral changes required for individuals is demanding and requires motivation. Modern child health care in theory has moved from treating life-threatening infections and illnesses to concern for the new morbidity in childhood, which includes behavioral and learning problems. Yet few practioners and health care delivery systems have shifted their model of service to a broader developmental, family, and community perspective.

To insure a healthy baby the preconceptual and prenatal period is an important time for encouraging healthy behavior such as good nutritional habits, moderate exercise, adequate rest, reduction of stress, and support of the parent(s). The psychological work the parents need to do, so the baby is accepted by them and other family members, begins in pregnancy and is important to encourage. It is even true that many teenage pregnancies are planned by the couple. Intercourse is deliberate; for the purpose of giving the mother and/or father a baby that they believe can change their unsatisfying lives. To reduce the occurrence of teenage pregnancies we need to seek effective means of improving the life experience of teenagers which would potentially improve their self-esteem, and school achievement. With the formation and realization of more satisfying life goals adolescent pregnancies could be prevented in many cases. Adolescence is not the time for taking on the challenge of parenting.

Adding to the general lack of a developmental and prevention focus in health care, individuals who are poor face other barriers in the health care delivery system. They frequently are not respected by providers. They have little priority in the system, having to often wait an excessively long time; first to be scheduled and then to be seen at their appointment. For this reason many clients use emergency rooms of hospitals for health care which reduces the opportunity for continuity of provider and for attention to health promotion and developmental issues of children. The restrictions in the Medicaid system, both for the client and provider, in terms of paper work and charges make it difficult to find good providers of health services for Medicaid clients. Health care reform is needed, however how it will affect the care received by poor families is at the best uncertain. Poverty is often associated with a lack of formal schooling which contributes to less ability to communicate with providers. It then becomes reciprocal with inadequate information going to the health care provider and the health care provider giving less information to the client.

A Preventive Intervention Model

How might a delivery system operate to deliver an effective program of developmental and preventive care to poor families. An important element in a effective system is the promotion of relationships. Caring relationships between consumer and provider, between consumer and family, and consumer, provider, family and community are all necessary. For instance it is important to start child health care with a relationship developed between provider and prospective parents during pregnancy.

The intent of this chapter is to describe interventions designed to deliver developmental preventive child health care beginning with pregnancy to a population of pregnant women who lacked resources, and then to examine the relationships among poverty, maternal risk, parenting, and child outcomes in this particular high risk sample.

In the mid-1980s we conducted an experimental study focused on evaluating the effectiveness of a relationship-oriented intervention with women who were pregnant and were judged as not having adequate support to successfully deal with the birth of a new infant. The evaluation of inadequate support considered both the emotional and financial resources available to the pregnant woman.

Preventive Intervention Begins during Pregnancy

Two approaches of prevention intervention were evaluated. Both interventions were based on the assertion that the best way to insure healthy development of the unborn child is to foster and nurture competence in the mother beginning even pre-conceptually. The two intervention approaches had several common features. First they both shared the same ultimate goal which was to prevent developmental delay or social-emotional disturbances in the child. Both programs used home visiting as the mode for delivering services and utilized professional nurses in the role of therapist. Both intervention strategies were complimented by medical care and nutritional supplements through the WIC program.

The two intervention strategies differed in their central organizing framework. The Mental Health intervention centered around the theme of establishing relationships, while the Information/Resource intervention was organized by the more traditional public health approach of providing the client access to information and support.

The Mental Health Model had as the primary focus the development of a therapeutic relationship with the pregnant woman. Through this relationship the objective sought was the development of other positive affiliative connections with the woman's family and friends. Nurses with graduate training in parent-child nursing were the providers of intervention. The nurse demonstrated, through the nurse-client relationship, ways of dealing with interpersonal situations and problem-solving. The client was seen as an active participant rather than as a passive learner or resource user. While a paramount goal was to increase the mother's social competence, the approach was not a literal social skills training model. Rather it was built around dealing with the daily life situations and structuring the environment so that the mother could be effective. In some cases this meant contacting another provider and actually bringing the mother and/or child to another resource. At other times, it meant role rehearsal for how to deal with partner conflict, or in pregnancy, helping the woman develop a birthing plan. The emphasis throughout the pregnancy and first year was on the process of dealing with family problems and developmental issues.

In both the Mental Health and Information Resource Models there were specific objectives that the nurse home-visitors hoped to achieve with each mother. However, each client was individually considered and the objectives favored by the mother figured most prominently in the intervention plan. We found that mothers in the Mental Health Model met more of their objectives than mothers in the Information Resource Model. The general objectives for each model are listed in Tables 1 and 2.

To illustrate how the objectives related to intervention strategies by home visitors, the antepartum objectives for the Mental Health Model will be presented and discussed. Objectives for the other time frames for the Mental Health Model and for the Information/Resource model followed the same pattern of activities related to specific objectives. In both models the objectives and activities were a guide that was individualized to the client's personal goals. The Mental Health Model antepartum objectives were:

> 1. *Increased support from the mother's affiliative system.* This was done by discussing support with the woman and getting her to identify the sources and meaning of support in her life. The woman was encouraged to keep in contact with her family and friends and to reach out to meet new people through prenatal classes. The women were receptive to the majority of the activities planned to help them meet this objective. However there was more evidence of mentally acknowledging the need for support than for the mother to seek out additional support.

> 2. *Decision-making of the mother in relation to delivery options.* This involved finding out about the available options for delivery, discussing them with the nurse, doctor, friends, and actually touring the delivery unit. The majority of the sample toured their delivering hospital. Many mothers developed a written birthing plan which they shared with their physician and the delivery room nurses.

> 3. *Dealing with situational anxieties and needs.* This again involved promoting the mother to think about her life demands and to strengthen her coping strategies and to prepare for labor.

TABLE 1

Objectives of the Mental Health Model

Antepartum
1. Increased support of the mother's affiliative system.
2. Foster decision-making of the mother in relation to delivery outcomes.
3. Dealing effectively with situational anxieties and needs.
4. Increasing self-image and confidence in the mother's ability to cope with childbirth.
5. Enhancing the mother-infant attachment

Intra-partum
1. Insure affiliative support during labor and delivery.
2. Enhance mother-infant acquaintance.
3. Modify the environment to enhance self-regulatory behaviors of the infant.

Newborn–3 months.
1. Increase self-regulating behavior of the infant in sleeping and eating.
2. Increase support of the mother's affiliative system.
3. Facilitate maternal adaptive behavior.
4. Enhance mother-infant interaction.
5. Minimize environmental disruptions for the infant and mother.

4 through 12 months
1. Maximize maternal affective involvement with the infant.
2. Facilitate provision of environmental input which insures for the infant a variety of sensory experiences and temporal organization.
3. Provide the mother with a basis of understanding the reciprocal nature of interaction.
4. Insure knowledge of realistic expectations for child development.
5. Facilitate mother's participation in community resources offering child care support.
6. Strengthen mother's affiliative relationships with others.
7. Increase the likelihood of child having trust in his/her environment.
8. Increase mother's ability to provide a safe environment for her child.
9. Avoid patterns of restrictive caregiving.

TABLE 2
Objectives of the Information/Resource Model

Antepartum

1. Continues or modifies diet to be adequate for pregnancy.
2. Keeps scheduled pregnancy care appointments.
3. Understands pregnancy symptoms of physical and mental changes.
4. Understands medical complications needing attention.
5. Decides on recourse for delivery by 28th week of gestation.
6. Understands risks associated with substance abuse.
7. Practices health habits that lead to optimum wellness.
8. Identifies adequate support system to meet needs.
9. Understands and utilizes community and personal resources for crisis and health promotion.
10. Understands anticipated course of labor and delivery.
11. Prepared for unexpected complications of labor and delivery.
12. Demonstrates knowledge and positive feeling toward pregnancy.
13. Demonstrates knowledge of physical and psychological postpartum recovery.
14. Reports to the primary nurse when she delivers.
15. Partner or significant other demonstrates support and caring.

Postpartum through 6 weeks

1. Understands physical care of self.
2. Understands emotional changes and stresses of postpartum period.
3. Recognizes complications of postpartum period and is prepared to take action.
4. Understands need for additional rest each day.
5. Understands nutritional needs.
6. Understands the impact of drugs and smoking on lactation.
7. Knowledge adequate to enhance post-partum recovery.
8. Demonstrates attachment and appropriate parenting.
9. Identifies a support system and includes family in infant care.
10. Recognizes and supports role adjustment of all family members.
11. Recognizes the need for support system to include plans for maternal relief.
12. Recognizes and deals constructively with sibling rivalry.

TABLE 2 (cont'd)

13. Practices safety measures, include car seats.
14. Knowledge and practice of appropriate infant care and stimulation.
15. Keeps 6–8 week post-partum medical check-up.
16. Understands birth control options.
17. Knowledge of community resources.

Newborn (0–6 weeks)

1. Newborn gains height and weight appropriately.
2. Newborn has at least one physical examination by six weeks.
3. Nutrition meets requirement for growth.
4. Receives safe care during feeding, changing, and transportation.
5. Mutuality is established by newborn giving clear cues and mother responding.
6. Given appropriate comfort measures when distressed.
7. Caregiver aware of signs and symptoms of illness in infant.
8. Caregiver will understand and give type of stimulation needed.
9. Comfort demonstrated in mother-child interaction and handling.
10. Caregiver asks relevant questions and uses new knowledge.

6 weeks through 12 months

1. Appropriate growth.
2. Immunizations appropriate.
3. Physical examination by 6 weeks and after 3 months.
4. Development in normal range at one year.
5. Environment is safe, including car seat.
6. Appropriate nutrition.
7. Caregiver finds pleasure in infant.
8. Parenting is competent and parent is confident.
9. Parent recognizes need for medical care for illnesses and injuries.
10. Recognizes changing developmental needs, especially related to safety.
11. Provides appropriate stimulation.
12. Infant has care and play time with both parents.

4. *Increased self-image and confidence in the woman's ability to cope with childbirth*. This involved helping her prepare for actually going to the hospital and in discussing both her fantasies and expectations of the baby and her mothering abilities.

5. *Enhancing mother-infant attachment*. Activities included getting the mother to relate to the fetus by identifying fetal body parts, to communicate with the fetus contingently through massage and talking, to record the pattern of fetal movements, and to discuss parenting values and beliefs.

The second model was developed around traditional public health notions of providing information and resources to clients for promoting and maintaining healthful lifestyles. The intervention, called the Information/Resource Model, was provided by nurses from the Seattle–King County Department of Public Health. The focus of this intervention strategy was centered on the physical and developmental health of the mother and child. The objective was to provide information, procedures, and practices to the mother in a straight-forward way. Table 2 presents the Information/Resource Model goals and objectives for the pregnancy, intrapartum, and child's first year of life. The nurse provided direct teaching as well as referrals to other agencies, thus serving both as a caregiver and a resource coordinator. This Information/Resource Model emphasized health promotion and disease prevention. It represented the closest approximation to existing community nursing services and resources for clients during pregnancy and early child-rearing years. While this model of care has existed in our communities in the past the availability of nursing visits is now severely restricted because of funding cuts. Only a small percentage of the most urgent cases are seen and then for one or two contacts, which we know is relatively useless.

The intervention study discussed here was conducted by the University of Washington, School of Nursing in cooperation with the Seattle–King County Health Department, and with support from the National Institute of Mental Health. Pregnant woman were recruited from the pregnancy detection and prenatal clinics of the southeast and southwest health districts of King County. These districts could be described as suburban-rural areas of the county. Transportation in the areas is by bus and the schedules are infrequent. Resources in the areas are widely scattered so, without personal transportation, individuals are isolated and dependent on friends or family for getting to the grocery store, health clinic, parent's group, or preschool.

Description of the Clinical Nursing Models Sample

The subjects in the intervention study were 147 high risk women who attended the clinics. Eligibility was established in in-person interview with the public health nurse. All study participants were 22 or fewer weeks pregnant and had one or more of the following risk factors: (a) alcohol or drug addiction (8%), (b) psychiatric diagnosis (4%), (c) previous child maltreatment (3%), (d) both low educational level and low social support (48%), (e) young and low social support (16%), (f) low income and low social support (67%), and (g) low educational level, young, and low income (24%).

The study women had a mean age of 21.2 (± 4.0) and had completed an average of 11.0 (± 1.5) years of school. Ninety percent were white. Only 25% were married and living with their spouses. Thirteen percent were working outside the home and the modal yearly family income was in the range of $5,000 to $7,500. Welfare status was collected at study intake and again when the baby was two years of age. Forty-nine percent of the families were receiving public assistance (welfare) at intake, and 41% at two years. Thirty-two percent were not on welfare at any time point, 23% were on welfare at all time points, and twenty-seven percent were on welfare at intake but off at two years. The average antepartum household size was 3.4 (± 1.7) persons. Forty- four percent of the mothers had at least one child younger than six years at home and three had at least one child older than six years.

The study infants were primarily full-term. Their mean gestational age of 39.7(± 1.6) weeks, the mean birth weight was 3409 (± 574.7) grams, and mean 5-minute Apgar was 8.9 (± 0.6). Most of the infants (78%) were delivered vaginally; 49% were male, and 50% were first born. By the time of birth, a number of women had dropped from the study, and the total sample size was 106. Attrition in the Mental Health group was primarily due to miscarriage and geographic relocation, while in the Information/Resource intervention group, more mothers elected to drop out, usually by avoiding the nurse by not being home at the time of the visit. In the Mental Health model, since the establishment of a relationship with the mother was paramount, the nurses were indefatigable—scheduling and rescheduling their home visits numerous times, especially in the early stages of the relationship. It was not uncommon for them to go to a home 5–6 times before the mother would be there and come to the door. Several mothers shared later that they had been testing out the nurse to see if she could be trusted to come back, to see, did she really care?

Overview of Results

A number of measures of the mother, child, and environment were collected during the course of the study of the intervention and have continued in follow-up studies. More complete reports of the data collection and treatment outcomes are available elsewhere (see, for example, Booth, Barnard, Mitchell, & Spieker, 1987; Barnard, Magyary, Sumner, Booth, Mitchell, & Spieker, 1988; Booth, Mitchell, Barnard, & Spieker, 1989; Morisset, Barnard, Greenberg, Booth, & Spieker, 1990). Briefly, the treatment differences can be summarized as follows: First, 80 percent of women in the Mental Health model completed the 18 months of intervention, whereas only 53 percent of mothers in the Information/Resource group did so. Second, there was differential attrition. Proportionately more of the less competent subjects dropped out of the Information/Resource group. The Mental Health Model, with its relationship focus, retained more of the depressed, low income, low education women. The Mental Health group mothers had more nurse contact, attained more of the treatment goals, and perceived more social support at the end of the intervention period. In the Mental Health group, more mothers who were initially low on social competencies improved their social skills, as measured by the Community Life and Social Skills Scales. The mothers who improved most in parenting competency as measured by mother-child interaction, regardless of their intervention group, were those whose social competency was low at intake but improved by the end of the intervention (Booth, et al., 1989).

Tests of treatment group differences revealed that the Mental Health Model mothers had higher scores on the NCAST Teaching Scale and the HOME inventory. There were no differences in child competency as reflected by 13- or 20-month infant-mother attachment, or the Bayley Mental and Physical Development scales at two years. The benefit of the intervention differed for different families. Analyses of group by initial maternal status (based on mothers' intelligence, reported depression, educational level, purity, or social skills) revealed that the less competent mothers and children did better in the Mental Health treatment group (Barnard et al., 1988).

Assessing the Effects of Poverty within the Context of Maternal Risk and Parenting: Describing Variables Used in the Analyses

For the purpose of analyzing the relationships among poverty, maternal risk, parenting, and child competence in the Clinical Nursing Models sample, summary variables were formed that reflect the following constructs: Family Social Status, Maternal Risk, and mother's Parenting Skill. Individual variables include measures of family income, socioeconomic status, mother's life stress, social and psychologic functioning, and her functioning within the role of parent. The child outcomes to be discussed reflect the child's cognitive-linguistic skill at ages 24, 30, 36, and 60 months. All variables are described in detail below. Tables 3 and 4 summarize the mean, standard deviation, and range for each variable and is limited to those families who continued with the study until their children were at least 30 months of age.

TABLE 3

Descriptive Statistics for Predictor Variables

Variable and Time of Assessment	Mean (*SD*)	Range
Poverty		
Social Status		
Intake	1.93 (.8)	10–30
2 Years	2.12 (.7)	10–30
Maternal Risk		
Depression		
6 weeks	9.8 (6.1)	1–24
1 Year	8.6 (8.1)	0–30
2 years	9.5 (7.2)	0–27
Negative Life Events		
3 months	12.9 (10.7)	0–53
1 year	9.6 (8.6)	0–41
2 years	9.3 (7.7)	0–33
Social Skills		
3 months	49.0 (5.6)	34–58
1 year	49.4 (4.8)	36–60
2 years	47.9 (7.2)	30–60
Personal Resources		
3 months	131.9 (23.3)	71–175
1 year	135.7 (25.9)	76–175
2 years	131.3 (22.6)	57 - 172
Community Life Skills		
1 year	26.6 (3.8)	17–35
2 years	27.1 (3.6)	17–34
Parenting Skill		
Teaching Scale (Mother)		
1 year	34.7 (.8.6)	9–49
2 years	31.5 (5.0)	19–43
HOME Inventory		
1 year	36.1 (4.2)	23–44
2 years	33.4 (4,8)	23–43
% Language Facilitating Speech		
13 Months	.72 (.14)	.31–.96
29 Months	.68 (.13)	.24–.95

TABLE 4

Assessments of Child Language and Cognition

Variable and Time of Assessment	Mean (*SD*)	Range	*n*
24-Month Bayley MDI	105.6 (15.7)	77–150	62
30- Month MLU-5	5.0 (1.7)	1–9	68
36-Month PLS Auditory	107.3 (17.8)	67–150	55
60-Month WPPSI IQ	102.2 (13.8)	71–135	29

Poverty

Social Status. Hollingshead's four-factor score was used to reflect family social status. The four factors used in computing the score are: education, occupation, marital status, and sex. Total scores can range from 8 to 66. At intake to the study, 35 percent of the families included in this report earned scores that reflect unemployed and unskilled laborers (Level V on the Hollingshead scale), 37 percent of the families' scores corresponded to semi-skilled employment (Level IV) and 28 percent to skilled or business occupations (Levels II and III). In contrast, when the children were three years of age, only 18 percent of the families were classified as unskilled and unemployed, 44 percent as semi-skilled, and 37 percent as skilled or above. Fourteen percent of the families fell in the lowest social stratum at both intake and (child's) age three years.

Income. Annual family income was collected on an interval scale that ranged from "less than $3,000" to "39,999." At intake to the study (in 1983), 80 percent of the sample had a yearly income of less than $10,000, when the children were two years of age (in 1986), 60 percent of the families earned less than $10,000 per year.

Comparing Income and Social Status as Predictor Variables

We examined the correlations between social status and income and parenting, maternal risk, and child outcomes. The only measure showing a relationship with income was the Home Inventory score at one and two years. In contrast, the Hollingshead score was correlated with multiple child outcomes: 2-year MDI ($r = .20$), 3-year Preschool Language Scale ($r = .35$ with the auditory language subscale), and with 5-year WPPSI IQ ($r = .56$) and consistently explained more variability in the parenting variables. For these reasons, we chose to use the Hollingshead score, representing socioeconomic status of the family, in subsequent analyses, but caution that a different pattern might be found in samples with greater variability in income. Parenthetically, future studies might consider adding a measure of social ordering to the assessment of "social status." It has been reported that conditions of the extra-familial environment, such as characteristics and stability of the neighborhood, influence individuals' health and well-being beyond that explained by more traditional SES indicators such as personal income and education (Alder, Boyce, Chesney, Cohen, Folkman, Kahn, & Syme, 1994).

Maternal Risk

Maternal depression. The Beck Depression Inventory was used (Beck, 1970). The inventory consists of 21 items, each of which was designed to represent an overt behavioral symptom of depression. The choices within each item are intended to gauge degrees of severity for each symptom. The total score, which can range from 0–63, reflects both the number and severity of symptoms. Data used in this analysis was collected at six weeks postpartum, and again when the children were one and two years of age.

Negative life events. The Life Experiences Survey (Sarason, Johnson, & Siegel, 1978) was used. This is a 61 item instrument that assesses changes in life events. The subject is asked to indicate which of the events occurred during the past year, to label them as good or bad, and then indicate the impact of each of the events using a 0 to 3 score. The survey yields both a positive and negative change score. The negative score was used in this analysis. The negative score has been shown to be a measure of stress for the individual. This variable was collected when the children were 3 months, one, and two years of age.

Personal Resources Questionnaire (PRQ). This questionnaire (Brandt & Weinert, 1981) is a 25-item Likert-type scale designed to assess the subject's perception of social support. It is based on Weiss's (1994) conceptualization of the functions of social relationships; sharing of concerns, intimacy, opportunity for nurturance, reassurance of worth, and assistance/guidance. Scores can range from 25 to 175. This measure was collected when the children were 3 months, one, and two years of age.

Social Skills. This is a 63 binary-item observational record of the mother's verbal and nonverbal interaction skills during conversation with an adult interviewer. The scale includes items related to: *greeting* (e.g., "Mother calls the visitor by name, after the visitor has introduced herself, at least once during the visit"), *nonverbal signals* (e.g., "Mother's upper body is turned no more than 45 degrees away from visitor at least 50% of the time"), *speech and conversation skills* (e.g., "Mother uses varied voice inflection"), *affect* (e.g., "Mother's face shows sadness at least once at an appropriate time"), and *communication skills* (e.g., "Mother attends to the interviewer's questions at least 80% of the time"). This measure was completed at 3 months, one and two years.

Community life skills. This is a 32 item binary scale that the evaluator completes on the basis of maternal report. The scale emphasized the social skills necessary for participation in group activities and community living in the areas of transportation, budgeting, support services, support-involvement, interests-hobbies, and regularity-organization-routines. This interview was done both at one and two years.

The above five measures were combined to reflect an overall measure of the mother's personal resources and stress. The combined measure is labeled maternal risk since it is composed of the number of times the mother had two or more extreme negative scores on any of the five measures at 3 months, 1, and 2 years. Extreme scores were defined by criterion, such as for the Beck Inventory score we used the clinical cut off score to define the extreme. In other measures we used the sample medium, so that scores below the medium were classified as extreme. In the total sample 14% had no extreme scores, 33% had extreme scores at one period, 12% had extreme scores at two times, 41% had extreme scores in all three time periods at 3 months, 1 and 2 years. The total maternal risk score was correlated with the three year measure of social status $r = -.32$. The total Maternal risk score was correlated with the NCATS mother score at 1 year $r = -.36$. Maternal risk was correlated with the HOME Inventory at 1 year $r = -.46$ and 2 years $r = -.39$. Maternal risk correlated with all child outcomes measures; with the MDI at 24 months $r = -.25$; with the MLU at 30 months $r = -.28$, with the Auditory comprehension score of the Preschool Language Test $r = -.41$, and with the 5 year IQ $r = -.46$

Parenting Skill

Nursing Child Assessment Teaching Scale (NCATS). The quality of parent-child interaction was assessed using a 76 item binary observation scale. The items of the scale describe both parental and child behaviors during an episode where the parent is asked to teach the child a task that the child does not yet perform. Example teaching tasks include stacking blocks, drawing lines, or stringing beads. Six underlying constructs are tapped by the scale; they are divided into four parent and two child subscales. The parent subscales are Sensitivity to Cues, Response to Distress, Social-Emotional Growth Fostering, and Cognitive Growth Fostering. The child subscales are Clarity of Cues and Child Responsiveness. (Barnard et al. 1989). The NCATS observations reported here occurred in the home when the children were 12 and 24 months of age. Evaluators were trained to at least 85% reliability.

Home Observation Measure of the Environment (HOME). The Caldwell HOME inventory (Bradley & Caldwell, 1976) was used to measure the overall organization of the child's home environment; this includes stimulation, maternal involvement, restriction and participation in family activities. The observers were trained and maintained a reliability of at least 85%. HOME scores were obtained when the children were 12 and 24 months of age. Only the total HOME score was used in the analyses reported here.

Maternal Language Facilitation (MLF). The measure was drawn from a snack interaction video taped during lab visits ages 13 and 20 months. Each maternal utterance was coded according to its underlying intention to promote verbal interaction through the use of questions and comments vs. to control or direct the child's behavior through the use of direct and indirect commands.

Child Cognitive and Language Outcomes

Bayley Scales of Infant Development. At 24 months, cognitive status was assessed with the Bayley Scales of Infant Development. (Bayley, 1969) The Mental Index of Development (MDI) was used in the present analysis.

Mean Length of Utterance of Longest 5 (MLU-5). At 30 months, mother-child conversation during a video-taped snack (part of a more extensive laboratory visit) was transcribed. A variety of child and maternal language variables were obtained from the transcripts, including mean length of utterance (MLU), a traditional measure of grammatical complexity. MLU was computed for the entire corpus and for the child's longest five utterances. It was computed based on morphemes and on words. The MLU measure included in the present discussion is MLU-5 based on words—that is, the average length of the child's longest five utterances, in words. Because the length of the snack, as well as the verbosity and intelligibility of the children varied greatly, MLU-5 is the most accurate and representative index of grammatical skill available from these data.

Preschool Language Scale (PLS). At 36 months, children's language ability was assessed with the PLS (Zimmerman, Steiner, & Pond, 1979). The PLS is an evaluation instrument that tests articulation, auditory comprehension, and verbal ability. For the present analyses we used the auditory comprehension subscale rather than the overall Language score because our prior experience is that the auditory subscale correlated most strongly with other cognitive measures.

WPPSI. At 60 months (5 years) the Wechsler Preschool and Primary Scale of Intelligence was administered to children who could be located and tested within 3 months of their 5th birthday; 29 subjects participated in this follow-up assessment. The WPPSI is designed for ages 4 to 6.5 years. It is composed of 11 subtests, grouped into Verbal and Performance scales, from which Verbal, Performance, and Full Scale IQs are found. In this study, we found that the pattern of correlations with the predictor variables was similar for the Verbal and Performance IQ scores, and so the summary Full Scale IQ score will be reported here.

The Relation of Poverty, Maternal Risk, and Parenting to Child Outcomes

We constructed two models to examine the relation of family social status and maternal functioning to child language and cognition at ages two through five years. Before discussing the models, a little more explanation of the predictor variables is warranted. In each of the explanatory models, social status and maternal psychosocial risk are represented by variables that aggregate family (or maternal) status over the child's first two years of life. With regard to social status, the "over time" variable indicates the number of times family social status is **not** the lowest stratum. The variable is based on two time points, intake (during pregnancy) and when the child was two years of age; thus it can range from 0–2. A score of "0" indicates that the family was in the lowest stratum at both time points; this was true of 14 percent of the sample. A score of "2" indicates that, at both time points family social status was that of semi-skilled employment or higher. This was true of 62% of the sample. The remaining 25 percent of the sample scored "1"—in the lowest stratum at one of the two time points.

The variable representing maternal psychosocial risk is also an aggregate representing the degree of risk over the child's first two years of life. It is based on three time points (3 months postpartum—except for depression which was collected at 6 weeks—when the child was one year and two-years old). Degree of risk "over time" is reflected in the number of time points in which at least two of the mother's psychosocial risk scores are extreme. Thus the aggregated risk variable can range from 0–3, with "0" indicating no time points with extreme scores (14% of the sample) and "3" indicating extremes at all three time points (41% of the sample).

Both models utilize hierarchical step-wise regression. We have maximized the predictive "power" of family social status by entering it first in each model. In both models, mother's psychosocial risk is entered on the second step. The models differ at the third step—the inclusion of the three parenting variables. In model number one, parenting skill reflects measures from when the child was about one-year of age. In model number two, the parenting variable reflects the child's second year. Entering the parenting variables last (on step 3) provides the most stringent test of their predictive capability because the amount of variance these variables "share" with the other independent variables has been removed.

Tables 5 and 6 summarize the results of the regressions. Column 1 of each table reports the variance accounted for by social status. Column 2 reports the R-squared change resulting from the addition of maternal risk. Column 3 reports the R-squared associated with the addition of the parenting construct. Column 4 reports the multiple R for each outcome.

The over all regression predicting the Bayley MDI, by either model is not significant. Table 5 shows that quality of parenting is the only significant predictor of 30-month MLU-5. In contrast, all three predictors are related to the PLS score; in combination, social status, maternal risk, and parenting account for 37% of the variance associated with the Preschool Language Auditory subscale. With regard to 5-year IQ, it is interesting to note that the first-year parenting variable explains more of the variance than either social status or maternal risk. Taken together, the three variables account for 61% of the variability in 5-year IQ.

TABLE 5

Model One

Dependent Variable	Social Status Step 1: R^2	Maternal Risk Step2: Change R^2	Parenting Skill 1-Yr Step 3: Change R^2	Overall R
24-Month Bayley MDI	.02	.06	.07	.40
30-Month MLU-5	.00	.07	.14[a]	.46[a]
36-Month PLS Auditory	.11[a]	.12[a]	.15[a]	.61[b]
60-Month WPPSI IQ	.18[a]	.15[a]	.29[b]	.78[b]

Note. Total sample size for each equation is: 53 (MDI), 55 (MLU-5), 46 (PLS), and 25 (IQ).

[a] $p < .05$; [b] $< .01$.

TABLE 6

Model Two

Dependent Variable	Social Status Step 1: R^2	Maternal Risk Step2: Change R^2	Parenting Skill 1-Yr Step 3: Change R^2	Overall R
24-Month Bayley MDI	.04	.04	.16[a]	.49
30-Month MLU-5	.00	.05	.19[b]	.49[a]
36-Month PLS Auditory	.10[a]	.17[b]	.23[b]	.71[c]
60-Month WPPSI IQ	.17[a]	.13[a]	.20	.70[b]

Note. Total sample size for each equation is: 49 (MDI), 50 (MLU-5), 44 (PLS), and 26 (IQ).

[a] $p < .05$; [b] $< .01$; [c] $p. < .001$.

The fact that Model One predicts language and cognitive outcomes after 30 months as well or better than Model Two suggests that the parent's role in mediating the young child's environment is even more important in the first year, when the child must depend on adults. At this age, few children use language well or locomote independently. Parenting skill at one year accounted for twice the amount of variance explained by social status and mother's psychosocial functioning.

What is equally interesting is the relative lack of prediction of 24-month MDI and 30-month MLU-5 from social status and maternal risk factors, while the parenting skill variables are predictive. It appears that parenting skill creates the most proximal environment for the young child and, while primarily within this relationship, the more distal environment has less impact on child development.

Since this sample is quite small and represents primarily Caucasian women and children, the results cannot be generalized. Similar analysis should be done where possible in other samples. However, because this is a racially homogeneous sample, it allows us to examine the relative contribution to child outcomes without the issue of disadvantaged minority group status. If similar analyses in other samples support these findings, there are important implications for early intervention.

It seems unlikely for the poorest and most at-risk parents, that interventions that solely concentrate on only one source of influence, e.g., poverty, or maternal risk, or parenting, will be successful in improving the lives of children. There must be equal attention to the social competency of the mother as reflected in her demands and resources, her parenting and the most distal factor of social economic status. The data presented with the 5-year IQ suggests all three factors influence the child's cognitive performance. At the minimum, an effective intervention must address each of the three constructs presented in these analyses. The Clinical Nursing Models Intervention concentrated on both maternal risk and parenting but was not designed to influence social economic status or the broader community and neighborhood contexts.

We did a further analysis of the 5-year extreme IQ groups. The low group (n = 3) had IQ scores below 85 and the high group's were above 115 (n = 5). In examining differences between the two groups, the greatest differences were in the parenting variables. The groups differed by 10 points on the mean HOME, and by 10 to 19 points on the NCATS Mother score—the proportion of mother's language facilitating speech was also greater in the high IQ group. Differences were also apparent in degree of psychosocial risk. In the low IQ group, there was no variability—each family was in the extreme-risk group at each of the three assessment times. In contrast, in the high IQ group, there was greater within and across time variability in degree of maternal risk. The same picture emerged regarding social status; mothers in the low child-IQ group had consistently lower SES scores. Maternal IQ as measured during pregnancy also differentiated the two child IQ groups. These data serve to remind us of the erosion in human potential that can result from chronic and compounding risks.

Our analyses suggest that for families characterized by multiple risks, preventive intervention needs to be comprehensive and deal with the range of factors which, in combination, influence children's development. We wonder whether infants and toddlers with extremely low-functioning parents would benefit from having additional, alternative caregivers provided in the form of therapeutic day care or Head Start. Ideally for parents with few resources, who are in poverty, with lack of education and support, the comprehensive, coordinated and continuous programs such as those being evaluated by the Administration on Children, Youth, and Families seem to model the ultimate answer. Yet it remains a question whether even the best, most comprehensive intervention program can reclaim all losses.

Our findings from the Clinical Nursing Models Intervention confirm the central importance of establishing a personal relationship with clients who have few social skills. In our study, women with few social competencies stayed longer, and gained more skills in the Mental Health intervention; an intervention that focused first on relationship-building. Our country's health and human services systems need to be reorganized around principles which help individuals feel connected, respected, and competent. If children have protection, support, and validation from their environment, they learn to trust the foundation their world gives them, and grow well.

The ultimate answer to changing the lives of children at risk due to poverty and inadequate parenting are intervention strategies that provide preventive interventions that begin in pregnancy and continue through the early years of the child's life. It is not enough to help the parent or child alone. These interventions must address the family as a whole and integrate health, behavioral, vocational, and educational services. There must be renewed attention to relationships in all these service systems, particularly for the socially at-risk client. Additionally, neighborhood and community contexts must be considered. Parents and children cannot thrive where family and community violence are a fact of daily life. Only by reducing the risk factors (poverty, stress, etc.) and increasing resistance through supportive services can we stop stealing developmental competence and health from our nation's children. Poverty of the individual is compounded by poverty of the neighborhood and community. We have experienced declines in the quality of our infrastructure and, at the same time, home-making and parenting skill have diminished in our young adults. We know the solution. Will we find the social will to act?

Acknowledgment

The authors acknowledge support from the MacArthur Foundation Network on the Transition from Infancy to Toddlerhood and the National Institute of Mental Health, Grant No. 5 RO1 MH-35894.

REFERENCES

Alder, N. E., Boyce, T., Chesney, M. A., Cohen, S., Folkman, S., Kahn, R. L., & Syme, S. L. (1994). Socioeconomic status and health: The challenge of the gradient. *American Psychologist*, 49, 14–24.

Barnard, K. E., Magyary, D., Sumner, G., Booth, C. L., Mitchell, S. K., & Spieker, S. J. (1988). Prevention of parenting alterations for women with low social support. *Psychiatry*, 51, 248–253.

Barnard, K. E., Hammond, M., Booth, C. L., Bee, H. L., Mitchell, S. K., & Spieker, S. J. (1989). Measurement and meaning of parent-child interaction. In F. J. Morrison, C. E. Lord D. P. Keating (EDS), *Applied developmental psychology* (Vol. 3). New York: Academic Press.

Bayley, N. (1969). *Bayley scales of infant development: Birth to two years.* New York: Psychological Corporation.

Beck, A. T. (1970). *Depression: Causes and treatments.* Philadelphia: University of Pennsylvania Press.

Booth, C. L., Barnard, K. E., Mitchell, S. K., & Spieker, S. J. (1987) Successful intervention with multi–problem mothers: Effects on mother-infant relationship. *Infant Mental Health Journal, 9*, 288–306.

Booth, C. L., Mitchell, S. K., Barnard, K. E., & Spieker, S. J. (1989) Development of Maternal Social Skills in Multiproblem Families: Effects on the Mother-Child Relationship. *Developmental Psychology, 25*, 403–412.

Bradley, R. H., & Caldwell, B. M. (1976) The relation of infants' home environments to mental test performance at fifty-four months: A follow-up study. *Child Development, 47*, 1172–1174.

Brandt, P. A., & Weinert, C. (1981). The PRQ—A social support measure. *Nursing Research, 30*, 277–280.

Halpern, R. (1993) . Poverty and infant development. In C. H. Zeanah (Ed.) *Handbook on Infant Mental Health*. New York: Guilford Press.

Mitchell, S. K. (1987) Maternal social skills related to mother-child interaction and child outcomes. Unpublished raw data.

Morisset, C. E., Barnard, K. E., Greenberg, M. T., Booth, C. L., & Spieker, S. J. (1990). Environmental influences on early language development: The context of social risk. *Development and Psychopathology, 2*, 127–149.

Sarason, I., Johnson, H., & Siegel, M. (1978). Assessing the impact of life changes: Development of the life experiences survey. *Journal of Consulting and Clinical Psychology, 46*, 932–946.

Weiss, R. (1974). The provision of social relationshiups. In Z. Rubin (ed.) *Doing unto others* (pp. 17–26). Englewood Cliffs, NJ: Prentice Hall.

Zimmerman, I. L., Stein, V. G., & Pond, R. E. (1979). *Preschool Language Scale*. Columbus, OH: Merrill.

* * *

Round Table Discussion

García-Coll. When there was an international meeting in South America about the world environment, one of the things talked about was that it was all coming down to women's issues and children's issues and population growth. They interviewed some young women in Kenya on NPR about what was being done in Kenya to reduce one of the highest birth rates in the world. They provided alternatives to having babies. If women have appealing alternatives, then they will choose not to get pregnant. They interviewed these 17 and 18 year-olds who represent the first generation of young women in Kenya who are not having children. They gave them an incentive that if they would earn a high school diploma they would be guaranteed a job. You could hear these women's excitement. These 17 and 18 year-olds saying, "Why would I have a child," "Why would I be home like my mom when I can have a job." So, it comes down to the notion that we are always trying to stop people from doing things, rather than giving alternatives that are real alternatives, that are perceived alternatives. So, that's one comment. The other comment concerns the notion of Hispanic women and infant mortality. We really have an incredible paradox in that highly acculturated women are worse off than less acculturated women. That, I think, is a very important phenomena. There's this notion that if you learn English you will have access to resources. Unfortunately, right now it seems to mean less resources.

Gadsden. First, there are some cross-cutting issues in both your talks. Policy has to focus on the institutions as well as the people. We're hearing that people simply don't want to go into these places which lead me to believe that there is this enormous possibility for this field to bring together some of the cross-cutting issues from other disciplines. When we ran literacy programs, people came in for a lot of different reasons. They came in to find out what to do with their babies. They came in to find out about prenatal care. They came to get information that could be rewritten so that they could read it. They came in to get information so that they could improve their own ability. So, I think that we need to think about the possibility of bringing all these disparate issues together into common issues. The second thing is the institution itself. I am appalled by health-care institutions. It is not simply their response to poor people; it's their response to all people. Here is a bit of anecdotal evidence. I had a stint in the hospital this past year. The fact that I got such incorrect information over time appalled me. Then, when I got into the hospital I saw how poor people were being treated, and how I was being treated, that is, until my name came up on the screen as Dr. Vivian Gadsden. The change in hospital behavior was amazing. All those poor people were treated as if they were relatively unimportant.

Lamberty. Kathy, you talk a lot about health care in relation to women, but you left out the other part of the equation, which is men.

Barnard. Yes, that's a whole separate talk! I agree with the importance of your point.

Kotelchuck. I think the undervaluing of men in our society is a very critical issue, particularly the undervaluing of minority men.

Lamberty. Well, also, the undervaluing of the nurturing contribution of men. For example, I think one of the greater things that I am proud of is having the experience of being a father. There are many contributions that men make to prenatal care as well as postnatal care.

Barnard. When you look at the value system of our society, there are many ways that our society is valuing not having a mother and a father. And, in fact, even at the older end of the life cycle, it's a great disadvantage for older people to marry, in terms of their economic status. So, we have, I think, a strong problem with our value system.

Kotelchuck. That was the topic I wanted to talk about, but I just wanted to follow up on the last comment on treatments. I do think that we could study much more how people are treated and not treated. But, I think, that's quantifying something that is well known. But, in terms of the actual public health issues that are fought out, the real question becomes, should physicians be expected to do all these things? Is that actually good use of physicians, or should this be a comprehensive team, or should we have a separate team that provides psychosocial services? That is actually how the debate is playing out. We already know there are problems. But, the solutions are less clear. The Europeans, for example, think that our desire to have our doctors learn to be sensitive to all these issues, is a complete waste of time. They want a specialist who can be seen for three minutes and then the patient is turned over to other supportive services.

Barnard. I don't think the physicians are going to be willing to accept the salaries that it's going to take for them to do the quality of work, because the broader work takes more time.

Kotelchuck. I don't disagree with you.

Ramey. I want to share an anecdote because I think the health care delivery systems are at the root cause of why many people don't use the systems. And, it is not something that is irremedial. When we began the infant-health development program, in all of the eight sites the follow-up clinics were lucky to get fifty percent of the kids back for the follow up. So you go to the clinics we are looking at and ask what is going on here? Well, there are two and three and four hour waits; they are not places where you would want to hang out with your children for any amount of time. We did a few simple things like chart and have the appointments made in such a way that they can be kept. How to cut down on the amount of waiting? We had in excess of ninety percent of all visits completed over a whole series of visits that were supposed to be made on the schedule as the American Academy of Pediatric and Small Child Care. So, when we deliver health care and, by implication, when we deliver educational services in the school systems, we create the most godawful services that one can imagine. You or I would not go there and spend any time if we had a choice. Until we make those services attractive, and we can do that, I believe, by bringing many of the behavioral principles that we know to bear, doesn't require new research. Until we do that, we are going to have people making rational choices to avoid a bad system.

Huston. I think part of the problem is that we started with the model, the medical model of the individual doctor-patient care and we sort of tinkered with that. And, maybe what we should do is to say we are dealing with something entirely different here. There are a lot of people who don't like current obstetrical care models who can come up with alternatives, such as a kind of educational model where you come into groups. I bet you could get six mothers to come in with their babies and talk together about a lot of . . .

Barnard. You can get educated mothers, but you can't get poor mothers.

Huston. There are probably lots of different ways to do it, especially if we begin to think about it from the point of view of a whole other model of education, rather than starting with the medical model and tinkering with it. We really have not begun to use television in the way that we could for reaching people with information.

Kotelchuck. We have to come up with models that are actually programs, that we could convert to programs. You can see how to take these possibilities and figure out a model that would work.

CHAPTER 8

Relationship between Risk and Protective Factors, Developmental Outcome, and the Home Environment at Four Years of Age in Term and Preterm Infants

Barry M. Lester, Margaret M. McGrath,
Cynthia García-Coll, Francine S. Brem,
Mary C. Sullivan, and Sara G. Mattis

The study of risk factors has become an important part of our understanding of child development. A high risk child is one who is at greater than average risk for later deviancies in behavior because of membership in some identifiable population (Sameroff & Seifer, 1983). Such populations could include infants with anomalous experiences including medical conditions such as low birth weight, disordered parentage, disturbed family and childrearing milieus and disadvantaged environments. However, we also know that many children do not succumb to deprivation, that even in the face of disorganized, impoverished homes, many children appear to develop normally; children who are referred to as "resilient" (Anthony, 1987; Werner, 1981; & Garmezy, 1981). This has lead to the study of protective factors; dispositional attributes, environmental conditions, biological predispositions and positive events that can act to contain the expression of deviance or pathology (Garmezy, Masten, & Tellegen, 1984; Fisher, Kokes, Cole, Perkins, & Wynee, 1987;

Murphy, 1987). Our models of development are now enriched by the concepts of resilience and protective factors as the positive counterparts to the constructs of vulnerability and risk factors (Werner, 1986).

In contrast to the large corpus of literature on risk factors, (Kopp & Drakow, 1983; Sameroff & Chandler, 1975), fewer studies have focused on protective factors in infants exposed to biological insult. These studies include infants with perinatal complications, congenital heart defects, cerebral palsy, down syndrome, and sensory deficits (Berry, 1987; Colona, 1981; Garmezy, 1987; Hrncir, 1987; Moriarty, 1987; O'Dougherty, Wright, Garmezy, Loewenson, & Torres, 1983; Werner & Smith, 1982; Williams, Williams, Landa, & Decena, 1987). Most studies of protective factors have focused on resilient children exposed to serious family caregiving deficits such as psychotic parents (Garmezy, 1974), alcoholism (Werner, 1986), child abuse (Egeland & Sroufe, 1986), or resiliency under conditions of poverty (Coles, 1967; Werner & Smith, 1982; Garmezy, 1981).

The Kauai Longitudinal Study is one of the few studies to prospectively follow the roots of resilience in infants (Werner, Bierman, & French, 1971; Werner & Smith, 1977; 1982). This study started in the prenatal period and monitored biological and social-environmental risk factors as well as protective factors in almost 700 Asian and Polynesian children born in 1955 on a rural Hawaiian island. Half of the children lived in poverty, the others in relative affluence. Multiple risk factors including perinatal complications, parental psychopathology, family instability and chronic poverty were related to later learning or behavior problems in approximately one-third of the subjects. However, there were 72 subjects who also experienced four or more of these risk factors and developed normally. The resilient subjects were also characterized by protective factors including positive temperament, favorable parental attitudes, low levels of family conflict, less life stress, smaller family size, counseling and remedial assistance.

Cumulative risk model. The idea that the number of biological and social-environmental factors is related to child outcome has been used to study risk factors but not protective factors. In early work, Parmelee (Parmelee & Haber, 1973) primarily used measures of child health and physical status to predict developmental outcome in infancy. Similarly, Rutter (1979) argued for the importance of the number of risk factors rather than the type of risk factor that contributes to child psychiatric disorder.

In reports from the Rochester Longitudinal Study (Sameroff, Seifer, Barocas, Zax, & Greenspan, 1987; Sameroff, Seifer, Baldwin, & Baldwin, 1993), Sameroff and colleagues calculated a multiple environmental risk score from ten factors and compared the intelligence of children with differing numbers of risks. They found a linear relationship between the number of risk factors and IQ at four years of age. Moreover, it was the total number of risk factors and not the kind of factor that affected the IQ scores. These results were replicated in a 13-year follow-up of these children. The cumulative risk score was related to IQ at 13 years of age and the pattern of risk, including poverty, was less important than the total amount of risk present in the child's context.

In the present study we used the cumulative factor approach. However, we applied this strategy to protective factors as well as biological and social risk factors. Our primary interest was in the interaction between risk and protective factors, that is, how do these factors interact; exacerbate or modify the effects of poverty on developmental outcome? To address these questions, we identified risk and protective factors in a sample of children followed longitudinally from birth to four years of age. Each subject was assigned a risk score and a protect score based on the total number of risk and protective factors. These scores were used to define four groups of children representing combinations of high and low risk and high and low protective factors. Developmental outcome was measured at four years of age in these four groups of children, and subsequently, after statistically controlling for poverty.

Methods

Sample. The sample included 134 subjects participating in a longitudinal study of development in term and preterm infants with complete developmental outcome at four years of age. Ninety-seven of the children had been born prematurely. The birth weight of the preterm infants ranged from 690–1820 grams (Mean = 1265, SD = 311), gestational age ranged from 25–35 weeks (Mean = 30, SD = 2.45). The preterm infants included subgroups of infants who were healthy and free of CNS insult (N = 30), sick infants, primarily with respiratory disease (N = 40), infants with CNS insult, primarily grade III or IV intraventricular hemorrhage (N = 15) and preterm infants who were also small for gestational age (N = 12). At the time of the infant's birth, mean four-factor Hollingshead (1975) scores were 2.69 (SD = 1.16) with all five SES categories represented, maternal age averaged 27.11 (SD = 5.19), 13.43% of the mothers were single, and most families (85.60%) were white.

Procedures. Demographic and medical information was collected during the infant's hospital stay in the neonatal period. A home visit was conducted when the infant was 9 months of age. At four years of age the children came to the hospital laboratory for a 2-hour testing session administered by an examiner unaware of the child's previous history. A second home visit was also conducted.

Measures. Two classes of measures were collected; the first class included demographic, medical, home environmental, maternal personality and parenting measures which were used to measure risk and protective factors. These measures were selected based, in part on previous work (Sameroff et al., 1987; Seifer, & Sameroff, 1987; Werner, 1986). Second, child developmental outcome, and temperament and home environmental measures were used to assess child outcome and to describe the home environment when child outcome was assessed. These two classes of measures are described below.

Risk and Protective Factors

Demographic. The Hollingshead four-factor index of social status was used to measure socioeconomic status based on parental education and occupation (Hollingshead, 1975). Other demographic factors included marital status, minority status, and maternal age.

Medical. The Hobel Medical Summary Score (HOME; Hobel, Hyvarinen, Okada, & Oh, 1973) was used to assess infant health status during the newborn period. The Hobel provides a weighted sum of the total number of medical complications. It is scored as an index of infant health, with higher scores reflecting increased risk status. In addition, preterm status, birth weight and the number of days the infant spent in the special care nursery were also used.

Home Environment. The Home Observation for Measurement of the Environment Inventory (Caldwell & Bradley, 1984) was administered when the infant was nine months of age. The HOME Inventory is designed to assess the quality of stimulation and support available to a child in the home environment. The infant version contains 45 binary-choice items clustered into six subscales: (a) parental responsibility, (b) acceptance of child, (c) organization of the environment, (d) play materials, (e) parental involvement, and (f) variety of stimulation.

Maternal personality. Two measures of maternal personality factors were administered when the infants were four years of age. Maternal personality variables of anxiety, depression, and other symptoms were rated on the Symptom Checklist—90-R (SCL-90-R; Derogatis, 1981). This measure produces ten factor scores: general anxiety, interpersonal sensitivity, phobic anxiety, depression, hostility, somatization, obsessive-compulsive, psychoticism, paranoid ideation, and problems/symptoms. Each symptom is rated on a Likert-type scale from "not at all" (0) to "extremely" (4).

Pre-school maternal self-esteem was assessed through a 26 item Likert-type scale developed for this study and based on the Maternal Self-Report Inventory (Shea & Tronick, 1988). The Maternal Self-Report Inventory was not appropriate for the present study as it is specific to the neonatal period, although it has also been used in early infancy. A relationship between this measure of pre-school maternal self-esteem and the Beck Depression Inventory (Beck, 1967) ($r = -.51$) was previously established. In the present study the Cronbach alpha coefficient for the preschool maternal self-esteem measure was .90, reflecting adequate internal consistency.

Family. These measures were also administered when the child was four years old. The Family Support Scale measures the helpfulness of sources of support to families with a young child (Dunst, Jenkins, & Trivette, 1984). Each item on this 18-item instrument is rated on a five-point scale ranging from "not at all helpful" (1) to "extremely helpful" (5). The Family Support Scale has been used in several studies investigating the relationship between social support and parental health or well-being, family integrity, parent's perceptions of child functioning, and parent-child styles of interaction (Dunst, 1985). The Family Resource Scale assesses the adequacy of various resources in households with young children (Dunst & Leet, 1987). It includes 31 items which are roughly ordered from the most to least basic and rated on a five-point scale ranging from "not at all adequate" (1) to "almost always adequate" (5). The Family Functioning Style Scale (Dunst, Trivette, & Deal, 1988) measures two aspects of family strengths: (1) the degree to which a family is characterized by different qualities and (2) the style in which various combinations of strengths define the unique functioning of a family. The items of the scale are divided into three categories thought to represent distinct facets of family functioning style: family identity, information sharing, and coping/resource mobilization. The Family Functioning Style Scale is a self-report instrument which may be completed by the family as a unit or by an individual family member. It includes 26 statements which the respondent rates on a five-point scale ranging from "not at all like my family" (0) to "almost always like my family" (4).

Outcome Measures

Developmental outcome. Cognitive and motor outcome variables were measured during the laboratory visit at four years of age. The McCarthy Scales of Children's Abilities (1972) were used to assess the child's cognitive ability. Eighteen separate subtests are summarized by an overall general cognitive index (GCI) and five major area scores: verbal, perceptual performance, quantitative, memory, and motor.

The Beery Developmental Test of Visual-Motor Integration, a test of geometrical form reproduction, is a measure of the integration of visuomotor functions (1967). The test has been standardized with a mean of 10 and a standard deviation of 3.

Receptive language was measured using the Peabody Picture Vocabulary Test-Revised (Dunn & Dunn, 1981). The Riley Motor Problems Inventory (1976) was used to identify neurological "soft" signs. It consists of ten tests which are summarized into scores for oral, fine motor, and gross motor subtests and a total cumulative score.

Temperament. Two measures of temperament were included, an observer rating and a parent rating. Temperament of the child during the testing session was rated by the examiner using a behavioral style assessment (Vohr, Garcia-Coll, & Oh, 1989). This instrument measures six dimensions: (1) approach-withdrawal, (2) activity, (3) attention, (4) co-operation, (5) mood, and (6) persistence. Children are scored on a scale ranging from 1 to 7 for each behavior characteristic observed during testing, with a score of 4 denoting average.

The EAS Temperament Survey of Children (Buss & Plomin, 1984) asks parents to rate twenty items on a five-point Likert-type scale reflecting the extent to which each item is typical of their child. Questions reflect three construct domains: emotionality, activity, and sociability.

Home environment. The HOME was also used in this study at the four year home visit (Caldwell & Bradley, 1984). This version contains 55 items forming eight subscales and a total score. The eight subscales are: Stimulation Through Toys, Games, and Reading Materials; Language Stimulation; Physical Environment: Safe, Clean, and Conducive to Development; Pride, Affection, and Warmth; Stimulation of Academic Behavior; Modeling and Encouragement of Social Maturity; Variety of Stimulation; and Physical Punishment.

Risk and Protective Factor Groups

Subjects were divided into four groups based on the number of risk and protective factors in each family. The four groups were; (1) Low risk-Low protect, (2) Low risk-High protect, (3) High risk-Low protect and (4) High risk-High protect. Fourteen variables were used as risk or protective factors shown in Table 1.

Table 1 also shows the cut-off values used for each variable as a High risk or High protective factor and the percentage of

TABLE 1

Criteria for risk and protective factors

Factor	Risk	Percent	Protect	Percent
Hollingshead	4 & 5	23.9	1	15.7
Maternal education (yrs.)	<12	14.3	>15	18.0
Maternal age (yrs.)	<20, >34	8.4, 6.2	20—34	85.4
Marital status	Single	13.4	Non-single	78.4
Ethnicity	B, H, O	14.4	—	—
Hobel	>160	24.6	<30	24.6
Birth weight (grams)	<1500	50.0	>2500	27.6
Days hospitalized	>61	24.6	<5	27.6
HOME (9 months)	<35	23.8	>41	30.3
Family support scale	<14	21.4	>27	23.7
Family resource scale	<103	24.4	>133	23.8
Family functioning style scale	<65	24.6	>86	23.7
Pre-school maternal self-esteem	<89	24.2	>108	22.0
SCL-90-R	>0.06	24.4	<0.01	20.6

subjects for each cut-off value. For most variables, values closest to the upper and lower 25th percentile were used as cut-off values for determining the High risk or High protective score.

For the variables of mother's age, marital status and birth weight, the cut-off values were determined a priori based on their documented importance in the literature (Sameroff et al., 1987). Membership in a minority ethnic group was considered a risk factor, but ethnicity was not used as a protective factor. Some factors were based on neonatal information. These were: infant birth weight, days of hospitalization prior to initial discharge from the nursery during the newborn period, the Hobel medical risk score, maternal age and education, Hollingshead score, ethnicity and marital status. The HOME score was based on the 9-month home visit. The remaining factors were based on information collected when the children were four years of age.

Each subject was assigned one point for each risk factor and one point for each protective factor. The number of risk and protect points were summed for each subject resulting in a total risk score and a total protect score. The mean risk score of the total sample was 3.16 (SD = 2.67); the mean protect score of the total sample was 4.13 (SD = 2.17). Subjects with a risk score <3 were assigned to the Low risk group (45.5%), subjects with scores of 3 or above were assigned to the High risk group (54.5%). Subjects with protect scores <5 were assigned to the low protect group (53%), subjects with scores of 5 and above were placed in the High protect group (47%). Subjects were then divided into the following four cells: Low risk-Low protect (N = 18, 13.43%), Low risk-High protect (N = 43, 32.09%), High risk-Low protect (N = 53, 39.55%) and High risk-High protect (N = 20, 14.93%).

Results

The means and standard deviations for the McCarthy, PPVT-R, Beery and Riley developmental outcome scores for the four groups of children with High and Low risk and protect factors are shown in Table 2.

TABLE 2

Means and Standard Deviations of Developmental Outcome Scores for the Four Groups of Children

	Lo-Risk/ Lo-Protect	Lo-Risk/ Hi-Protect	Hi-Risk/ Lo-Protect	Hi-Risk/ Hi-Protect
	Mean (S.D.)	Mean (S.D.)	Mean (S.D.)	Mean (S.D.)
McCarthy				
General Cognitive Index	100.58 (12.13)	110.37 (13.07)	92.24 (13.75)	101.05 (22.41)
Verbal	51.64 (9.52)	54.32 (9.57)	46.22 (8.80)	50.70 (13.18)
Perceptual Performance	47.17 (9.12)	54.90 (9.95)	44.43 (8.44)	47.45 (11.03)
Quantitative	53.17 (5.24)	56.09 (9.41)	46.34 (8.82)	51.25 (11.48)
Memory	51.52 (9.04)	55.44 (9.28)	48.07 (9.13)	52.05 (13.17)
Motor	45.00 (8.13)	50.74 (8.99)	40.26 (8.50)	42.00 (12.03)
PPVT-R	103.23 (10.01)	111.52 (12.48)	97.80 (17.75)	103.15 (13.72)
Beery Developmental Test of Visual-motor Integration	8.23 (1.64)	9.86 (2.41)	8.50 (1.73)	8.75 (2.97)
Riley motor problems inventory Total score	11.94 (3.66)	9.72 (3.69)	12.56 (3.90)	12.40 (3.70)
Oral	3.29 (1.86)	3.16 (1.77)	3.62 (1.63)	3.20 (1.88)
Fine motor	4.23 (1.56)	2.95 (1.60)	4.09 (1.57)	4.20 (1.32)
Gross motor	4.41 (1.77)	3.60 (1.77)	4.83 (1.94)	5.00 (1.83)

The four groups were compared using analysis of variance followed by the Duncan multiple range test for individual cell comparisons. On the McCarthy scales significant effects were found on the general cognitive index and on all five subscales. On the general cognitive index, $F(3, 129) = 11.61$, $p<.0001$, children in the Low risk-Hi protect group scored higher than children in the other three groups ($p<.05$). In addition, children in the Low risk- Low protect and High risk-High protect groups scored higher than children in the High risk-Low protect group, $p<.05$.

The effects on the verbal subscale, $F(3, 129) = 5.48$, $p<.001$, were due to higher scores in the Low risk-High protect group than the High risk-Low protect group, $p<.05$.

On the memory subscale, similar effects were observed, $F(3, 128) = 4.43$, $p<.005$; children in the Low risk-High protect group scored higher than children in the High risk-Low protect group, $p<.05$. On the perceptual-performance subscale, $F(3, 129) = 10.05$, $p<.0001$, children in the Low risk-High protect group scored higher than children in the other three groups, $p<.05$. Significant effects on the quantitative subscale, $F(3, 129) = 9.41$, $p<.0001$, were due to higher scores in the Low risk-High protect and Low risk-Low protect groups than in the High risk-Low protect group, $p<.05$. On the motor subscale, $F(3, 129) = 10.79$, $p<.0001$, children in the Low risk-High protect group received higher scores than children in the other three groups, $p<.05$.

There were significant effects on the PPVT receptive language test, $F(3, 127) = 6.71$, $p<.0003$. Children in the Low risk-High protect group showed higher scores than children in the High risk-Low protect group, $p<.05$. On the Beery test, significant effects were observed, $F(3, 129) = 3.89$, $p<.01$, due to higher scores in the Low risk-High protect group compared to both the High risk-Low protect group and the Low risk-Low protect group, $p<.05$. The Riley showed significant effects on three of the four scales, fine motor, $F(3, 129) = 5.80$, $p<.001$, gross motor, $F(3, 129) = 4.28$, $p<.006$, and the total score, $F(3, 129) = 5.04$, $p<.002$. No differences were observed on the oral scale. The differences on the fine motor and total scales were both due to fewer problems (lower scores) in the Low risk-High protect than in the other three groups (both p's$<.05$). On the gross motor scale, children in the Low risk-High protect group showed fewer problems than children in the High risk-Low protect group and the High risk-High protect group. On the behavioral style assessment, significant effects were found on two scales, attention, F(3, 129) = 4.15, $p<.007$, and persistence/distractibility, F(3, 129) = 6.06, $p<.0007$. Children in the Low risk-High protect group showed higher attention ($p<.05$) and more persistence ratings ($p<.05$) than children in the High risk-Low protect group.

On the HOME Inventory, significant differences were found on the total score, F(3, 130) = 8.07, $p<.0001$, with lower scores in the High risk-Low protect group than in the other three groups, $p<.05$, and on six of the eight subscales. The learning stimulation scale, F(3, 129) = 6.85, $p<.0003$, showed less stimulation in the homes of children in the High risk-Low protect group than in the other three groups, $p<.05$. Language stimulation, F(3, 129) = 3.88, $p<.01$, was higher in the Low risk-High protect than in the High risk-Low protect group, $p<.05$. On the physical environment scale, F(3, 129) = 10.72, $p<.0001$, a less adequate environment was found in the High risk-Low protect group than in the other three groups, $p<.05$. The modeling scale, F(3, 129) = 4.01, $p<.009$, showed more modeling in the Low risk-High protect group than in the High risk-Low protect group, $p<.05$. Variety of experience, F(3, 129) = 4.80, $p<.003$, was less in the High risk-Low protect group than in the three other groups, p's$<.05$. Similarly, acceptance, F(3, 129) = 4.09, $p<.008$, was less in the High risk-Low protect group than in the other three groups, $p<.05$. There were no significant differences on the warmth and affection and academic stimulation subscales.

Group differences in risk and protective factors. The findings reported above show group differences as a function of combinations of risk and protect scores. To determine which risk and protect factors differed among the four groups, we compared the High and Low risk and protect groups on the individual variables used to calculate the risk and protect scores.

The distribution of subject characteristics in the four groups for categorical variables is shown in Table 3. The distribution of preterm infants in the four groups was not evenly distributed. Preterm infants represented over 90% of the subjects

TABLE 3

Subject Characteristics for Categorical Variables Used in the Risk and Protective Scores

	Lo-Risk/ Lo-Protect N (%)	Lo-Risk/ Hi-Protect N (%)	Hi-Risk/ Lo-Protect N (%)	Hi-Risk/ Hi-Protect N (%)
Birth Status				
Full Term	1 (5.56)	23 (53.49)	4 (7.55)	9 (45.00)
Preterm	17 (94.44)	20 (46.51)	49 (92.45)	11 (55.00)
Marital Status				
Single	0 (0.00)	0 (0.00)	17 (32.08)	1 (5.00)
Non-Single	18 (100.00)	43 (100.00)	36 (67.92)	19 (95.00)
Ethnicity				
Black	0 (0.00)	1 (2.38)	12 (24.00)	0 (0.00)
Hispanic	0 (0.00)	0 (0.00)	1 (2.00)	0 (0.00)
White	15 (100.00)	41 (97.62)	34 (68.00)	17 (94.44)
Other	0 (0.00)	0 (0.00)	3 (6.00)	1 (5.56)

in the two Low protect groups and approximately 50% of the subjects in the two High protect groups. Of the 18 single mothers in the sample, 17 were in the High risk-Low protect group. This group also included 16 of the 18 minority subjects in the sample.

The means and standard deviations for the continuous variables used in the risk and protect scores are shown in Table 4. On the infant medical variables, the differences in infant birth weight, $F(3, 130) = 14.25$, $p<.0001$, were due to higher birth weight in the two High protect groups than in the two Low protect groups $p<.05$. The number of days of hospitalization prior to initial discharge from the newborn nursery, $F(3, 130) = 10.90$, $p<.0001$, was lower in the Low risk-High protect group than in the three other groups, $p<.05$. On the Hobel medical risk score, significant differences, $F(3, 130) = 8.12$, $p<.0001$, were due to a lower medical risk score in the two High protect groups than in the two High risk groups, $p<.05$.

In terms of demographic and maternal characteristics, on the Hollingshead scale, $F(3, 130) = 15.78$, $p<.0001$, the mean SES was highest in the Low risk-High protect group, $p<.05$. The SES level of the Low risk-Low protect and High risk-High protect groups did not differ from each other but was higher than the SES of the High risk-Low protect group, $p<.05$. The effect for maternal education, $F(3, 129) = 11.51$, $p<.0001$, was due to a lower education achieved by mothers in the High risk-Low protect group than by mothers in the three other groups, $p<.05$. Maternal age did not differ among the four groups. There were significant differences for maternal self esteem, $F(3, 128) = 6.21$, $p<.0006$. Maternal self-esteem was higher in the Low risk groups than in the two High risk groups, $p<.05$.

The total score on the SCL-90-R measure of maternal psychological distress was significant, $F(3, 127) = 11.51$, $p<.0001$; mothers in the two Low risk groups reported less overall psychological distress than mothers in the High risk-High protect group, $p<.05$. There were also significant effects on the SCL-90-R subscales. The effects on three of the subscales, somatic, $F(3, 127) = 4.52$, $p<.005$, obsessive compulsive, $F(3, 128) = 8.64$, $p<.0001$, and anxiety, $F(3, 128) = 10.48$, $p<.0001$ were due to differences between the High risk-High protect group and the

TABLE 4

Means and Standard Deviations of Continuous Variables Used in the Risk and Protect Scores

	Lo-Risk/ Lo-Protect	Lo-Risk/ Hi-Protect	Hi-Risk/ Lo-Protect	Hi-Risk/ Hi-Protect
Birth Weight	1506.11	2549.47	1376.60	2071.60
	(572.51)	(1105.75)	(664.75)	(1244.75)
Days of Hospitalization	38.83	20.23	51.85	41.90
	(19.67)	(22.40)	(28.13)	(37.51)
Hobel	117.75	73.13	133.12	99.45
	(46.50)	(62.02)	(52.15)	(83.86)
Hollingshead	2.56	1.98	3.38	2.55
	(0.78)	(0.83)	(1.06)	(1.32)
Maternal Education	14.11	14.40	12.08	13.25
	(1.60)	(1.75)	(2.10)	(2.61)
Maternal Age	28.44	28.07	25.57	27.85
	(3.68)	(3.90)	(6.25)	(5.00)
Pre-School Maternal Self-Esteem	103.19	103.05	93.55	96.00
	(9.40)	(9.90)	(14.40)	(10.28)
SCL90-R	0.03	0.02	0.05	0.07
	(0.01)	(0.02)	(0.03)	(0.05)
HOME	39.69	41.02	34.62	36.45
	(3.66)	(2.04)	(6.68)	(6.89)
Family Support Scale	19.31	25.07	16.58	30.10
	(7.38)	(10.36)	(6.87)	(13.09)
Family Resource Scale	123.31	128.79	102.87	116.25
	(14.95)	(13.68)	(23.33)	(30.97)
Family Functioning Scale	76.06	84.33	65.12	77.25
	(6.37)	(10.94)	(16.88)	(20.78)

other three groups. Mothers in the High risk-High protect group showed more somatic complaints, $p<.05$, more obsessive compulsive symptoms, $p<.05$, and more anxiety, $p<.05$ than mothers in the other groups. On the interpersonal sensitivity scale, $F(3, 128) = 6.73$, $p<.003$, mothers in the two Low risk groups showed more interpersonal sensitivity than mothers in the two High risk groups, $p<.05$. The effects on the depression scale, $F(3, 128) = 10.90$, $p<.0001$, showed lower levels of depression in the two Low risk groups, $p<.05$, with the most depressive symptomatology shown by mothers in the High risk-High protect group, $p<.05$. On the hostility scale, $F(3, 128) = 7.04$, $p<.0002$, mothers in the two Low risk groups showed less hostility than mothers in the two High risk groups, $p<.05$. The phobic anxiety scale, $F(3, 128) = 4.14$, $p<.008$, revealed less phobic anxiety in the Low risk-Low protect group than in the High risk-High protect group, $p<.05$. Effects on the paranoid ideation scale $F(3, 128) = 6.75$, $p<.0003$, and on the psychotic symptom scales, $F(3, 128) = 4.75$, $p<.004$, showed more paranoid ideation, $p<.05$ and more psychotic symptomatology, $p<.05$, in the High risk-High protect group than in the Low risk-High protect group, $p<.05$. Finally, on the additional problems scale, $F(3, 128) = 9.26$, $p<.0001$, mothers in the two High risk groups reported more problems than did mothers in the two Low risk groups, $p<.05$.

On the home and family measures, group differences on the 9 month HOME Inventory, $F(3, 129) = 11.85$, $p<.0001$, were due to higher HOME total scores in the two Low risk groups than in the two High risk groups, $p<.05$. The effects on the Family Resources Scale, $F(3, 126) = 12.30$, $p<.0001$, showed more family resources in the two Low risk groups than in the two High risk groups, $p<.05$. However, the High risk-Low protect group showed fewer resources than the other three groups, $p<.05$. The effects on the Family Support Scale, $F(3, 127) = 12.93$, $p<.0001$, showed that families in the two High protect groups reported more social support than families in the two Low protect groups, $p<.05$. The results of the Family Functioning Style Scale, $F(3, 127) = 13.31$, $p<.0001$, showed lower functioning in the High risk-Low protect group than in the other three groups, $p<.05$.

Analysis of poverty effects. The data reported here suggest that developmental outcome, temperament and home environment scores are related to many variables in the social context. However, it is still possible that poverty may be the overriding factor. To test for this possibility, the group comparisons on the outcome measures were recomputed using analysis of covariance with the Hollingshead SES level as the covariate.

Table 5 shows the adjusted means for the outcome measures with SES removed. The table also shows F values and significance level following the analysis of covariance. Controlling for SES did not alter the finding of group differences on the McCarthy, PPVT-R, Beery, or Riley tests. All F tests on these measures that were statistically significant with SES included were still significant with SES removed. The significant effect on the temperament measure of attention was marginally significant with SES controlled. In contrast, none of the previously significant effects on the four year HOME scale were significant with SES removed.

Discussion

This study examined the interaction between risk and protective factors in relation to four-year developmental outcome in term and preterm infants. We utilized the multiple risk strategy of assigning one point for each risk factor and computing a summary risk score and extended this method to compute a counterpart summary protective factor score.

By dividing families into groups with High and Low risk and protective scores, we were able to determine differences in child developmental outcome as a function of the interaction between the number of risk and protective factors.

It may seem obvious that, in general, children in the Low risk-High protect group showed the best overall performance and that children in the High risk-Low protect group showed the worst overall performance. These findings were consistently observed on the McCarthy, Peabody, Beery, and Riley tests. The

TABLE 5

Mean Outcome Scores Adjusted for SES

	Lo-Risk/ Lo-Protect	Lo-Risk/ Hi-Protect	Hi-Risk/ Lo-Protect	Hi-Risk/ Hi-Protect	$F(1,3)$	$P<$
McCarthy						
GCI	100.15	108.90	93.68	100.77	6.10	.0006
Verbal	51.42	53.59	46.95	50.56	2.69	.049
Perceptual-Performance	47.19	54.96	44.38	47.46	7.73	.0001
Quantitative	52.96	55.37	47.05	51.11	5.04	.0025
Memory	51.42	55.09	48.42	51.98	2.65	.051
Motor	45.23	51.41	39.61	42.12	10.20	.0001
PPVT-R	102.81	110.13	99.18	102.88	3.34	.021
Beery	8.21	9.79	8.58	8.74	2.83	.041
Riley						
Oral	3.27	3.08	3.71	3.18	.86	N.S.
Fine Motor	4.21	2.88	4.16	4.19	5.62	.001
Gross Motor	4.40	3.58	4.85	5.00	3.63	.014
Total	11.88	9.53	12.75	12.36	4.85	.003

	Lo-Risk/ Lo-Protect	Lo-Risk/ Hi-Protect	Hi-Risk/ Lo-Protect	Hi-Risk/ Hi-Protect	$F(1,3)$	$P<$
Behavioral Style Assessment						
Approach-Withdrawal	2.79	3.36	3.38	3.01	.51	N.S.
Activity	4.15	3.82	4.15	4.57	.88	N.S.
Attention	3.63	3.89	2.89	3.09	2.55	.059
Co-Operation	4.52	5.01	4.11	4.65	1.51	N.S.
Mood	4.75	4.92	4.41	4.64	.62	N.S.
Persistence/ Distractibility	3.97	3.45	4.68	4.12	3.28	.023
4 Year HOME						
Learning Stimulation	8.92	9.13	8.20	9.36	1.81	N.S.
Language Stimulation	6.47	6.58	6.28	6.21	.77	N.S.
Physical Environment	6.36	6.48	5.88	6.33	2.14	N.S.
Warmth and Affection	6.33	6.36	5.85	6.13	1.04	N.S.
Academic Stimulation	4.02	4.51	4.23	4.13	1.29	N.S.
Modeling	3.39	3.79	3.57	3.55	.70	N.S.
Variety in Experience	7.27	7.23	6.71	7.65	1.66	N.S.
Acceptance	3.80	3.70	3.41	3.88	1.92	N.S.
Total	46.63	47.63	43.92	47.17	1.82	N.S.

effects were robust and not specific to any one domain; they were seen across a range of cognitive and intellectual abilities and motor function.

One could suggest that risk and protective factors merely represent opposite ends of the same continuum such that the presence of one implies the absence of the other. If this were true, one could simply use a risk score or a protect score and the results should be comparable. However, our results did not show main effects for either "risk" or "protect": the two High risk groups did not show worse scores than the two High protect groups. The scores of the children in the High risk-High protect and Low risk-Low protect groups were between the scores of the children in the High risk-Low protect and Low risk-High protect groups. For example, in terms of IQ, the McCarthy GCI showed almost a twenty point difference between the two extreme groups (90 in the High risk-Low protect group versus 110 in the High protect-Low risk group) but only a ten point difference between either extreme group and the two groups where the interaction between risk and protective factors could be seen. In other words, half of the differences could be explained if either the effects of protective factors were diminished by risk factors or if the effects of risk factors were attenuated by protective factors.

The results show that the interaction between risk and protective factors is a better predictor of child developmental outcome, than the presence of other factors per se. It is not simply the presence or absence of risk or protective factors but the combination of these factors that mediates child outcome. From this perspective we can understand the importance of the context of development in determining child outcome. Organismic and contextualist world views stress the importance of experience in explaining child outcome (Sameroff, 1982; Bronfenbrenner, 1979; Rutter, 1979). The environment has also been described as a dynamic system that interacts with the regulatory capacities of the child (Sameroff, 1982). The interaction between risk and protective factors may be a dynamic aspect of the environment that mediates child outcome. Risk factors may serve as de-regulators that destabilize child regulatory capacities, whereas protective factors may be re-regulators that stabilize child regulatory capacities.

We saw good evidence of this phenomenon in the current study. In the High risk-High protect group, protective factors buffered the child against the effects of high risk factors alone. These children did not do as poorly as the children in the High risk-Low protect group. It is also interesting that in the absence of risk and protective factors, the children perform at about the same level as when both risk and protective factors are present. In other words, there are no environmental factors to enhance or attenuate performance.

Temperament and Home Measures

There were no differences on the EAS parent report temperament measure. If the mothers do not perceive temperament differences between children in the four groups, it may be that observed differences in the children are not due to differential treatment by the mothers as a function of her perceived temperament of the child. Temperament differences were observed during the laboratory visit based on rating by an examiner. The differences that were observed were on dimensions of attention and persistence. These dimensions are theoretically linked to cognitive performance and the differences observed were consistent with the findings on the cognitive outcome measures.

Differences on the HOME Inventory at four years of age were found on six of the eight subscales as well as on the total score. Most of the findings suggested that the environment of the children in the High risk-Low protect group was less adequate than the home environment of the children in the three other groups.

Specific Risk and Protective Factors

Comparisons of the four groups on the 14 risk and protective factors suggested that it is the combination of risk and protective factors rather than the presence of any specific factor that explains the four year developmental outcome of these children.

The medical risk measures showed an interesting pattern of results on three of the four variables: preterm infants were over-represented in the two Low protect groups. We typically think of preterm infants as being over-represented in high risk environments. In this study the cells with the most preterm infants were the low protect cells not the high risk cells. The study of both risk and protective factors may lead to a better understanding of biologically at-risk populations.

Not surprisingly, the two Low protect groups with mostly preterm infants had lower birth weights and more medical complications than the two High protect groups. The number of days to hospital discharge, however, was only different between the Low risk-High protect group and the other three groups, suggesting that medical illness played a similar role in three of the four groups.

From a strictly medical risk perspective, one might have predicted that the Low protect groups, with over 90% preterm infants would have worse developmental outcome than the two High protect groups with approximately half preterm infants. Yet we have learned from a number of longitudinal studies with preterm infants that prematurity or even prematurity coupled with illness and other medical risk factors in the newborn period is not necessarily a harbinger of poor developmental outcome (Sameroff & Chandler, 1975; Werner et al., 1971). Rather it is the socio-environmental context within which the preterm infant develops that determines the outcome of these children. In this case, it was the combination of Low protective and High risk factors that seems to predispose the preterm infants to poor developmental outcome; preterm infants in low protective environment in which High risk factors are not operative show better developmental outcome scores.

The demographic features of the sample showed that single, less educated mothers, minorities and families with a lower SES characterized the High risk-Low protect group. Mothers in the High risk groups showed a lower self esteem than mothers in the Low risk groups, but the overall psychological distress of the mother was highest in the High risk-High protect group and lowest in the two Low risk groups. Mothers in the High risk-High protect group also showed the most psychological disturbances including somatic, obsessive-compulsive, anxiety, insensitivity, depression, hostility, paranoid ideation, psychotic symptomatology, and psychological problems. If maternal psychological factors were the major determinant of child outcome, we would have expected children in the High risk-High protect group to show the worst performance.

On the 9-month HOME scale, both risk groups showed less adequate home characteristics than both protective groups. Thus, a compromised home environment contributed to the poorer outcome of children in the High risk-Low protect group, but the home alone was not sufficient to account for the performance of these children. It is the combination of an inadequate home environment in conjunction with other factors that explains poor outcome.

The results of the social support measure showed less family resources and poorer family functioning in the two High risk groups; the two High protect groups showed more social support than the two Low protect groups. Less social support in the context of less resources and poorer family functioning has a more negative effect than less social support with more resources and higher levels of family functioning.

The general finding from the analysis of the specific risk and protective factors suggests that the effects of risk and protective factors are cumulative and interactive. Risk factors in the absence of protective factors deter child outcome, protective factors in the absence of risk factors enhance child outcome, when both are present or neither are present, risk and protective factors seem to offset each other. This appears to be a dynamic system in which risk and protective factors act as check and balance factors that regulate child outcome. It is not the presence or absence of one factor that has a positive or negative consequence for the child. Rather, it is the presence of a factor given the presence or absence of other factors that facilitate or retard child developmental outcome.

Summary of Risk and Protective Effects

The four groups that we studied represent different combinations of risk and protective factors. In some ways, the Low risk-High protect and High risk-Low protect groups represent rather classic familial patterns with classic child outcomes. The Low risk-High protect group included higher SES families with a good home environment, high social support and family resources and mothers with a good self concept and low levels of psychological distress. Their children showed the best developmental outcome. The High risk-Low protect group consisted of families with mostly preterm infants, a lower SES, more single mothers and minorities, lower maternal education, lack of family resources and lower family function, a less adequate home environment, and mothers with a lower self concept and less sensitivity, more hostility and more psychological problems. Their children showed the poorest developmental outcome.

Of greater scientific interest are the families in the other two groups. Like the High risk-Low protect group, the Low risk-Low protect group included mostly preterm infants, with similar birth weights and medical complications and illness. What protected these infants from the poor outcome of their counterparts in the High risk-Low protect group? On the one hand, they were protected by the absence of other risk factors: low SES, less maternal education, minority status, single mothers. On the other hand, they had more protective factors; higher maternal self-esteem and sensitivity, less overall maternal psychological distress, depression, hostility and anxiety, more family resources and a better home environment. These preterm infants grew up in supportive environments with protective factors to buffer the negative impact of risk factors and facilitate recovery from medical illness. Yet their recovery was probably dampened by the combination of their medical history and an environment that was not as high in protective factors as we saw in the Low risk-High protect group.

Finally, the High risk-High protect group shared a similar number and type of protective factors with the Low risk-High protect group. Half of the infants were term, SES was middle or higher, and there was a high level of social support. However, the development of these infants was attenuated by risk factors: an adequate home environment, fewer family resources, lower maternal self-esteem and psychological disturbances in the mother. This group of mothers was distinct in their self-reported psychological distress that included the most severe symptomatology of the four groups. Perhaps these were resilient children who did reasonably well despite maternal psychological factors that could have been expected to have a more negative impact on their development. Perhaps some of the resiliency came from the biological integrity of the infant, the middle class environment in which they thrived and a strong social support system. These may have been the protective factors that buffered the children against the negative impact of maternal psychological disturbance.

Effects of Poverty

Analysis of outcome scores controlling for the effects of SES showed virtually no effects on the cognitive and motor outcome scores. For example, adjusting for SES only increased the mean GCI from 92.24 to 93.68 in the High risk-Low protect group and only decreased the mean from 110.37 to 108.90 in the Low risk-High protect group. This provides strong evidence that the poor performance of the children in the High risk-Low protect group was not due to the overriding effects of low social class. Poverty is one of a number of risk factors that, combined with the absence of protective factors to buffer the child, can result in poor developmental outcome.

Social class had a marginal effect on the attentional measure of temperament and no effect on the persistence/distractibility measure. SES had a strong impact on the four year HOME scores—none of the significant group differences remained when SES was controlled. This suggests that although the HOME appears to be strongly related to social class, the differences in developmental outcome do not appear to be due only to contemporaneous differences in the home environment.

Methodological Issues

The definitions that we used to assign risk or protect scores to each family were based primarily on the upper or lower quartile of the distribution of each variable. This is important because it leaves open the possibility for a family to not be assigned a risk or protective score. Thus, the presence of a protective factor does not simply mean the absence of a risk factor and vice versa.

There are two methodological limitations of this study. First, risk and protective variables included measures at various points in time including the newborn period, nine months and four years. Thus, we were not able to predict longer term developmental outcome scores since some of the variables used to define the groups were contemporaneous with the child's outcome scores.

Second, although we support the construct that contextual factors are dynamic and operate in transaction with the regulatory capacities of the child over time, we were not able to measure the dynamic aspect of this process. Ours is a single analysis in which data from multiple time points were used to define families with High and Low risk and protective factors. Future studies need to include measurement at several points in time and to include changes in child characteristics to truly describe the dynamic nature of how risk and protective factors combine to determine child outcome.

Implications for Our Understanding of Poverty. Previous studies have drawn attention to the importance of environmental factors and the compounding of environmental risk, including low SES, in predicting later child outcome. In particular, Sameroff et al. (1987) identified ten risk factors and found that it was the accumulation of risk variables rather than the action of specific factors that affected child outcome. The ten risk factors were predominantly found in lower SES families but affected outcome in all social classes. Poverty, when treated as one of many contextual factors, had no individual effect.

Our results support these previous findings; the compounding of risk factors relates to child outcome and, when viewed in the larger contextual framework, there are no individual effects for poverty. Poverty is best viewed as a marker variable for social status factors that are likely to impact on child outcome, and research has begun to identify the important factors and how they combine to affect child outcome.

In this study we were also able to add a protective factor dimension that is not simply the reciprocal of risk but seems to interact with risk factors in determining child outcome. As with risk factors, protective factors also seem to have a cumulative effect that regulates the child in the face of environmental stress. In this light it is useful to point out that not only was lower SES independently unrelated to poor outcome, but higher SES by itself was also unrelated to better outcome. We have already seen social status described as a nonspecific descriptor of negative individual, family and social forces—social status may also be a nondescriptor of positive forces as well. In this study we operationalized some aspects of social status that can foster child outcome and mediate environmental risk.

The phrase "children in poverty" is chilling and rightly so. However, as we learn about environmental strengths and the forces in the individual, the family and the culture that can mediate "poverty" effects, we learn more about the processes that determine child outcome and we are better positioned to target those aspects of the environment that are susceptible to intervention.

Acknowledgment

Supported by grants from the NICHD grant RO1HD21013 and the National Institute For Nursing Research grant R29 NR02263. Send requests for reprints to Barry M. Lester, Division of Child and Adolescent Psychiatry, Bradley Hospital, 1011 Veterans Memorial Parkway, E., Providence, RI 02915

REFERENCES

Anthony, E. J. (1987). Risk, Vulnerability, and Resilience: An Overview. In E. J. Anthony & B. Cohler (Eds.), *The Invulnerable Child* (pp. 3–48). New York: Guilford Press.

Beck, A. T. (1967). *Depression: Clinical, Experimental and Theoretical Aspects.* New York: Harper & Row.

Beery K. E. (1967). *Developmental Test of Visual-Motor Integration.* Chicago: Follett Publishing Co.

Berry, P. (1987, July). *Risk and Protective Factors in the Development of Down's Syndrome Children and Adolescents.* Paper presented at the Ninth Biennial Meeting of the International Society for the Study of Behavioral Development, Tokyo, Japan.

Bronfenbrenner, U. (1979). Contexts of child rearing: Problems and Prospects. *American Psychologist, 34* (10), 844–850.

Buss, A.H. & Plomin, R. (1984). *Temperament: Early Developing Personality Traits.* Hillsdale, NJ: Lawrence Erlbaum.

Cadwell, B. & Bradley, R. (1984). *Home Observation for Measurement of the Environment.* Little Rock:Center for Early Development and Education.

Coles, R. (1967). *Children of Crisis: Vol. 1. A study of courage and fear.* Boston: Little, Brown.

Colona, A. (1981). Success through their own efforts. *Psychoanalytic Study of the Child, 36,* 33–44.

Derogatis, L. (1981). Description and Bibliography for the SCL-90-R. Unpublished manuscript.

Dunn, L. M. & Dunn, L. M. (1981). *Peabody Picture Vocabulary Test-Revised: Manual for Forms L and M.* Circle Pines, Minnesota: American Guidance Service.

Dunst, C. J. (1985). Rethinking early intervention. *Analysis and Intervention in Developmental Disabilities, 5,* 165–201.

Dunst, C. J., Jenkins, V., & Trivette, C. M. (1984). Family Support Scale: Reliability and validity. *Journal of Individual, Family, and Community Wellness, 1,* 45–52.

Dunst, C. J. & Leet, H. E. (1987). Measuring the adequacy of resources in households with young children. *Child: Care, Health and Development, 13,* 111–125.

Dunst, C. J., Trivette, C. M., & Deal, A. G. (1988). *Enabling and empowering families: Principles and guidelines for practice.* Cambridge, MA: Brookline Books.

Egeland, B. & Sroufe, A. (1986, August). Stressful Life Events and School Outcome: A Study of Protective Factors. Paper presented at the American Psychological Association Meeting, Washington, DC.

Fisher, L., Kokes, R. F., Cole, R. E, Perkins, P. M., & Wynee, L. C. (1987). Competent children at risk: A study of well-functioning offspring of disturbed parents. In E. J. Anthony & B. Cohler (Eds.), *The invulnerable child* (pp. 221–228). New York: Guilford Press.

Garmezy, N. (1974). The study of competence in children at risk for severe psychopathology. In E. J. Anthony & C. Koupernick (Eds.), *The child in his family: Children at psychiatric risk, 3,* 77–98. New York: McGraw-Hill.

————. (1981). Children under stress: Perspectives on antecedents and correlates of vulnerability and resistance to psychopathology. In A. I. Rabin, J. Aronoff, A. M. Barclay, & R. A. Zucker (Eds.), *Further explorations in personality* (pp. 196–269). New York: Wiley.

————. (1987). Stress, competence, and development: Continuities in the study of schizophrenic adults, children vulnerable to psychopathology, and the search for stress resistant children. *American Journal of Orthopsychiatry, 52,* 159–174.

Garmezy, N., Masten, A., & Tellegen, A. (1984). The study of stress and competence in children: A building block for developmental psychopathology. *Child Development 55,* 97–111.

Hobel, C. J., Hyvarinen, M., Okada, D., & Oh, W. (1973). Prenatal and intrapartum high risk screening. *American Journal of Obstetrics and Gynecology, 1,* 117.

Hollingshead, A. (1975). "Four-Factor Index of Social Status." Unpublished paper, Yale University, New Haven, CT.

Hrncir, E. J. (1987, May). Mother and Infant Affective Contributors to Resiliency in At-Risk and Non-Risk Infants. Paper presented at the Fifth International Conference on Early Identification of Children at Risk, Durango, CO.

Koop, C. B., & Drakow, J. B. (1983). The developmentalist and the study of biological risk: A view of the past with an eye toward the future. *Child Development, 54,* 1086–1108.

McCarthy, D. (1972). *The Manual for McCarthy Scales of Children's Ability.* New York: The Psychological Corporation.

Moriarty, A. E. (1987). John, a boy who acquired resilience. In E. J. Anthony & B. Cohler (Eds.), *The invulnerable child* (pp. 106–144). New York: Guilford Press.

Murphy, L. B. (1987). Further reflections on resilience. In E. J. Anthony & B. Cohler (Eds.), *The invulnerable child* (pp. 84–105). New York: Guilford Press.

O'Dougherty, M., Wright, F. S., Garmezy, N., Loewenson, R. B., & Torres, F. (1983). Later competence and adaptation in infants who survive severe heart defects. *Child Development, 54,* 1129–1142.

Parmelee, A. H. & Haber, A. (1973). Who is the at risk infant? *Clinical Obstetrics and Gynecology, 16,* 376–387.

Riley, G. G. (1976). *Riley Motor Problems Inventory*. Los Angeles, CA:Western Psychological Services.

Rutter, M. (1979). Protective factors in children's responses to stress and disadvantage. In M. W. Kent & J. E. Rolf (Eds.), *Primary prevention of psychopathology: Social competence in children* (pp. 49–74). Hanover, NH: University Press of New England.

Sameroff, A. J. (1982). Development and the dialectic: The need for a systems approach. In W. A. Collins (Ed.), *Minnesota symposium on child psychology,* Vol. 15 (pp. 83–103). Hillsdale, N.J: Erlbaum.

Sameroff, A. J. & Chandler, M. J. (1975). Reproductive risk and the continuum of caretaking casualty. In F. D. Horowitz, M. Hetherington, S. Scarr-Salapatek, & G. Siegel (Eds.), *Review of child development research, 4* (pp. 187–244). Chicago, IL: University of Chicago Press.

Sameroff, A. J. & Seifer, R. (1983). Familial risk and child competence. *Child Development, 54,* 1254–1268.

Sameroff, A. J., Seifer, R., Barocas, R., Zax, M., & Greenspan, S. (1987). Intelligence quotient scores of 4-year-old children: Social environmental risk factors. *Pediatrics, 79,* 343–350.

Sameroff, A. J., Seifer, R., Baldwin, A., & Baldwin, C. (1993). Stability of intelligence from preschool to adolescence: The influence of social and family risk factors. *Child Development, 64,* 80–97.

Seifer, R. & Sameroff, A. J. (1987). Multiple determinants of risk and invulnerability. In E. J. Anthony & B. Cohler (Eds.), *The invulnerable child* (pp. 51–69). New York: Guilford Press.

Shea, E. & Tronick, E. (1988). The Maternal Self-Report Inventory: A research and clinical instrument for assessing maternal self-esteem. In H. E. Fitzgerald, B. M. Lester, & M. W. Yogman (Eds.), *Theory and research in behavioral pediatrics*. Boston: Plenum.

Vohr, B. R., García-Coll, C. T., & Oh, W. (1989). Language and neurodevelopmental outcome of low-birthweight infants at three years. *Developmental Medicine and Child Neurology, 31,* 582–590.

Werner, E. E., (1986). Resilient offspring of alcoholics: A longitudinal study from birth to age 18. *Journal of Studies on Alcohol, 47,* 34–40.

Werner, E. E., & Bierman, J. M., & French, F. E. (1971). *The children of Kauai: A longitudinal study from the prenatal period to age ten.* Honolulu: University of Hawaii Press.

Werner, E. E. & Smith, R. S. (1977). *Kauai's children come of age.* Honolulu: University of Hawaii Press.

Werner, E. E. & Smith, R. S. (1982). *Vulnerable but invincible: A longitudinal study of resilient children and youth.* New York: McGraw-Hill.

Williams, P. D., Williams, A. R., Landa, A., & Decena, A. (May 1987). *Risk and resilience: Another look at the excluded child.* Paper presented at the Fifth International Conference on Early Identification of Children at Risk, Durango, CO.

* * *

Round Table Commentary

Sameroff. Michael Rutter has argued that protective factors are not the opposite of risk factors, but rather are interactive factors that operate primarily under conditions of stress or risk. If this definition is accepted, one would expect to see in your data that the difference between the scores of the high and low protective groups would be greater in the high risk condition than in the low risk condition. In fact, your data show the opposite; this is particularly obvious for the perceptual score, the PPVT, the Beery, and the Riley. In each case, the high protection seems to have a greater enhancing effect in the low risk group. How do you explain these differential effects? Is Rutter wrong?

Lester et al. I suspect this is one of those areas in which conceptualization is way ahead of methodology The short answer to this question is that it probably cannot be directly addressed given our current understanding and methodology.

We are attempting to test complex, multivariate, highly sophisticated constructs using fairly simplistic measures. If we look at our present state of understanding, it is clear that we are just beginning to understand what are risk factors and how they operate without even asking the question of protective factors. There is substantial disagreement in the literature about various approaches to the study of risk factors, including whether it is the number or type and how they are combined etc. Then we bring in the concept of protective factors and we need to ask the same questions as we ask about risk factors, but there are prior questions such as do protective factors really exist or are they simply the absence of risk factors? If they are not the absence of risk factors, how can they be defined separately from risk factors? Then, assuming we can argue for the independent existence of risk factors there is the important issue that this question addresses, which is how do risk and protective factors interact. This is relatively new territory.

In our study, we chose the most simplistic approach, to assign a single point to each risk factor and each protective factor and use the number of risk and protective factors to define subject groups. The problem with this method is that it assigns the same weight to each factor, risk and protective, and assumes that the number of factors represents the strength of the construct. We cannot tell if any factors contribute more than others, if it is the number rather than the individual factor. Nor can we determine how individual factors interact, and that is the key to the issue raised about Rutter's model. Even though the number of factors may be the same in the risk and protect groups, the specific factors may not be the same and *how* risk and protective factors interact within a given risk protect group may not be the same. In addition, we may want to consider other classes of factors not even included in our analysis. For example, there is no consideration here of the possible role of the child as a contributor to his or her own developmental outcome. We know from developmental research that characteristics of the infant, including physical and behavioral characteristics such as temperament, can affect how the infant is treated by the caregiving environment. A more complete analysis would add the infant and determine how risk and protective factors operate at various levels of infant characteristics. Caregivers respond differently to physical characteristics of infants and to perceived conditions of infants. Our study includes mostly preterm infants. These infants vary in their behavioral style, and their behavioral and medical fragility. The caregiving environment has different perceptions of preterm infants, different expectations for the developmental outcome of these infants and perceptions of what are their needs.

In our data the greater differences between the low risk groups than between the high risk groups are probably due to the specific risk and protective factors that characterize these groups. The Lo Risk-High Protect group includes mostly term infants with a healthier medical course, higher SES and a more optimal caregiving environment. Where we can see the protective factors working in a high risk situation is in the High Risk-Hi Protect group. The fact that these infants do better than their counterparts in the High Risk-Low Protect group and as well as infants in the Lo Risk-Lo Protect group shows how protective factors can operate in a high risk environment However, it is important to understand that the risk and protective factors that are operating are not the same in the four groups, and we do not understand how different combinations of risk and protective factors interact with each other in affecting the child.

Zuckerman. Barry, this paper represents an important contribution to our understanding of the interplay and contribution of risk and protective factors to children's developmental functioning. However, I would like you to share your thoughts on a couple of questions. First, on what theoretical or empirical basis did you decide that each protective factor was approximately equal to each other or to one unit? Why did you decide to use temperament as an outcome measure instead of a possible risk or protective factor?

Lester et al. The decision to assign one point to each risk and protective factor was based on work suggesting that the number of risk factors was related to developmental outcome. It seemed to be a logical starting point and to extend previous work by adding the dimension of protective factors to what had already been published with respect to risk factors. There is also a methodological advantage to this approach in that single scores can be readily obtained for risk and protective factors and the four groups that we wanted to study could be constructed in a straightforward manner. The drawbacks of this approach, as mentioned above, are that we lose the ability to determine the relative impact of individual factors and how specific risk and protective factors interact to determine child outcome. With larger data sets one could compare the utility of the approach we used with approaches that include a more thorough exploration of the role of specific risk and protective factors.

We decided to use temperament as an outcome variable rather than as a risk or protective factor primarily to reduce the complexity of what we were doing and because we did not have the statistical power to include temperament as a third dimension. From a conceptual point of view, temperament belongs not as a risk or protective factor, but as a third dimension in which we could study the child's contribution to his or her developmental outcome at various levels of risk and protective factors. It would be very interesting to determine how risk and protective factors interact with temperament factors and determine child outcome. Practically speaking in our data we did not have enough subjects to conduct a 3×3 (temperament $\times$ risk $\times$ protective) analysis. Also, given that we felt that we were venturing into relatively new territory with risk and protective groups, we felt that it would be too much to try and add temperament as a third dimension. But it is definitely the way to go.

Zuckerman. Your model is more sophisticated than previous studies that assess the impact of cumulative risk. However, in this sample of premature babies, are you able to replicate the findings of those studies? Are the number of risk factors related to 4-year developmental outcome?

Lester et al. The same trend appears in our data as has been reported in previous studies relating the number of risk factors to developmental outcome The easiest way to appreciate this is to look at the means in Table 2 and collapse the protect groups, leaving a high risk and a low risk group. You can see that the mean scores for the high risk group are generally lower than the means for the low risk group. For example, on the McCarthy GCI, the mean for the high risk group is 96 compared with a mean of 105 for the low risk group. On the PPVT, the means are 107 for low risk infants and 100 for high risk infants. However, what you can also see if you compare these means with the means of the four groups in Table 2 is that by excluding the protective factors we have narrowed the range of mean group differences. When the protective factors are included, the range of mean scores among the four groups is 92–110 for the GCI and 97–111 for the PPVT. You can see how the addition of protective factors explains more of the variation or more of the distribution of outcome performance than does their exclusion. While it seems to be true that, as in previous work, the number of risk factors is related to developmental outcome, it also seems that risk factors alone only tell a partial story and explain a narrower range of outcome than does the inclusion of both risk and protective factors.

CHAPTER 9

Accumulation of Environmental Risk and Child Mental Health

Arnold J. Sameroff and Ronald Seifer

Poverty is a major factor influencing the development of children. For developmental psychologists understanding this simple fact leads to many complicated analyses. Whereas there are few, relatively speaking, children who are so destitute as to be without food or shelter, there are many who suffer less direct consequences of economic deprivation in the form of poor psychological development. Questions about the effects of poverty on children must be further differentiated into whether the question is an academic, social, or political one. Each of these questions will have a different answer. An academic interest is centered on understanding the processes by which disadvantaged environments place children at risk for poor intellectual and emotional development and the processes that act as protective factors against these risks. A social interest is centered on using this information to change conditions so that more children can grow in conditions of lower environmental risk or conditions where protective factors are more powerful. A political interest is to identify the factors in our society that prevent or permit beneficial changes in the life of children. This presentation will focus on all of these questions. We will begin with the academic question by discussing the factors that affect childrens' development, then discuss the social question with implications for interventions and conclude with the political question by discussing who is to blame.

Risk and Protection

Despite the nominal interest of developmentalists in the effects of the environment, the analysis and assessment of context has fallen more in the domain of sociology than of developmental psychology (Clausen, 1968; Elder, 1984; Kohn & Schooler, 1983; Mayer & Jencks, 1989). The magnitude of a social ecological analysis involving multiple settings and multiple systems (Bronfenbrenner, 1979) has daunted researchers primarily trained to focus on individual behavioral processes. A further daunting factor has been the increasing necessity to use multicausal models to explain developmental phenomena (Sameroff, 1983).

In a study to examine the relation between early characteristics of the child and the environment and later mental health we began an investigation of the development of a group of children from the prenatal period through adolescence living in a socially heterogeneous set of family circumstances—the Rochester Longitudinal Study (RLS). We began the study with the idea that parental mental illness was a major risk factor for child development. As the study progressed we had to modify this belief.

During the first part of the RLS (Sameroff, Seifer, & Zax, 1982) we assessed children and their families at birth, and then at 4, 12, 30, and 48 months of age both in the home and in the laboratory. At each age we assessed two major indicators of developmental status, the child's IQ and social-emotional competence. In our search for family risk factors that would adversely affect the children's growth we considered three major hypotheses: (1) that problem behavior would be related to a specific parental psychiatric diagnosis, e.g., schizophrenia; (2) that problem behavior would be attributable to variables associated with parental mental illness in general, especially severity and chronicity of disorder, but no diagnosis in particular; and (3) that problem behavior in the children would be associated with other aspects of the family's condition, especially socioeconomic status. Because many of the families had single parents we focused our assessments of characteristics of the mother. This approach was taken not because we believed that fathers were unimportant, but because there were too few available for participation in our study.

When we examined the results of our study we found little support for the first hypothesis. There was no effect of the parent's specific psychiatric diagnosis on the behavior of her offspring during early childhood. The second hypothesis, that mental illness in general would produce substantial effects, was supported more strongly. General effects of parental psychopathology, i.e., severity and chronicity, were ubiquitous throughout the study. Children of more severely or chronically ill mothers had poorer obstetric and newborn status. At four months they had more difficult temperaments, lower developmental scores, and less adaptive behavior. At home these mothers were less involved and more negative in affect during home observations. At twelve months their infants were less spontaneous and mobile when observed in the home and less responsive in the laboratory. The ill mothers remained less involved and less affectionate during home observations. At thirty and forty-eight months their children were again less responsive in the laboratory, had lower developmental test scores, and were reported by their others as having a variety of nonadaptive behavior patterns at home.

Our third hypothesis that differences in family social status would produce differences in child behavior was also strongly supported. The social status effects were apparent throughout the first four years of life. Children from the poorest families in our sample exhibited the poorest development. Specifically, the low-SES children had poorer obstetrical status, more difficult temperaments and lower developmental test scores at four months, less responsivity during the home and laboratory observations at twelve months, and less adaptive behavior in the home and laboratory at thirty and forty-eight months of age. Like their children, the low-SES mothers were less positive in affect and less involved with their children during our observations.

When the number of differences in child behavior was compared for the diagnostic, mental illness, and social status dimensions, the highest density was found in the social status contrasts (Sameroff & Seifer, 1983). Family factors of socioeconomic status and parental factors of severity and chronicity of mental disturbance were more powerful risks than the specific psychiatric diagnoses we examined.

At that point in our study we had discovered, on the one hand, if the only developmental risk for a child was a mother with a psychiatric diagnosis, that child was doing fine. On the other hand, if the child had a mother who was schizophrenic, who was also poor, uneducated, without social supports, and with many stressful life events, that child was doing poorly. But, we also found that children whose mothers were poor, uneducated, without social supports, and with many stressful life events had bad outcomes, even if the mother did not have a psychiatric diagnosis. What was learned in the RLS was the overriding importance of attending to the context of the children in the study in order to understand their development. In the RLS social status was a more powerful risk factor than any of the mental illness measures. To better understand the role of social status, more differentiated views of environmental influences needed to be taken. In order to translate a sociological measure into something that would have direct impact on the child, we needed to analyze the socioeconomic factor into variables that would have a more direct influence on the child. We had to discover what was different about the experience of children raised in different socioeconomic environments. But first let us review the efforts of others to find early characteristics of the child that would predict later developmental problems.

Longitudinal Studies of Early Risk

In an effort to discover the causes of a major developmental disability, cerebral palsy, the federal government funded a large longitudinal study of 26,760 children from the National Institute of Neurological and Communicative Disorders and Stroke Collaborative Perinatal Project. Most of the factors examined in this project were physical but there were a few environmental measures. Broman, Nicholls, & Kennedy (1975) compared the effects of 169 individual biomedical and behavioral variables during infancy on 4-year intellectual performance in a sample. Although only 11 (7%) of these variables could be said to constitute social or family behavioral factors, two of these, SES and mother's education, were the most predictive of outcome of all the variables. This study demonstrated the importance of early environmental factors but did not reveal the aspects of the environment that were the most salient predictors.

Another study that contrasted the effects of early biological and social conditions on later development was the Louisville Twin Study (Wilson, 1985). The developmental status of several hundred infants was assessed from birth to 6 years of age and correlated with early biological and social factors. Although the two social factors of mother's education and SES were not correlated with developmental quotients during the first year of life, by the second year and thereafter they became the most potent predictors of the child's intelligence.

The Kauai study of Werner and her colleagues (Werner, Bierman, & French, 1971; Werner & Smith, 1977; Werner & Smith, 1982) provides a more elaborate description of the interplay among risk factors in the child and those in the environment. When this predominantly lower SES sample of children was followed from birth through adolescence, more than half had learning or emotional problems by 18 years of age. But in the main these developmental problems did not result from early medical conditions like birth and pregnancy complications. Infants with severe early trauma frequently showed no later deficits unless the problems were combined with persistently poor environmental circumstances such as chronic poverty, family instability, or maternal mental health problems.

The Kauai study is in tune with many others (Sameroff & Chandler, 1975) in targeting SES and family mental health variables, such as parental attitudes, family conflict, family size, stressful life events, and the utilization of counseling and remedial assistance, as important moderators of child development. In the analyses comparing children from various groups of mothers in the RLS we also were able to demonstrate that both parental mental illness and social status factors were directly related to child performance (Sameroff et al. 1982).

Although these analyses were helpful, they did not fully address the issue of what psychological mechanisms are responsible for the individual and group variation observed in the children's development. It was necessary to identify which factors in the family and social environment of the children in the RLS were associated with developmental risk.

Environmental Conditions as Developmental Risks

Although SES is the best single variable for predicting children's cognitive competence, we decided to add more psychological content to this sociological variable. We subdivided the global variable of social class to see if we could identify factors that acted as environmental risks more directly connected to the child. The factors we chose ranged from proximal variables like the mother's interaction with the child, to intermediate variables like the mother's mental health, to distal variables such as the financial resources of the family.

From the 4-year assessment of the children in the RLS we chose a set of 10 environmental variables that are correlates of SES but not equivalents (Sameroff, Seifer, Barocas, Zax, & Greenspan, 1987). We then tested whether poor cognitive and social-emotional development in our pre-school children was a function of low SES or the compounding of environmental risk factors found in low-SES groups. The ten environmental risk variables, as can be seen in Table 1, were (1) a history of maternal mental illness, (2) high maternal anxiety, (3) a parental perspectives score derived from a combination of measures that reflected rigidity in the attitudes, beliefs, and values that mothers had in regard to their child's development, (4) few positive maternal interactions with the child observed during infancy, (5) head of household in unskilled occupations, (6) minimal maternal education, (7) disadvantaged minority status, (8) reduced family support, (9) stressful life events, and (10) large family size.

TABLE 1

Summary of Risk Variables
(Sameroff, Seifer, Barocas, Zax, & Greenspan, 1987)

Risk Variables	Low Risk	High Risk
Mental Illness	0–1 psychiatric contact	More than 1 contact
Anxiety	75% least	25% most
Parental perspectives	75% highest	25% lowest
Spontaneous interaction	75% most	25% least
Education	High school	No high school
Occupation	Skilled	Semi- or unskilled
Minority status	No	Yes
Family support	Father present	Father absent
Stressful life events	75% fewest	25% most
Family size	1–3 children	4 or more children

To determine whether each of these factors was indeed an environmental risk condition we compared the high-risk and low-risk group for each variable separately. For the cognitive outcomes, in all cases the low risk group had higher scores than the high risk group. Most of the differences were about 7 to 10 IQ points, about H to O of a standard deviation. On the social-emotional competence comparisons the low risk group performed significantly better than the high risk group for all but one of the comparisons. The differences between groups on these comparisons was generally about $1/2$ of a standard deviation.

Although there were significant effects for the individual risk factors it is clear that with only a single risk factor most children would not end up with major developmental problems. But what would be the result if a comparison was made between children growing up in environments with many risk factors compared to children with very few. A multiple risk score was created that was the total number of risks for each individual family. In the RLS the range was well distributed between scores of 0 and 8, with one family having as many as 9 risks. When these risk factors were related to the child's intelligence and social competence, major differences were found between those children with few risks and those with many. On an intelligence test children with no environmental risks scored more than 30 points higher than children with 8 or 9 risk factors as can be seen in Figure 1. On average, each risk factor reduced the child's IQ score by 4 points.

The relation between the multiple risk scores and the social-emotional outcome can be seen in Figure 2. It is clear that the effect of combining the 10 risk variables was to strongly accentuate the differences noted for the individual scores described above. As the number of risk factors increases, performance decreases for children at 4 years of age. For the social-emotional scores, the difference between the lowest and highest groups was more than one standard deviation. Thus the combination of risk factors resulted in a nearly three-fold increase in the magnitude of differences found among groups of children relative to the effect of single variables (Sameroff, Seifer, Zax, & Barocas, 1987).

These data support the view that the behavior of 4-year-old children is strongly affected by many variables in the social context, but the possibility exists that poverty may still be an overriding variable. To test for this possibility, two additional analyses were attempted. The first analysis was to determine if the relation between more risk factors and worse performance was to be found in high-SES as well as low-SES families. The second analysis was to determine if there were consistencies in the distribution of risk factors, that is, were there always the same factors present?

For the first analysis, the families were divided into high and low SES groups and the effect of increased number of risks was examined within each social class group. The effects of the multiple risk score were as clear within SES groups as well as for the population at large. The more risk factors the worse the child outcomes for both high and low SES families.

For the second type of analysis the data from the families that had a moderate score of 3, 4, or 5 risk factors were cluster analyzed. The families fell into five clusters with different sets of high-risk conditions that are listed in Table 2. Different

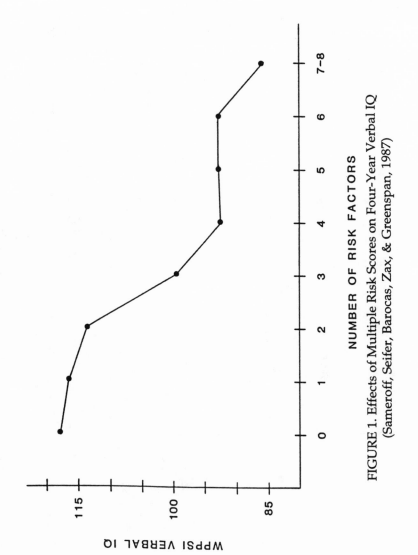

FIGURE 1. Effects of Multiple Risk Scores on Four-Year Verbal IQ
(Sameroff, Seifer, Barocas, Zax, & Greenspan, 1987)

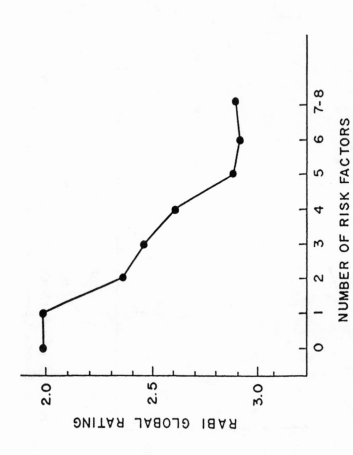

FIGURE 2. Effects of Multiple Risk Scores on Four-Year Social-Emotional Competence (Sameroff, Seifer, Zax, & Barocas, 1987)

combinations of factors appear in each cluster. Cluster 2 has no overlapping variables with clusters 3, 4, or 5. Minority status is a risk variable in clusters 3, 4, and 5, but does not appear in clusters 1 or 2. Despite these differences in the specific risks among families, the mean IQs were not different for children in the five clusters, ranging from 92.8 to 97.7. Thus, it seems that it was not any single variable but the combination of multiple variables that reduced the child's intellectual performance. In every family situation a unique set of risk or protective factors was related to child outcome.

TABLE 2

Cluster Analysis of Families with Moderate Multiple–Risk Scores
(Sameroff, Seifer, Barocas, Zax, & Greenspan, 1987)

Cluster 1	Mental Health
	Family Support
	Mother Education
	Anxiety
Cluster 2	Mother–Infant Interaction
	Mental Health
	Anxiety
Cluster 3	Family Support
	Minority Status
Cluster 4	Mother Education
	Minority Status
	Occupation
Cluster 5	Parental Perspectives
	Minority Status
	Mother Education

These analyses of the RLS data were attempts to elaborate environmental risk factors by reducing global measures such as SES to component social and behavioral variables. We were able to identify a set of risk factors that were predominantly found in lower SES groups, but affected child outcomes in all social classes. Moreover, no single variable was determinant of outcome. Only in families with multiple risk factors was the child's competence placed in jeopardy.

The multiple pressures of environmental context in terms of amount of stress from the environment, the family's resources for coping with that stress, the number of children that must share those resources, and the parents' flexibility in understanding and dealing with their children all play a role in the fostering or hindrance of child mental health.

Continuity of Environmental Risk

The studies that explored the effects of environmental risk factors on early development have shown major consequences for children living in multi-problem families. What are the long term consequences of these early adverse circumstances? Will later conditions alter the course for such children or will early experiences lock children into pathways of deviance?

Within the RLS our attention has been devoted to the source of continuities and discontinuities in child performance. We have recently completed a new assessment of the sample when the children were 13 years of age (Sameroff, Seifer, Baldwin, & Baldwin, 1993). Because of the potent effects of our multiple risk index at 4 years, we calculated a new multiple environmental risk score for each family based on their situation nine years later. To our surprise there were very few families that showed major shifts in the number of risk factors across the nine-year intervening period. The correlation in number of risks was .77. The factor that showed the most improvement was maternal education where the number of mothers who had not gotten a high school diploma or equivalent decreased from 33 to 22% of the sample. The risk factor that increased the most was single parenthood with the number of children being raised by their mothers alone increasing from 24 to 41%.

Because of the very high stability in the number of risks experienced by these families it was impossible to determine if the effects of early adversity were affecting the later behavior of these children. Those children who had been living in high risk environments at 4-years of age were still living in them at 13-years of age. Moreover, these contemporary high-risk contexts were producing the same negative effects on behavior as the earlier ones had done. We found the same relationship between the number of risk factors and the child's intellectual competence; those children from families with no risk factors scored more than 30 points higher on intelligence tests than those with the most risk factors.

The typical statistic reported in longitudinal research is the correlation between early and later performance of the children. We too found such correlations. Intelligence at 4 years correlated .72 with intelligence at 13 years. The usual interpretation of such a number is that there is a continuity of competence or incompetence in the child. Such a conclusion cannot be challenged if the only assessments in the study are of the children. In the RLS we examined environmental as well as child factors. We were able to correlate environmental characteristics across time as well as child ones. We found that the .77 correlation between environmental risk scores at the two ages was as great or greater than any continuity within the child. Whatever the child's ability for achieving high levels of competence, it was severely undermined by the continuing paucity of environmental support. Whatever the capabilities provided to the child by individual factors, it was the environment that limited the opportunities for development.

Secular Trends

The thrust of a contextual analysis of developmental regulation is not that individual factors in the child are non-existent or irrelevant but that they must be studied in a context larger than the single child. The risk analyses discussed so far have implicated parent characteristics and the immediate social conditions of family support and life event stress as important moderators of healthy psychological growth in the child. To this list of risks must be added changes in the historical supports for families in a given society. The importance of this added level of complexity was emphasized when we examined secular trends in the economic well-being of families in the United States.

At 4-years we had divided the sample into high, medium, and low risk groups based on the number of cumulative risks: 0 or 1 in the low-risk group, 2 or 3 in the medium risk group, and 4 or more in the high-risk group. We found that 22% of the high risk group had IQs below 85 whereas none of the low-risk sample did. Conversely, 59% of the low-risk group had IQs above 115 but only 4% of the high risk sample did.

After the 13-year assessment we made the same breakdown into high, medium and low-risk groups and examined the distribution of IQs within risk groups. Again we found a preponderance of low IQ scores in the high risk group and a preponderance of high IQ scores in the low risk group indicating the continuing negative effects of an unfavorable environment. But strikingly, the number of children in the high-risk group with IQs below 85 had increased from 22% to 46%, more than doubling. If our analysis was restricted to the level of the child and family, we would hypothesize that high-risk environments operate synergistically to further worsen the intellectual standing of these children during the period from pre-school to adolescence, placing them in a downward spiral of increasing incompetence.

An alternative hypothesis was that society was changing during the nine years between the RLS assessments. In a study completed by the House of Representatives Ways and Means Committee (Passel, 1989) it was found that between the years 1973 to 1987, during which time we were doing this study, the average household income of the poorest fifth of Americans fell 12% while the income of the richest fifth increased 24%. Elder (1984) has made a strong case for attending to major changes in society as determinants of the life course for growing children. His work centered on the great depression of the 1930s. Similar effects seem to be apparent in our own times.

Many factors have been identified as possibly having protective quality in children at risk. Garmezy (1985) emphasizes three classes of variables ranging from stable individual traits to dynamic contextual interactions: personality dispositions, family interaction, and social support.

Protective factors and resilient children. We have documented above that the accumulation of risk factors has a deleterious impact on the development of children. A different perspective has been taken by researchers seeking forces that offset the action of such risk factors. The search for such variables has included characteristics of the child and characteristics of the context. Personality dispositions such as temperament, locus of control, or perceived competence are individual cognitive and behavioral styles of children that are thought to protect them from risk (Rae-Gant, Thomas, Offord, & Boyle, 1989; Rutter, 1987). The issue of locus of control has traditionally been formulated in terms of internal versus external attributions (Rotter, 1966). More recently, Connell (1985) and Peterson and Seligman (1984) have expanded the construct to include features such as unknown locus of control where the child cannot attribute cause to either internal or external sources. These recent formulations may be more relevant to the study of stress-resistance because they differentiate between those children who have a focused view of what controls their lives versus those who have no such perspective.

Social support of the parents is a major contextual variable that has been identified as a protective factor for children of depressed parents (Pellegrini, Kosisky, Nackman, Cytryn, McKnew, Gershon, Hamovit, & Cammuso, 1986), children with handicaps, or preterm infants (Crnic, Greenberg, Ragozin, Robinson, & Basham, 1983; Greenberg & Crnic, 1988).

Family interaction styles, particularly expressed emotion (Vaughn & Leff, 1972) have been strongly implicated in relapse rates for those at highest risk for serious mental disorder as well as for initial onset of a variety of emotional disorders (Doane, West, Goldstein, Rodnick, & Jones, 1981; Rae-Gant, Thomas, Offord, & Boyle, 1989). Specific patterns of social interaction are also important.

When examining protective factors, one strategy would be to use final outcome levels as the criteria to identify those factors that ameliorate risk. However, this approach may obscure positive effects by failing to consider that children at risk often have initial levels of function well below established norms. Therefore, their outcome scores, even after improvement, could be below average. It is more appropriate to examine the relation of protective factors to the change in status between the time risk is identified and final assessments are made. As Werner (1989) noted, protection is not a static phenomenon, but one that may occur even after poor interim outcomes have been attained. We looked at the change in cognitive performance and social emotional competence of the children in the RLS between preschool and adolescence (Seifer, Sameroff, Baldwin, & Baldwin, 1992).

To examine outcomes in our sample of children, we looked at the relation of protective factors to change in cognitive status and change in social-emotional status during the period from 4 through 13 years of age. Put another way—given their functioning at 4 years, what factors differentiated high-risk children and their families who improved most between 4 or 13 years of age from those who did not improve or became worse? We thought that the following protective factors would be related to the better outcomes in the face of high levels of risk: children who had high perceived competence, more social support, and low levels of unknown locus of control; families where mother-child interactions had low levels of expressed emotion or required sophisticated cognitive operations by the children; and contexts with high social support. Further, we hypothesized that many of the relations would be characterized by interaction effects where impact was greater in high-risk individuals.

Many of the protective factors we examined proved to be associated with change in child status from 4 to 13 years of age. Helpful qualities included individual child characteristics such as self-esteem, social support, and low external or unknown locus of control; family characteristics such as self-directing parental values, good parent teaching strategies, and low rates of parental criticism and maternal depressed mood; and contextual characteristics of good social support and few life events. Conversely, little self-worth, unknown locus of control, parental criticism, conforming values, poor parenting styles, many life events, and little social support predicted less than optimal outcomes. Some of these findings were strong indicators of protective factors in the sense that interaction effects of protective factor and risk status were observed in the prediction of change in outcome status, indicating a greater positive impact of the protective factor in the high-risk group (Jenkins & Smith, 1990; Rutter, 1991).

Unfortunately, all of the child characteristics that were related to improved outcomes were 13-year variables; none of the child's characteristics that we examined at 4 years were predictive. As a consequence we cannot tell if what we are calling the protective child characteristics are merely correlates of competence at 13 years. The direction of effects between predictors and outcomes were clearer for parent interaction variables where we did find that interactive style at 4 years was predictive of 13-year cognitive competence.

Protective Factors and Individual Families

When studies are successful in identifying protective factors, the issue is raised of identification on an individual basis of resilient (or protected) individuals. The analysis strategy of this study obscured the absolute level of functioning at the last assessment. Ideally, one would like to identify a substantial subset of children who by any measure of competence were doing better than average, despite the adversity they faced in daily life. We selected a high risk subsample of children who had four or more environmental risks to determine the characteristics of those who were doing better than expected. Only three of the fifty high-risk children were above the total sample mean on our 13-year child outcome measures; but all three had also improved in their risk status. They had been in the highest risk category at 4 years of age, but by 13 years were doing better. Thus, it is unclear whether the more favorable outcomes in these children were due to protective factors or to a lessening of risk.

When we examined the whole sample to see what the consequences of moving from high (four or more) to low (0 or 1) environmental risk or from low to high risk was for children in the study we found major effects. The group that changed from high risk at 4 years to low risk at 13 years improved in IQ by 13 points. In contrast the group that changed from low risk at 4 years to high risk at 13 years dropped in IQ by 15 points. These findings make a strong case for the powerful effects of environmental risks on the children. Unfortunately, such changes in number of risk factors are not common. We discussed above the stability of risk factors from early childhood to adolescence. Only one child was in the group that went from high to low risk and there was only one child in the group that went from low to high risk.

Social and Political Agendas

What we have described above are the results of an academic agenda for understanding the effects of poverty on children. There are many who argue that children do poorly in conditions of poverty because they don't have individual characteristics that would promote resilience, overcome challenge, and eventuate in productive work and family life. By identifying characteristics of children who achieve despite adverse circumstances, some hope that we could instill those characteristics in other children to help them overcome environmental adversity. In contrast is the position that environmental risks are so pervasive that opportunities do not exist for positive development even if the child does have excellent coping skills.

The holocaust was a major environmental event from which there were few survivors. If one were a scientist seeking methods to survive the holocaust, a resilience strategy would be to determine the characteristics of those who survived and then instill those characteristics in the rest of the affected population. The stories of how these survivors overcame adversity usually is remarkable. If they weren't remarkable there would not have been survival. One example is of someone who was in the last row of a group being shot and survived because the rest of the bodies fell on top of him so the Nazis didn't notice that he was still alive. Other examples are of individuals who worked for the Nazis to administer the other inmates of the concentration camps. What can we learn from such stories? Are there lessons that could have been used to save the rest of the victims of the holocaust? Unfortunately not. Not everyone can stand in the last row. Not everyone can be an administrator. A much more fruitful strategy would have been to change the risk factors, to get rid of the holocaust.

In the current discussions about the consequences of poverty a focus on resiliency can take the form of blaming the victims. If a child shows poor outcomes it is because they weren't resilient. The political agenda is to identify programs for changing the outcomes of children raised in poverty. Clearly if one believes it is the resiliency of the individual child that is the determining factor then the political agenda will be different than if one believes it is social and familial risk factors that are more important.

We have indicated that there are many environmental risk factors associated with poor developmental outcomes. These risk factors can be found in all socioeconomic strata but are most concentrated in areas of poverty. There may be social consequences of this research if changes can be made in the number of risk factors experienced by families. In the natural course of time in the sample we studied, there were few such changes. High risk families remained high risk and low risk families remained low risk. A number of intervention programs have demonstrated some capacity for making changes in children's lives (Ramey & Ramey, 1992). The social and political agendas of our society will determine if the results of our academic agenda can be extended to making differences in the lives of children living in conditions of poverty.

REFERENCES

Broman, S. H., Nichols, P. L., & Kennedy, W. A. (1975). *Preschool IQ: prenatal and early developmental correlates.* New York: Erlbaum.

Bronfenbrenner, U. (1979). *The Ecology of Human Development.* Cambridge: Harvard University Press.

Clausen, J.A. (1968). *Socialization and Society*. Boston: Little, Brown and Company.

Connell, J. P. (1985). A new multidimensional measure of children's perceptions of control. *Child Development, 56,* 1018–1041.

Crnic, K. A., Greenberg, M. T., Ragozin, A. S, Robinson, N. S., & Basham, R. B. (1983). Effects of stress and social support on mothers and preterm and full-term infants, *Child Development*, 54, 209–217.

Doane, J. A., West, K. L., Goldstein, M. J., Rodnick, E. H., & Jones, J. E. (1981). Parental communication deviance and affective style: Predictors of subsequent schizophrenia spectrum disorders in vulnerable adolescents. *Archives of General Psychiatry, 38,* 679–685.

Elder, G. H., Jr. (1984). Families, kin and the life course: A sociological perspective. In R. D. Parke (Ed.), *Review of Child Development Research: The Family* (Vol. 7). Chicago: University of Chicago Press.

Garmezy, N. (1985). Stress-resistant children: The search for protective factors. In J. E. Stevenson (Ed.), *Recent research in developmental psychopathology* (pp. 213–233). Oxford: Pergamon Press.

Greenberg, M. T., & Crnic, K. A. (1988). Longitudinal predictors of developmental status and social interaction in premature and full-term infants at age two. *Child Development, 59,* 554–570.

Jenkins, J. M., & Smith, M. A. (1990). Factors protecting children living in disharmonious homes: Maternal reports. *Journal of the American Academy of Child and Adolescent Psychiatry, 29,* 60–69.

Kohn, M., & Schooler, C. (1983). *Work and personality: An inquiry into the impact of social stratification*. Norwood, NJ: Ablex.

Mayer, S. E., & Jencks, C. (1989). Growing up in poor neighborhoods: How much does it matter? *Science, 243,* 1441–1445.

Passell, P. "Forces In Society And Reaganism, Helped By Deep Hole For Poor." *New York Times,* 16 July 1989, p.1, 20.

Pellegrini, D., Kosisky, S., Nackman, D., Cytryn, L., McKnew, D. H., Gershon, E., Hamovit, J., & Cammuso, K. (1986). Personal and social resources in children of patients with bipolar affective disorder and children of normal control subjects. *American Journal of Psychiatry, 143,* 856–861.

Peterson, C., & Seligman, M. E. P. (1984). Causal explanations as a risk factor for depression: Theory and evidence. *Psychological Review, 91,* 347–374.

Rae-Gant, N., Thomas, B. H., Offord, D. R., & Boyle, M. H. (1989). Risk, protective factors, and the prevalence of behavioral and emotional disorders in children and adolescents. *Journal of the American Academy of Child and Adolescent Psychiatry, 28*, 262–268.

Ramey, C. T., & Ramey, S. L. (1992). Effective early intervention. *Mental Retardation, 30*, 1–9.

Rotter, J. B. (1966). Generalized expectancies for internal versus external control of reinforcement. *Psychological Monographs, 80*, (Whole No. 609).

Rutter, M. (1987). Psychosocial resilience and protective mechanisms. *American Journal of Orthopsychiatry, 57*, 316–331.

———. (1991). Protective factors: Independent or interactive? (Letter to the editor). *Journal of the American Academy of Child and Adolescent Psychiatry, 30*, 151–152.

Sameroff, A. J. (1983). Developmental systems: Contexts and evolution. In W. Kessen (Ed.). *History, theories, and methods*. Volume I of Ph. H. Mussen (Ed.), *Handbook of Child Psychology* (pp. 237–294). New York: Wiley.

Sameroff, A. J. & Chandler, M. J. (1975). Reproductive risk and the continuum of caretaking casualty. In F. D. Horowitz, M. Hetherington, S. Scarr-Salapatek, & G. Siegel (Eds.), *Review of Child Development Research* (Vol. 4, pp. 187–244). Chicago: University of Chicago.

Sameroff, A. J. & Seifer, R. (1983). *Sources of continuity in parent-child relationships*. Paper presented at the meeting of the Society for Research in Child Development. Detroit.

Sameroff, A. J., Seifer, R., Baldwin, A. & Baldwin, C. (1993). Stability of intelligence from preschool to adolescence: The influence of social and family risk factors. *Child Development, 64*, 80–97.

Sameroff, A. J., Seifer, R., Barocas, R., Zax, M., & Greenspan, S. (1987). Intelligence quotient scores of 4-year-old children: Social environmental risk factors. *Pediatrics, 79*, 343–350.

Sameroff, A. J., Seifer, R., & Zax, M. (1982). Early development of children at risk for emotional disorder. *Monographs of the Society for Research in Child Development, 47*, Serial No. 199).

Sameroff, A. J., Seifer, R., Zax, M., & Barocas, R. (1987) Early indicators of developmental risk: The Rochester Longitudinal Study. *Schizophrenia Bulletin, 13*, 383–393.

Seifer, R., Sameroff, A. J., Baldwin, C. P., & Baldwin, A. (1992). Child and family factors that ameliorate risk between 4 and 13 years of age. *Journal of the American Academy of Child Psychiatry, 31,* 893–903

Vaughn, C. E., & Leff, J. P. (1972). The influence of family and social factors on the course of psychiatric illness. *British Journal of Psychiatry, 129,* 125–137.

Werner, E. E. & Smith, R. S. (1977). *Kauai's children come of age.* Honolulu: University of Hawaii Press.

———— (1982). *Vulnerable but invincible: A longitudinal study of resilient children and youth.* New York: McGraw Hill.

Werner, E. E. (1989). High-risk children in young adulthood: A longitudinal study from birth to 32 years. *American Journal of Orthopsychiatry, 59,* 72–81.

Werner, E. E., Bierman, J. M. & French, F. E. (1971). *The children of Kauai.* Honolulu: University of Hawaii Press.

Wilson, R. S. (1985). Risk and resilience in early mental development. *Developmental Psychology, 21,* 795–805.

* * *

Round Table Discussion

Lester. Have you been able to identify any potentially protective factors in this sample. For example, some of the factors that explain why not all children do poorly? Or, do you think that's just a function of less risk?

Sameroff. There are articles about complicated models of risk and protective factors. I'm still on that simple level of protective as the other side of risk. Being poor is a risk, being rich is protective. If you look at the resilient studies, they typically look at a sample of children who are at risk and then pick some out and see how many of those children who are at risk are doing better than average. Then they ask what is different about the group that is doing better than average, compared to the group who is worse than average. Typically, what they call a risk group is a poor group. For us, that's one risk factor, you don't have money. If you just took one risk factor, and that was all that was going on in that family, those kids would be doing fine. The problem is that most of those families have more than one risk factor. When I think about these issues, the metaphor I like is the holocaust. What were the protective factors for people in the holocaust? If you think about those ways of surviving and the lessons you learned from that, those are not lessons that can be applied to the rest of society. You go into high schools where they have intervention programs for kids who aren't making it. They always have some great name like the "High Fives" or something like that. You talk to these kids and ask, why are you in this program? They say, "Well, we don't want to end up like the rest of the kids in this school. We don't want to end up like the rest of the kids in our neighborhood. We want to make it." When you stop to think about it, that's terrific for them. We want to give them credit. We have to foster them as much as possible. But, what's going to happen to the rest of the people.

Zuckerman. Some thoughts while looking at your risk factors. What do you think about the list you generated? Would you do it differently now?

Sameroff. One has to be really environmentally based. We were very lucky because most other researchers were working with poor samples. But because of the nature of our samples, which were wide-ranging in social class from very rich kids to very poor kids, we got correlations across time. If you're only looking within the poor population or only looking within the middle class population, you don't see these trends. What we found in our sample, at thirteen, was that there was a group of kids who were doing better than expected in a multi-risk environment. When we looked at the differences between these kids and other kids, their parents were more restrictive. That is, they were saying here are the rules. You have to live by the rules. You come home from school. The difference between that and the standard authoritarian family as described by Baumrind, is that these families accompanied their authoritarianism with warmth. They said we don't want to argue about it. We're doing this for your own good. It also seems to be tied up with religion. They clearly were strongly religious families; they had a reason for being in this world. There was a purpose to these kids' lives and they were doing better than average. But, just consider the psychological measure, restrictiveness. We look at the low-risk sample and see the effect of restrictiveness is just the opposite. Restrictive parenting in a low-risk environment was related to poorer children's performance. If you're restricting those children in a benign environment, you are limiting their experiences, you are limiting their opportunities.

Huston. You may also be responding to the fact that they are doing so well in the first place.

Sameroff. That may be.

Lamberty. Was race or ethnicity part of your risk?

Sameroff. Yes. But we considered it an environmental variable rather than an individual one. In that sense it was assumed that the ethnic groups in our sample, African American and Puerto Rican, were subject to discrimination.

Brooks-Gunn. Policy question. If the stability is .7, .8 and I think you find that in other studies, what does that mean for policy for trying to alter poverty levels by getting mothers off welfare and into the workforce? Or, some of the other suggestions that have been made for trying to alter the lives of poor children. If there's such stability are we going to make much difference. That would be the question that the stability of the environment makes. Pretend that I can change welfare status, I might not change some of those other risk factors. What does it mean for policy or what would we suggest on the parents' side?

Sameroff. The way we got into this twenty-five years ago was that we were just looking at one risk factor—maternal pathology—and we said if you have a mentally ill mother the kid's going to end up having all kinds of problems. That's when we discovered that if all you have is a mother with some kind of psychiatric diagnosis, the kid does fine. But if the mother's psychiatric diagnosis is compounded with four kids in the family, no husband, no job, and variety of other things, then those kids turn out to have problems, even if the mother was not mentally ill, in some sense. So, now we get into the multiple issue. Remember when the government got into intervention research, you had to demonstrate that the population was at very high risk before you could get funded. We didn't learn anything, because even though you had an effect of intervention and you may have changed something about getting off welfare for some people, because you were working in a population where there were twelve other things going on, you wouldn't show a big effect. If you want to demonstrate scientifically how things work, you have to find a range where you can find that risk factor unaccompanied by a variety of other risk factors. But, then, if you find a family with many high-risk factors, you're going to have to work on five of them. Just changing one thing is not going to affect the others.

Huston. You may have answered this already, but Lee Shorr argues in her book that the data shows that risks are multiplicative, not additive. So part of my question is, do you think your data support that assumption. Secondly, she argues that reducing the number by one or two should lower the risk significantly, because it takes out multiples and not just an add on? I think that really is an important issue for intervention.

Sameroff. A couple of things. One is I don't think we have a good enough data base to really answer that question. Rutter's data show a linear effect occurs between zero and four, but with more than four, there's no further effect. So, what are the four that he used? a parent in jail, a kid in a foster home for a year or more, mother in a mental institution. I think that's an important question but we can't answer that right now.

The other point I want to make is that as the longitudinal study moves on, some of the risk factors do not seem to be impacting on child outcomes. One of the interesting ones is life events stress. For some reason, by 13 to 18, the kids are insulated in some way from this.

Zuckerman. This session served the purpose of laying the groundwork. I think as we go along, we can encourage people who have a developmental background and who think about the paradigms they have to help with a lot of the issues we're addressing both in terms of understanding processes, as well as developing and evaluating interventions with impact on child health. These outcomes go together. We need to think about which factors affect which outcomes, whether it's health, development, or behavior, in order to understand those potentially different processes because they all have implications for how we think about interventions.

PART THREE

Public Policy Agenda

CHAPTER 10

Setting Research Priorities for Poverty Children at Risk for Adverse Outcomes

Craig T. Ramey

Not all children who are economically poor are at risk for adverse developmental outcomes. Nevertheless poverty does take a significant toll on the development of some, unknown, percentage of poor children and we, as a resourceful society, have a moral and practical obligation to reduce that toll, if reduction is feasible.

In this paper I am going to make four major points that if acted upon would help us to better understand the relationships between poverty and development. I'll label these points as problems to be solved. *The first* one concerns the lack of a federal process for setting research priorities. At present I believe that we do not have an adequate federal mechanism to serve as a focal point or clearing house for research dealing with children of poverty. The federal effort is fragmented across multiple agencies and uncoordinated. It is a little in NIMH, a little in NICHD, a little bit here and there. Given the magnitude of the poverty problem, which we know to affect at least 25 percent of the child population at any given point in time, that mystifies me. Any other condition that affected that many people would certainly have a clear focal point, and would be given high priority.

We can take a lesson from some other agencies, for example, the Agency on Health Care Policy and Research as to how such a research effort might be structured. This agency works systematically, through a variety of mechanisms, to provide syntheses of existing knowledge and to formulate by professional consensus a strategy for original research that needs to be done on topics of high priority. The conduct of this original research is then facilitated through a competitive bid process that involves peer review. This approach allows the careful targeting of resources on areas of agreed upon importance in a timely manner.

Second problem. I believe that there is a glaring need for clearer and more understandable indicators of the adverse conditions associated with poverty. These indicators need to be widely reported and disseminated on a regular basis. We need information that pertains, of course, to topics such as mortality. We also need indices that pertain to labile conditions such as untreated chronic diseases, delayed development, and learning disorders. Equally importantly, we need good understandable measures that make sense to the general public. I believe that we need both absolute measures of poverty as well as measures that emphasize the relativistic nature of poverty such as the 50% of median income measure.

To collect clear and understandable indicators, we need a governmental body that is charged with collecting and disseminating this information. We need the equivalent of a National Center for Health Statistics or a National Center for Educational Statistics. But one that is particularly concerned with poverty. Again, if 25 percent of our child population is affected, that is more than is affected by almost any other condition that we know of in this country, and I think that it is realistic and important to ask for adequate research tools to address this issue.

The third problem is that we need more epidemiological research on poverty. We need population based, catchment-area research that is large scale, systematic, ongoing and meets the current standards of high quality developmental epidemiology. We need to bring to bear techniques, widely known in other areas, so that we do appropriate case-control studies, so that we do appropriate randomized control trials of interventions and other forms of information-gathering that are regarded as *de rigueur* in more mature life sciences. I think if we duck the issue of appropriate scale of the research effort, if we try to get by on a shoestring, we won't have a chance of delivering findings with significant clarity so that Congress will act to reduce the burdens of poverty. I believe that many of the numbers that the child development community has brought to the table in policy circles have simply been too weak to do the job that we want to have done. This weakness is frequently due to samples that are too small or unrepresentative of the poverty population.

The fourth problem is that we need to do more multi-site studies. What we find in Chapel Hill, Birmingham, Rochester, New Haven, or Berkeley, may indeed be conditioned by the local ecology and therefore not representative of the universe of poverty. We need to understand better via multisite studies so that we get replicable findings in ways that give us clear insights into the magnitude of the problem and the controlling processes. There is nothing fundamentally new about this issue. Systematic multi-site work is done in other fields as a matter of routine. I think we need to say clearly that we need the resources to do this more frequently in the field of child development. Single-site studies will continue to have their place but when we want to deal with populations, when we want to deal with replicability of findings, there simply is no substitute for multi-site trials. I believe that we must also be more systematic in doing comparative trials of various prevention and treatment approaches and to do that within an explicit developmental framework using randomized controlled multi-site trials where appropriate—where the knowledge base suggests that it is time for a critical test. I will give just a few examples of studies that are ongoing in the country now which I believe provide some evidence for movement in these recommended directions. I suggest that we in the scientific community take the appropriate actions to ensure that such studies are done more frequently as a matter of routine.

The "Infant Health and Development Program" the "8-Site Randomized Intervention Trial" for 985 low birthweight infants is one such effort. The Centers for Disease Control has recently launched a follow-up study to that effort. This follow-up effort known as Project Begin is scaling up the intervention to whole geographical catchment areas and comparing the yield in reducing mild mental retardation by bringing high intensity sustained developmental interventions to bear to support poverty families and their children who are at risk for mild mental retardation.

There is also now underway a 32-site randomized trial of the Head Start/Public School Transition Program which is altering both what Head Start delivers during the time children are in Head Start and then altering in pre-planned ways what public schools provide during kindergarten, 1st, 2nd, and 3rd grades.

In addition there are approximately thirty sites funded by the Administration on Children, Youth and Families in a trial called the Comprehensive Child Development Program, to improve the child outcomes during the first three years of life for children from poor families.

I will conclude by noting that Dr. Frances Campbell, my colleague from North Carolina is going to report here at SRCD on this notion of doing comparative trials of various interventions. Frances is going to give a paper in which we have compared intensive interventions over the first five years of life for individuals, all of whom are from poor and under-educated families with interventions beginning when children enter public schools, in kindergarten. The program is called the "Abecedarian Project." Results indicate that early intervention is much more important than later intervention with respect to positively altering cognitive performance and academic achievement. And, that at age 15, at least seven years after any intervention has been delivered to any of these families, there are residual effects of early intervention in five developmental domains that I think are important to note.

1. Children who have preschool intervention have higher cognitive scores by standardized tests.
2. They have higher scores in reading achievement.
3. They have higher scores in mathematics achievement.
4. They are less likely to be retained in grade.
5. And, they are less likely to have been placed in special education.

The findings replicate, but with a larger magnitude of effect, the Consortium for Longitudinal Studies' findings on

Special Education and grade retention reduction, and extend the findings to show that there are cognitive and economic achievement results that seem to undergird those more positive academic outcomes.

I believe we need to be involved in many more systemic comparisons of different forms of intervention, and different forms of health-care and other service systems to reduce the adverse effects of poverty on development outcomes for children and families.

*   *   *

Round Table Discussion

Huston. It strikes me that one of the things that would be helpful would be to have some centralized way of trying to define a way of research agenda in this area. Is there an agency probably in the Federal bureaucracy somewhere that deals which these issues that you think would be an appropriate one to try to do this?

Ramey. I think this would be very appropriate for the National Academy of Sciences. I think it's the most prestigious group of scientists in the country. It can and should focus on this and then from that would come the involvement of various agencies . . . NIMH, various NIH's, and other groups including education, I believe have major roles to play. I would not house this effort in a single agency. I believe that would balkanize the overall effort. It needs an umbrella organization that speaks broadly for society as a whole and I cannot think of a more prestigious group to take on what I believe is a highly complex task than the National Academy of Sciences.

Zuckerman. I would like to share with you a project that I am involved with at the American Academy of Arts and Science. The goal of this effort is to increase investment in children and one of the important projects is to develop new indicators for children's wellbeing. We are discussing the possibility of combining a number of parameters regarding children's health, education, leisure time, etc. in order to present a picture of different aspects of children's lives. The next step will be to link these indicators with interventions that affect them; understanding what public policies and programs affect the indicators that will help us improve the wellbeing of children.

Kotelchuck. I don't disagree with your sense that our research isn't as strong as it could be, but at the same time I wonder if it's our lack of rigor that's making the political process not listen to us. I'm curious from the IHDP or anybody, how expensive would such a program be, how likely is such a program to be implementable in any broad-scaled way. I guess that's what worries me, is it the rigor or is it someone's political judgment of the likelihood of that being made into a larger program.

Ramey. I have a couple of responses. One is I believe we are much too timid in asking for the resources to do what I believe we need to be doing, that is developing and testing programs and tying them into epidemiology. We don't raise the question in the same way if we talk about cancer, if we talk about heart disease. We somehow have assumed the burden as part of the child development community that we have to do this on the cheap. And, I think that we have made a profound mistake in doing that. We know that many of these risk factors are highly interrelated and that diet and life style and environmental strategies get linked in pervasive ways both in innercity environments and low resource rural environments. And, I for one, am not going to play the cost benefit analysis game because I think that is a game designed to rig the deck against us. I think we have to say what needs to be done and why it is important and let's talk about comparing the various approaches we already have, let's just say within NIH. I don't think that we should allow ourselves to be maneuvered into a defensive posture.

Brooks-Gunn. It's particularly important if you think about high quality childcare costs, given what we know are good ratios and given what we know from, not just IHDP or Abecedarian, but the studies that have gone on and have looked at high-quality childcare as it exists in communities. The fact is almost no studies have looked at how many kids actually attend on a day-to-day basis until Craig's at Frank Porter Graham did that in IHDP. Without transportation you are not going to get poor families to consistently bring their kids into a center. If they don't come into the center, you are not going to show the effects. I really agree with Craig if we are talking about believing from the data that high quality childcare during the first years of the child's life makes a difference then you are going to probably have to offer transportation. But, it means that IHDP wasn't that expensive. The evaluation was expensive. But, if you are talking about implementation, you are not having people filling out records daily and all of the careful controls that we have done. So, I think Craig's really right. You can try to do it on the cheap, but there is no quick fix for those families. And, it's true if we look at child care and it's true if we look at the kinds of programs we offer to mothers to get them off welfare. Some night course on getting your literacy scores up is not going to do the trick. It's absolutely no different than the child side. People haven't come to grips with that either, with what it takes to really help these mothers. All through their life circumstances, it's not easy.

Ramey. I'd like to conclude with this point. I think we have been led into a losing game in which we have been encouraged to bring forth interventions that allow various administrations to argue that more people are being served and that we are addressing this problem when, in fact, there's not much chance that these interventions are big enough or powerful enough to bring about meaningful change in the lives of individuals. If we think that we can make four or six home visits to a desperately poor family living in the middle of a ghetto and that will alter the mother's desire for more education, provide her children with better healthcare and allow her to be a more effective parent, I think that is cynicism of the worst kind. It defies credulity that it can bring about the kind of changes that we have allowed the public to believe might occur. I don't think we ought to do it. I don't think we should be afraid to ask for the level of resources to do it right.

CHAPTER 11

Poverty, Parenting, and Policy: Meeting the Support Needs of Poor Parents

Vonnie C. McLoyd

Lower class life is marked by an over-representation of a broad range of frustration-producing life events and chronic conditions outside personal control (Liem & Liem, 1978). Individuals who are poor are confronted with an unremitting succession of negative life events (e.g., eviction, physical illness, criminal assault) in the context of chronically stressful, ongoing life conditions such as inadequate housing and dangerous neighborhoods. Furthermore, stressors in the context of poverty are highly contagious. Because of limited financial resources, negative life events often precipitate additional crises (Makosky, 1982).

Adults who are poor also have more mental health problems than their economically advantaged counterparts. For example, McAdoo (1986) found perceived psychological distress to be significantly higher among single African American women with lower incomes, compared to those with higher incomes. The inverse relation between socioeconomic status and various forms of psychological distress and mental disorder is due in part to the increased exposure of the poor to chronic and acute stressors (Liem & Liem, 1978; Neff & Husaini, 1980). This relation also reflects the fact that stressors experienced by poor individuals, compared to those experienced by more affluent individuals, are more likely to be outside personal control. Catastrophic events not under the control of the individual, compared to those with greater elements of personal control, have been linked with more severe psychological impairment (Liem & Liem, 1978). In addition, ongoing stressful conditions associated with poverty such as inadequate housing and shortfalls of money have been found to be more debilitating than acute crises and negative events (Belle, 1984; Brown, Bhrolchain, & Harris, 1975; Makosky, 1982). In some studies, after chronic stressors are controlled, the effects of life events on psychological distress are diminished to borderline significance (Dressler, 1985; Gersten, Langner, Eisenberg, & Simcha-Fagan, 1977; Pearlin, Lieberman, Menaghan, & Mullan, 1981).

In addition to exposing the individual to more acute and chronic stressors, poverty weakens the individual's ability to cope with new problems and difficulties which, consequently, have more debilitating effects. Individuals who are poor are more likely than higher-status persons to suffer mental health problems following negative life events, a conclusion based on the fact that the positive relation between life-change scores and impairment is strongest in the lower-class. This relation is even stronger when events outside the control of the individual are analyzed separately (Kessler & Cleary, 1980; Liem & Liem, 1978). Differences in the occurrence of stressful life events only partially account for the link between social class and psychological distress, and this too has prompted questions about the existence of greater responsiveness or vulnerability to stress among lower-class persons (Turner & Noh, 1983). Social class differences in responsiveness to stress may stem from differences in social and economic resources. They also may be due to the excessive severity and chronicity of stressors in the lives of poor people, combined with the high frequency of negative life events over long periods of time. The rapid succession of negative life events leaves little time for recuperation after each occurrence (Belle, 1984) and, over time, these events in conjunction with stressful chronic conditions grind away and deplete emotional reserves.

Race and Marital Status as Risk Factors
for Mental Health Problems.

Vulnerability to stress following negative life events is reported to be higher among African Americans than whites (Neff, 1984, 1985). Controlling for social class generally attenuates, but does not eliminate race differences in psychological distress (Neff, 1984), suggesting that there may be true effects of race on psychological distress. This is the conclusion drawn by Kessler and Neighbors (1986) on the bases of analyses of eight different surveys encompassing more than 22,000 African American and white respondents. The indicators of psychological distress in the surveys were depression and somatic complaints associated with anxiety and depression. Race differences in distress were consistently and markedly greater among individuals with low incomes compared to those with higher ones. Moreover, these researchers found that the true effect of race is suppressed, and the true effect of social class is magnified, in models that fail to take the interaction of race and social class into consideration.

The factors responsible for this interaction between race and social class are not well understood, but might involve differences in the perception of threat posed by stressors, differences in availability of financial and social resources that blunt the impact of stressors, and increased vulnerability. African Americans may be more distressed than whites at low levels of income because their caste-like inferiorized status thwarts mobility aspirations and results in greater exposure to chronic, ongoing stressors (Dowhrenwend & Dowhrenwend, 1969; Pierce, 1975; Powell, 1982) and higher levels of resource deprivation (Kessler & Neighbors, 1986; Ogbu, 1978). This combination of factors may put lower class African American parents at higher risk for mental health problems. In keeping with this explanation, Myers and King (1983) suggest that the confluence of racism and the stressors resulting from chronic, urban poverty leads poor African Americans to function at a higher basal stress level than the norm. That is, it primes individuals physiologically and psychologically to perceive a wider range of stimuli as stressful.

For at least three reasons, single mother families deserve special attention in discussions of the relation of poverty to mental health and parenting. First, the risk of poverty in single mother families is high as a result of several factors including low wages for women, unfavorable economic conditions, the low educational attainment of many single mothers, and the large number of adolescent mothers who are single (Huston, McLoyd, & García Coll, in press). In 1990, the poverty rates for African American, Hispanic American and white families with a female householder and no husband present was 48.1%, 48.3%, and 27%, respectively. The corresponding figures in 1990 for married-couple families were 13%, 14%, and 5%, respectively (Reddy, 1993; U.S. Bureau of the Census, 1992). Second, single custodial parents are overwhelmingly female. Third, whether it is a consequence of divorce or nonformation of marital bonds, single motherhood is a risk factor for mental health problems. Single mothers are at greater risk of anxiety, depression, and health problems than other marital status groups and this risk is intensified if they are poor and live alone with their children (Belle, 1984; Guttentag, Salasin, & Belle, 1980; McAdoo, 1986; Pearlin & Johnson, 1977).

Some of the psychological distress associated with single parenthood is rooted in the burdens and responsibilities of solo parenting, as evidenced by the fact that the younger the child and the greater the number of children in the households, the greater is the association between marital status and mental health problems (Pearlin & Johnson, 1977). Adding to their plight is the fact that poor single mothers are more socially isolated and generally experience their interaction with the public welfare system as demeaning and dehumanizing (Goodban, 1985; Marshall, 1982; Popkin, 1990). In addition, lower-class women are more likely to experience the illness or death of children, the imprisonment of husbands, and privation and major losses in childhood which may make coping with new losses even more difficult (Belle, 1984; Brown et al., 1975; Reese, 1982; Wortman, 1981). Even when income is controlled, families headed by single mothers are more likely than two-parent, "male-headed" families to experience stressful life events such as changes in income, job, residence, and household composition, and for those in the labor force, unemployment (McLanahan, 1983; Weinraub & Wolf, 1983). Taken together, these findings suggest that the co-existence and co-occurrence of difficult life circumstances and events associated with poverty exact an extraordinarily high toll on mental health. As Pearlin and Johnson (1977) succinctly put it, "The combination most productive of psychological distress is to be simultaneously single, isolated, exposed to burdensome parental obligations and—most serious of all—poor" (p. 714).

The Consequences of Psychological Distress and Negative Life Events for Parenting Behavior

Psychological distress and negative emotional states (e.g., depression, anxiety) have significant implications for parenting. Among both poor and economically advantaged parents, psychological distress and negative emotional states are predictive of less positive attitudes regarding their parental role and increased punitiveness, inconsistency, and insensitivity to children's needs (McLoyd, 1990). Mothers experiencing higher levels of psychological distress perceive parenting as more difficult and less satisfying (Crnic & Greenberg, 1987; McLoyd & Wilson, 1990) and exhibit less positive behavior (hugs, praise, supportive statements) and more negative behavior toward the child (e.g., threats, derogatory statements). They tend to be more critical, less affectionate, less responsive to the child's overtures, and less active and spontaneous. They are more likely to choose conflict resolution solutions that require little effort, such as dropping initial demands when the child is resistant or enforcing obedience unilaterally, rather than negotiating or reasoning with the child (Conger, McCarty, Yang, Lahey, & Kropp, 1984; Davenport, Zahn-Waxler, Adland, & Mayfield, 1984; Radke-Yarrow, Richters, & Wilson, 1988; Longfellow, Zelkowitz, & Saunders, 1982; Zelkowitz, 1982). Parental depression also has been linked to physical abuse (Daniel, Hampton, & Newberger, 1983; Downey & Coyne, 1990).

These patterns of parenting associated with psychological distress resemble those linked to negative life events. For example, the occurrence of undesirable life events was found by Gersten et al. (1977) to correlate positively with affectively distant, restrictive, and punitive parenting. Similarly, Weinraub and Wolf (1983) reported that mothers who experienced more stressful life events were less nurturant toward their children and, in the case of single mothers, were less at ease, less spontaneous, and less responsive to their children's communications. Even ephemeral, relatively minor hassles produce detectable changes in maternal behavior. Patterson's (1988) observations of mother-child dyads over the course of several days indicate that day-to-day fluctuations in mothers' tendency to initiate and continue an aversive exchange with their children were systematically related to the daily frequency of hassles or crises the mother experienced.

Given that parents who are poor experience both more psychological distress and more chronic and acute stressors than their advantaged counterparts, it is not surprising that they tend to be less nurturant, supportive, and sensitive in their interactions with their children than middle-class parents. Numerous studies report that mothers who are poor, as compared to their economically advantaged counterparts, are more likely to use power-assertive techniques in disciplinary encounters and are generally less supportive of their children. They value obedience more, are less likely to use reasoning, and more likely to use physical punishment as a means of disciplining and controlling the child. Lower-class parents are more likely to issue commands without explanation, less likely to consult the child about his or her wishes, and less likely to reward the child verbally for behavior in desirable ways. Poverty also has been associated with diminished expression of affection and lesser responsiveness to the socioemotional needs explicitly expressed by the child (Conger et al., 1984; Gecas, 1979; Hess, 1970; Kamii & Radin, 1967; Kriesberg, 1970; Langner, Herson, Greene, Jameson, & Goff, 1970; Peterson & Peters, 1985; Portes, Dunham, & Williams, 1986; Wilson, 1974). These class-linked patterns of parenting discussed above parallel both event-linked and affect-linked patterns of parenting, lending strong support for the argument that differences in the parenting of poor versus nonpoor adults are partly the result of differences in the level of environmental stress and, hence, the degree of psychological distress, experienced by these two groups. Recently, McLeod and Shanahan (1993) questioned whether the distal, environmental reasons for harsh discipline are the same for poor minority parents as they are for poor white parents. They speculated that for poor African American and Hispanic parents, frequent use of harsh discipline may stem from the fact that they enter poverty with less and live in more impoverished neighborhoods, whereas for poor white parents, it may be precipitated by negative social comparisons resulting from living among wealthier peers. This is an interesting issue that merits systematic study.

Child abuse: an extreme form of punitive parenting. Although it is indisputable that only a small proportion of poor parents are even alleged to abuse their children, strong evidence exists that child abuse occurs more frequently in poor families than in more affluent families (e.g., Daniel et al., 1983; Garbarino, 1976; Pelton, 1989). Indeed, poverty is the single most prevalent characteristic of abusing parents (Pelton, 1989). Some have claimed that the relation between child abuse and social class is spurious owing to bias in detection and in the records of child welfare agencies typically used to estimate the occurrence of child abuse. It is asserted that poor people's behavior is more open to scrutiny (e.g., the poor have more contact with public agencies and are less likely to live in isolated single-family dwellings), making detection of child abuse more likely among them than among more affluent individuals. Furthermore, critics argue, known cases of child abuse are more likely to be reported to agencies and agencies are more likely to intervene if the family is poor (Wright, 1982). Although these biases may inflate the estimates, several trends suggests that a true relation exists between poverty and abuse. First, although greater public awareness and new reporting laws resulted in a significant increase in official reporting in recent years, the socioeconomic pattern of these reports has not changed (Pelton, 1989). Second, child abuse is related to degrees of poverty even within the lower class which admittedly is more open to public scrutiny; abusing parents tend to be the poorest of the poor (Horowitz & Wolock, 1985; Wolock & Horowitz, 1979). Third, the severest injuries occur within the poorest families, even among the reported cases (Pelton, 1989).

The relation between poverty and child abuse appears to be explained, in part, by elevated levels of psychological distress in economically deprived parents and relatedly, an abundance of negative life events and a paucity of social support. In their study of African American families, for instance, Daniel et al. (1983) found that abusive mothers not only were more likely than nonabusive mothers to be very poor, but suffered more losses due to recent deaths in their families, more recent changes in their life situations, and generally more negative family stress. As noted previously, even within poor abusive families, material deprivation is associated with severity of maltreatment. In addition, research with African American and Anglo American samples indicate that, compared to nonabusing parents, parents who abuse their children are more isolated from formal and informal support networks, are less likely to have a relative living nearby, and have lived in their neighborhoods for shorter periods of time (Cazenave & Straus, 1979; Daniel et al., 1983; Gelles, 1980; Trickett & Susman, 1988). The isolation of abusive families may be partly self-imposed owing to perceptions of the worlds as hostile and threatening, but it is unlikely that the relation between child abuse and low integration into support networks is due entirely to self-selection factors (Trickett & Susman, 1988).

Parenting and Children's Socioemotional Functioning

Poverty has been linked to a variety of socioemotional problems in both African American and white children of varying ages including such difficulties as depression (Gibbs, 1986), strained peer relations (Langner et al., 1970), low self-confidence, conduct disorders, and higher levels of overall social maladaptation and psychological disorder (Kellam, Ensminger, & Turner, 1977; Langner, Greene, Herson, Jameson, Goff, Rostkowski, & Zykorie, 1969; Levinson, 1969; Myers & King, 1983). Both indirect, and more recently, direct empirical evidence suggest that at least some of these problems are mediated by punitive and harsh parental discipline brought on by economic hardship.

With respect to indirect evidence, childrearing practices that are more prevalent among impoverished or economically pressed parents are predictive of a number of socioemotional problems in children. For example, punitive, inconsistent discipline by parents is associated with increased rates of delinquency, drug use, and socioemotional distress (e.g., depressive symptoms, moodiness, hypersensitivity, feelings of inadequacy) among adolescents, and more quarrelsome, negativistic, and explosive behavior among younger children (Elder, 1979; Elder, Nguyen, & Caspi, 1985; Lempers, Clark-Lempers, & Simons, 1989; McLoyd, Jayaratne, Ceballo, & Borquez, in press). Patterson (1986) has shown that preadolescent and adolescent children are at high risk of becoming antisocial and highly aggressive if they are temperamentally difficult and have parents who are highly irritable, erratic, and punitive. A recent investigation by Dodge, Pettit, and Bates (in press) indicated that harsh parenting during the preschool years predicted externalizing behavior problems in children as much as four years later. Children who have been neglected or physically abused, compared to children with no history of neglect or abuse, exhibit more anger, aggression, frustration, and noncompliance in problem-solving situations (Egeland & Sroufe, 1981a), behave more aggressively toward their peers and their caregivers, and reciprocate friendly overtures less frequently (George & Main, 1979). Finally, research indicates that harsh discipline and low levels of positive responsiveness to children's needs are key mediators of the link between maternal depression and child maladjustment (Downey & Coyne, 1990).

A vast literature also exists concerning consequences for children's socioemotional functioning of nonsupportive behavior in parents, defined as low levels of behavior that make the child feel comfortable in the presence of the parent and communicate to the child that he or she is basically accepted and approved (Rollins & Thomas, 1979). Research consistently shows that children whose parents are nonsupportive have lower self-esteem (Coopersmith, 1967; Gecas, 1979; Rollins & Thomas, 1979) and more psychological disorders, exhibit more antisocial aggression and behavioral problems (Rollins & Thomas, 1979), and are more likely to show arrested ego development (Powers, Hauser, & Kilner, 1989). Adding to this picture is recent evidence that across all social classes, adolescents with nonsupportive parents report more psychological distress and engage in more delinquent activities in comparison to adolescents whose parents are warm and democratic, but firm in disciplinary encounters (Steinberg, Mounts, Lamborn, & Dornbusch, 1991).

A few recent, process-focused studies provide direct evidence that an increase in harsh, punitive, and inconsistent discipline, parental hostility, and parent-child conflict in response to elevated levels of psychological distress in parents is one of the pathways by which poverty adversely and indirectly affects children's socioemotional functioning. McLoyd et al. (in press) found that the adverse effects of poverty and unemployment among single-parent African American mothers adversely affected adolescents' socioemotional functioning by increasing maternal depression and, in turn, increasing punishment of the adolescent. The relation between maternal punishment and adolescents' socioemotional functioning was partially mediated by adolescents' perceptions of the quality of relations with their mothers.

McLeod and Shanahan's (1993) recent study of 4- to 8-year-olds further elaborates on the mediational role of parenting behavior by distinguishing between current and persistent poverty. Mothers' weak emotional responsiveness to their children's needs and frequent use of physical punishment explained the effect of current poverty on children's mental health (i.e., internalizing and externalizing symptoms), but not the effect of persistent poverty. Length of time spent in poverty neither increased the frequency of physical punishment nor decreased mothers' emotional responsiveness, perhaps indicating that family interactions stabilize as the duration of poverty increases and the family adapts to economic deprivation. However, McLeod and Shanahan point out that other forms of harsh discipline may be more common in persistently poor families and may account for children's mental health problems. The relations among poverty, parenting behavior, and children's mental health did not vary by race/ethnicity (African Americans and Hispanics versus non-Hispanic whites).

Social Support and Attitudes: Effects on Psychological Functioning and Parenting Behavior

Considerable variation exists in the extent to which individuals succumb to the debilitating effects of stress brought on by poverty and economic hardship. Social support, which refers to a vast array of different types of assistance including instrumental, informational, emotional, and parenting support, among others, contributes to this variation. Social support buffers feelings of depression in mothers on welfare (Colletta & Lee, 1983; Zur-Szpiro & Longfellow, 1982) and feelings of psychological distress among unemployed adults (Gore, 1978; Kasl & Cobb, 1979; Kessler et al., 1987; Kessler, Turner, & House, 1988). However, it is far less effective in buffering the psychological distress associated with chronic economic stressors than that induced by negative life events, especially among young African American women (Dressler, 1985).

Another potent protective factor consists of the individual's attributional biases. Poor women who do not blame themselves for being on welfare (Goodban, 1985) tend to have fewer psychological problems than those who blame themselves for their economic difficulties. Similarly, unemployed African Americans who more frequently perceive themselves to be victims of racial discrimination report higher levels of psychological well-being than unemployed African Americans whose perceived experience with racial discrimination is lower. Religiosity also is associated with lower distress among unemployed African Americans (Barbarin, in press).

A burgeoning body of literature indicates that social support not only improves parents' dispositions, but in turn, lessens their tendency toward insensitivity and coercive discipline. Both poor and more affluent mothers receiving higher levels of emotional support (i.e., companionship, expressions of affection, availability of a confidant) report being less likely to nag, scold, ridicule, or threaten their children and are observed to interact in a more nurturant, sensitive fashion with their children. They report feeling less overwhelmed by their parenting situation, more gratified by the maternal role, and more satisfied with their children (Crnic & Greenberg, 1987; Zur-Szpiro & Longfellow, 1982), factors that may both instigate as well as result from more positive parenting behavior. Parenting support also has salutary effects on parenting behavior. Crockenberg's (1987) observational study of impoverished adolescent mothers indicated that maternal sensitivity and accessibility to the baby, as well as promptness in responding to the infant's cries, increased with an increase in the number of family members who helped with various household and child-care chores. This is consistent with reports from poor mothers that they are warmer and less rejecting of their preschool children when given an opportunity to break continuous interactions with them for more than two hours (Colletta, 1979).

Because psychological distress among mothers is a risk factor for difficulties in children's socioemotional functioning, factors that protect against maternal distress may bolster the probability of adaptive resilience in the child. There are hints of this in existing research, but more evidence is needed before strong conclusions can be drawn. For example, the availability of child care support to the primary caregiver, both generally and specifically from the father, has been found to distinguish stress-resilient from stress-affected children (Cowen, Wyman, Work, & Parker, 1990). The presence of an adult male in the home predicts secure attachment in impoverished infants (Vaughn, Gove, & Egeland, 1980), and the presence of a supportive family member, usually the grandmother, shows a weak association with secure attachment in poor infants who have been abused or neglected by their mothers (Egeland & Sroufe, 1981b). These findings are consistent with evidence that emotional adjustment in poor

African American children living in mother/grandmother
families is almost as high as that of children living in
mother/father families, and significantly higher than that of
children living alone with the mother (Kellam et al., 1977). It is
unclear from these studies, however, whether these reported
relations are the result of support to the primary caregiver, direct
support to the child, or both.

Meeting the Support Needs of Poor Parents: Policy Considerations

The research reviewed above provides compelling
evidence that poverty and its attendant chronic and acute
environmental stressors are major contributors to depression,
psychological distress, insensitive or abusive parenting and
negative child outcomes in low-income populations. It follows,
therefore, that alleviation of such stressors is likely to reduce
mental health problems in mothers, enhance parenting, and
contribute to positive socioemotional functioning in children.
Existing research is inadequate to determine whether counseling
and parenting education alone, without supporting
interventions, produce positive and enduring changes in
parenting behavior in low-income populations (Dornbusch, Barr,
& Seer, 1993). Nonetheless, in view of the strong linkages among
these variables, we believe that intervention and prevention
strategies that focus exclusively on intrapsychic flaws and parent
education, while ignoring the environmental difficulties that
undermine psychological and parental functioning, are likely to
be of limited usefulness and, indeed, may engender more, rather
than less, passivity, guilt, and depression (Belle, 1984). This
position is in accord with Schorr's (1989) research indicating that
intervention programs that are successful in changing outcomes
for high risk children typically adopt a comprehensive, rather
than fragmented, piece-meal approach, offering a broad
spectrum of services. The prevailing wisdom of these programs
is that social and emotional support and immediate, concrete

help are usually necessary before families can make use of interventions with long-range, developmental goals.

Given research on the link between attributional biases and psychological well-being, as well as research on the relation between members of the helping profession and their clients, we also believe that blaming poor mothers for their economic and psychological plight will exacerbate their psychological problems, heighten mistrust and apprehension, and undercut the professional's role as facilitator and helper (Belle, 1984; Crockenberg, 1987). On these grounds, we argue that programmatic efforts to ameliorate or prevent negative outcomes in parental functioning, parental psychological well-being, or children's socioemotional functioning, whether targeted at the general population of poor parents or particular segments of the poverty population (e.g., adolescent mothers, poor mothers at high risk of child abuse), should be unambivalently supportive, rather than punitive in nature, reflect a knowledge of and sensitivity to the cultural characteristics of the families to be served (Gray & Nybell, 1990; Slaughter-Defoe, 1993), and encompass delivery of a broad range of concrete services that ease the negative life conditions experienced by poor families.

The first requisite poses a particularly formidable challenge because of an historically rooted, deeply etched, and widespread value among Americans for independence and self-sufficiency and a resulting ambivalence toward and suspicion of poor people in trouble. Our sense of morality, ethics, and magnanimity moves us to help them, but our steadfast ideological commitment to individualism, self-sufficiency, and person-blame explanations of poverty compels us to punish them (Pelton, 1989; Halpern, 1991). We suspect them of sloth, guile, loose living, and individual culpability and worry that they are more interested in exploiting than contributing to society. Because of racism, cultural ethnocentrism, and ignorance of non-Anglo American cultural traditions, these attitudes are intensified when the poor in question are non-white. Agents of intervention and prevention must confront and seek to minimize ambivalence about the character and worth of poor people and the causes and meaning of their plight, lest it corrode the integrity of their efforts. Achieving an intimacy with the ongoing struggles and environmental stressors impinging on poor families and the coping strategies of these families is a first step in this process. Because the typical middle-class therapist or mental health worker has never experienced the stressors that poor parents routinely confront, concerted efforts are essential on the part of therapists and mental health workers to bridge the class- and culture-linked chasms between them and the poor. Visits to clients' neighborhoods and homes, when undertaken as an educational rather than evaluative process, can help interventionists appreciate clients' ongoing struggles to survive and raise their children in the midst of daunting environmental realities (Belle, 1984).

Although family support services are emphasized here as a mechanism to address the problems of poor parents discussed in this paper, it is crucial to acknowledge the limits of what such services can accomplish. Many of the causes of difficult life conditions confronting poor families (e.g., racism in labor market and lending institutions, low wages paid by traditionally "female" jobs, unavailability of affordable, high-quality child care, unjust housing policies) are impervious to family-level interventions (Halpern, 1990a). As Halpern (1991) has pointed out, there has been an over-reliance on services to address problems created by poverty "due to an unwillingness to acknowledge that many of our most serious problems are a result of chosen social and economic arrangements and a reluctance to use the political process to alter arrangements even when it is acknowledged that they are harmful" (p. 344).

The case for community-based early intervention. Halpern (1990a) identifies two major practices that have been developed to address parenting and related support needs of poor families with young children: (a) clinical, therapeutic strategies in which trained professional teams work with families manifesting problematic parent-child interaction, and (b) community-based interventions targeting any family with young children in a specific population of poor families (e.g., adolescent parents). Although there is variation in how the problems of individuals and families are conceptualized (e.g., behavioral versus psychoanalytic perspectives), the former strategies typically have their roots in a medical or disease model and share a common emphasis on locating and treating the problem within the "mini-systems" of the individual or the family.

Community-based interventions, in contrast, are based on a "mega-system" perspective that extends the helpers' view beyond the individual or family to the broader ecological context (Conte, 1983). Among the other distinguishing features of most community-based interventions is use of lay family workers (sometimes in conjunction with professionals) by neighborhood-based agencies to provide a range of support services and to locate and press into service helping resources in low income communities. These service strategies aim to promote "family conditions, parental competencies, and behaviors that contribute to maternal and infant health, maternal personal development, and healthy child development" (Halpern, 1990a, p. 470). Familial stressors as well as extrafamilial stressors and negative life conditions impinging on the family are seen as obstacles to nurturant, sensitive, and stimulating parenting. This ecologically-oriented diagnostic approach dictates the provision of a broad range of services. Therapeutic, individual-focused services such as information, guidance and feedback, joint problem solving, encouragement, and psychological support are complemented by practical assistance (e.g., help in securing entitlements and tangible services) in solving concrete problems and effecting environmental changes. The mechanisms for providing support are also varied and include individualized (e.g., home visiting) as well as group formats (e.g., peer support groups and parent education classes).

Halpern (1990a) credits four recent developments with stimulating interest in community-based interventions as a promising strategy to address the complex of problems and support needs of poor families and children: (a) the deteriorating social and economic well-being of young families (e.g., Wilson, 1987; William T. Grant Commission on Work, Family and Citizenship, 1988); (b) the growing recognition that mainstream public and private services, whether because of mandate, caseload, location, or ill-suited practice modalities, are not equipped to provide young, stress-burdened families with sustained, multifaceted, and nonstigmatizing support; (c) the increasing recognition of the limitations of informal social supports to address chronic, pressing needs and the potential for informal support to exact greater costs than benefits in resource-scare environments; and (d) the growing appreciation of the need for models of practice that address not only psychological and interpersonal problems, but adverse life conditions confronting poor families as well.

Although not abundant, evidence exists of positive effects of community-based interventions from studies of randomly assigned program and control groups. Extensive reviews of the effects of these and other more narrowly focused parenting education programs can be found elsewhere (Dornbusch et al., 1993; Halpern, 1988, 1990a, 1990b). Detailed discussion of these programs is beyond the scope of this paper, but it is instructive to examine a few model programs. Among the most impressive of community-based interventions are three Parent Child Development Center (PCDC) programs conducted under the U.S. Office of Economic Opportunity (Andrews et al., 1982). These programs included the following core components: (a) a comprehensive curriculum for mothers consisting of information on child development and child rearing practices, home management, nutrition and health, mothers' personal development, and government and community resources and how to use them; (b) a simultaneous program for the children of these women (ranging in age from 2- to 12-months at the time of entry into the program); and (c) extensive supportive services for participating families including transportation, some meals, family health and social services, peer support groups, and a small, daily stipend. The programs ended when the child was 36 months of age and varied in the amount of weekly participation expected. Although the measures and variables assessed differed across sites, at graduation, program mothers in all three sites scored significantly higher than controls overall on dimensions of positive maternal behavior (e.g., giving child praise and emotional support, being affectionate and accepting, encouraging children's verbal communications, participating actively in child's activities, greater use of language to inform, rather than restrict and control children). In addition, in the one site where a graduation interview was conducted, mothers who participated in the intervention reported higher levels of general life satisfaction and greater use of positive child-control techniques than mothers in the control group (e.g., greater use of reasoning, less use of physical punishment). In all three programs, program children scored higher than control children on the Stanford-Binet, although this difference reached statistical significance in only two of the three sites. In general, the intervention program had more positive effects on mothers than children.

Notwithstanding these positive effects, generalizability, cost, and burgeoning need for services have been cited as problems that dampen the potential of PCDC programs as a dominant strategy to meet the needs of large numbers of low-income parents. Halpern (1988) warns that ". . . effects potent enough to leave a meaningful residue in parents' and children's lives may depend on interventions of such skill, expense, and intensity as to be unreplicable in the average practice context; unaffordable without a significant redeployment of public resources toward prevention; and unmanageable by the growing proportion of low-income parents facing overwhelming personal, familial, and situational problems" (pp. 297–298). In light of evidence that informal support systems are increasingly strained, that growing numbers of young families are in need of support due to structural changes in the economy, and that parent support combined with parent education for poor families can improve parenting, family functioning, and children's development, increased private and public funding to support high-quality, community-based intervention programs as a central component of an overall prevention strategy seems to be an essential and sound investment in the future.

Targeting abusing parents and parents at high risk of child abuse. Because child abuse poses a serious threat to children's basic survival, its amelioration and prevention deserve special attention. The public institution charged to protect the welfare of dependent, neglected, and abused children is the public child welfare system. Family preservation has been the avowed and uncontested bedrock of this institution since the 1909 White Conference on the Care of Dependent Children pronounced that:

Children should not be deprived of home life with their parents except for urgent and compelling reasons. Children of parents of worthy character, suffering from temporary misfortune, and children of reasonably efficient and deserving mothers who are without support of the normal breadwinner, should as a rule be kept with their parents, such aid being given as may be necessary to maintain suitable homes for the rearing of the children. Except in unusual circumstances, the home should not be broken up for reasons of poverty, but only for considerations of inefficiency or immorality. (Pelton, 1989, p. 2)

Policy and rhetoric aside, research conducted by Pelton (1989) indicates that child removal is the primary strategy used to deal with cases of abuse and neglect, and, relatedly, that woefully few supports are offered to remediate poverty-related environmental, situational, and personal problems and to obviate child placement. This contradiction between policy and practice was present from the very inception of the public child welfare system. By the mid-1960s, psychological and personality deficits had replaced moral turpitude as the accepted cause of child abuse and neglect. This view, which essentially dismissed the role of poverty and poverty-related stressors, dovetailed another specious claim that gained currency during the same period, namely that child abuse and neglect are distributed proportionately across social classes (Pelton, 1989).

The claim that poverty and child abuse, or poverty and child neglect, are unrelated has the effect of encouraging case workers to search solely for psychological defects in parents accused of child neglect and abuse. This makes it easier for them to decide to remove the child from the home rather than to provide concrete services in the home to alleviate adverse circumstances. Nonetheless, caseworkers are less villains than hapless victims themselves, caught as they are between the proverbial "rock and a hard place." They are confronted with ambiguous policies and guidelines for action, severely limited supportive services to offer and most importantly, contradictory role demands (Pelton, 1989).

It seems obvious that caseworkers can most effectively fulfill their charge to offer treatment and services in the interest of family preservation by forming trusting, supportive, and cooperative relationships with the parents. However, according to Pelton (1989), their ability to do so is undermined by a bureaucracy that typically accords more resources for punitive intervention and child rescue than prevention, positive assistance, and family preservation and by the repertoire of actions they must undertake to fulfill their responsibility to investigate allegations of child abuse and neglect. This repertoire includes asking probing, intrusive questions of parents; questioning neighbors; taking the child for a medical examination, and making unannounced visits—all actions that are likely to antagonize parents and, if the child is removed from the home, hamper the caseworker's ability to work effectively with parents toward the goal of returning the child (Pelton, 1989). The gravity of these contradictions is underscored by research findings on the effects of foster care, serial foster placement, and recidivism on parent-child relationships and children's emotional well-being, although it should be noted that the studies on these issues tend to be methodologically weak and few in number (Wald, 1988; Pelton, 1989). It is arguable that reunifying children with their parents after they have been placed in foster care is more difficult to achieve than the prevention of placement in the first place.

The Adoption Assistance and Child Welfare Act of 1980 and accompanying legislation at the state level were partly in response to the criticism that child welfare agencies devote insufficient effort to placement prevention and provide care of questionable quality to children who have been removed from their own homes. This law mandates that a certain portion of funding must go toward services aimed at placement prevention, family reunification, and permanency planning for children who cannot return home. Reimbursement for foster care is subject to review aimed at determining whether agencies have made sufficient efforts toward these goals (Frankel, 1988). Family-centered, home-based service programs are among the options available to meet these requirements. These programs focus on the family system (not just the mother) and its social and physical context as the target for change. Counseling and concrete services such as homemakers and day care are provided. Unfortunately, very few well-designed studies exist of the effectiveness of this approach versus more traditional approaches in preventing child placement. Existing evaluations tend to be seriously flawed (e.g., lack of comparison or control groups, inadequate descriptions of service activities). Furthermore, almost no research has been done to determine if these programs affect family functioning or to assess the relation between changes in family functioning and placement. This is a glaring gap given the assumption that family-centered, home-based services prevent placement by improving family functioning (Frankel, 1988).

Parents accused of child abuse and neglect often are required by public welfare agencies to undergo therapeutic counseling focusing on intrapsychic processes and/or enter educational programs focusing on parenting and knowledge about child development. It is questionable whether parenting education *alone* is a sufficient antidote to the reoccurrence or prevention of child abuse. To some extent, this is a moot issue because rarely does intervention targeted toward abusing parents or parents with high child-abuse potential consist solely of parenting education. Parenting education, if mandated, usually is mixed with other services, however meager. The more policy-relevant question is whether parenting education combined with support services is more effective in preventing child abuse and placement than support services alone. Recent evidence favors the former strategy. Wolfe, Edwards, Manion, & Koverola (1988) conducted a study of the effects of a parenting education intervention for mothers and children who were under supervision from a child protective service agency because public health nurses who visited the family expressed concerns that the child was at risk of maltreatment. The intervention provided mothers with instruction, modeling, and rehearsal procedures to increase positive child management skills (e.g., rewarding compliance, using more praise and less criticism, giving concise demands). Compared to a comparison group of families who received standard agency services (i.e., informal discussion of topics related to health and family, social activities, periodic home visits from caseworkers), mothers in the parenting group had more positive attitudes and feelings about parenting and reported less depressive symptomatology, but their child rearing methods as assessed by home observation did not differ. One year following treatment, caseworkers rated mothers in the parenting training group as managing their children significantly better and at lower risk of maltreatment than mothers in the comparison group.

These findings are in general accord with those from a randomized trial of nurse home visitation conducted by Olds, Henderson, Chamberlin, and Tatelbaum (1986). During their home visits, nurses provided mothers with information about infants' development and socioemotional and cognitive needs, encouraged involvement of relatives and friends in child care and support of the mother, and connected families with community health and human service agencies. Among poor, unmarried teenage mothers, those who were visited by a nurse had fewer instances of confirmed child abuse and neglect, reported less conflict with and scolding of their 6-month-old infants, and were observed in their homes to restrict and punish their children (10- and 22-month-olds) less frequently, compared to those who received either no services or only free transportation to medical offices for prenatal and well-child care. In addition, the babies of nurse-visited women were seen in the emergency room less frequently during the first year of life.

Pelton (1989) has argued that irrespective of the type of service programs instituted to prevent abuse and obviate placement, the public child welfare system will remain hobbled in its ability to promote family preservation because of its contradictory roles. In keeping with Ghandi's claim that "a reformer cannot afford to be an informer," he proposes disentanglement of the investigatory/coercive role and the helping/supportive role by shifting the investigatory/coercive role, along with the foster care system, from public child welfare agencies to law enforcement agencies and the courts. Theoretically, this would free the child welfare system to pursue its helping role unencumbered by internal contradictions. Moreover, under this kind of reform, agencies could more easily expand beyond their crisis orientation and emergency services to *primary prevention*. Rather than operating in accordance with a narrow medical or psychodynamic model that prescribes changing individual behavior, the public child welfare system could function according to a multiple-causation model, removing causative factors through environmental changes (e.g., eliminating poverty-related safety and health hazards in the household) and delivery of a broad range of concrete services (e.g., housing assistance, emergency caretakers and homemakers, visiting nurses, home safety instruction). Pelton's prescription is eminently reasonable and merits careful consideration, based as it is on a careful and trenchant analysis of the problems besetting the current system. Research that assesses the effectiveness of these reforms relative to the current system would be essential in guiding future policy decisions.

Acknowledgment

Portions of this paper were presented at the Society for Research on Child Development Preconference Round Table on Child Development I: Children of Poverty, New Orleans, LA., March 24, 1993, Hiram Fitzgerald, B. Lester, & B. Zuckerman, Co-organizers, and adapted from a review paper by the author that appeared in *Child Development*, 1990, *61*, 311–346.

References

Andrews, S. R., Blumenthal, J. B., Johnson, D. L., Kahn, A. J., Ferguson, C. J., Lasater, T. M., Malone, P. E., & Wallace, D. B. (1982). The skills of mothering: A study of parent child development centers. *Monographs of the Society for Research in Child Development, 47,* Serial No. 198.

Barbarin, O. (in press). Coping by blacks with joblessness: Relationships among stress, attributions, and mental health outcomes. In J. Jackson & P. Bowman (Eds.), *Coping with stress in black America.*

Belle, D. (1984). Inequality and mental health: Low income and minority women. In L. Walker (Eds.), *Women and mental health policy* (pp. 135–150). Beverly Hills: Sage.

Brown, G., Bhrolchain, M., & Harris, T. (1975). Social class and psychiatric disturbance among women in an urban population. *Sociology, 9 , 225–254.

Cazenave, N., & Straus, M. (1979). Race, class, network embeddedness and family violence: A search for potent support systems. *Journal of Comparative Family Studies, 10,* 281–300.

Colletta, N. (1979). Support systems after divorce: Incidence and impact. *Journal of Marriage and the Family, 41,* 837–846.

Colletta, N., & Lee, D. (1983). The impact of support for black adolescent mothers. *Journal of Family Issues, 4,* 127–143.

Conger, R., McCarty, J., Yang, R., Lahey, B., & Kropp, J. (1984). Perception of child, child-rearing values, and emotional distress as mediating links between environmental stressors and observed maternal behavior. *Child Development, 54,* 2234–2247.

Conte, J. (1983). Service provision to enhance family functioning. In W. Meezan & B. McGowan (Eds.), *Child welfare: Current dilemmas, future directions* (pp. 171–209). Itasca, IL: Peacock Publishers.

Coopersmith, S. (1967). *The antecedents of self-esteem.* San Francisco: Freeman.

Cowen, E. L., Wyman, P. A., Work, W. C., & Parker, G. R. (1990). The Rochester child resilience project: Overview and summary of first year findings. *Development and Psychopathology, 2,* 193–212.

Crnic, K., & Greenberg, M. (1987). Maternal stress, social support, and coping: Influences on early mother–child relationship. In C. Boukydis (Eds.), *Research on support for parents and infants in the postnatal period* (pp. 25–40). Norwood, NJ: Ablex.

Crockenberg, S. (1987). Support for adolescent mother during the postnatal period: Theory and research. In C. Boukydis (Eds.), *Research on support for parents and infants in the postnatal period* (pp. 3–24). Norwood, NJ: Ablex.

Daniel, J., Hampton, R., & Newberger, E. (1983). Child abuse and accidents in black families: A controlled comparative study. *American Journal of Orthopsychiatry, 53,* 645–653.

Davenport, Y. B., Zahn-Waxler, C., Adland, M. L., & Mayfield, A. (1984). Early child rearing practices in families with a manic-depressive parent. *American Journal of Psychiatry, 142,* 230–235.

Dodge, K., Pettit, G., & Bates, J. (in press). Socialization mediators of the relation between socioeconomic status and child conduct problems. *Child Development.*

Dornbusch, S. M., Barr, J. A., & Seer, N. A. (1993, June). The impact of education for parenting upon parents, children and family systems. A report to the Carnegie Task Force on Meeting the Needs of Young Children. Stanford Center for the Study of Families, Children, and Youth, Stanford CA.

Dowhrenwend, B. P., & Dowhrenwend, B. S. (1969). *Social status and psychological disorder.* New York: Wiley.

Downey, G., & Coyne, J. (1990). Children of depressed parents: An integrative review. *Psychological Bulletin, 108,* 50–76.

Dressler, W. (1985). Extended family relationships, social support, and mental health in a southern black community. *Journal of Health and Social Behavior, 26,* 39–48.

Egeland, B., & Sroufe, A. (1981a). Developmental sequelae of maltreatment in infancy. In R. Rizley & D. Cicchetti (Eds.), *New Directions for Child Development: Vol 11. Developmental perspectives on child maltreatment* (pp. 77–92). San Francisco: Jossey-Bass.

———. (1981b). Attachment and early maltreatment. *Child Development, 52,* 44–52.

Elder, G. (1979). Historical change in life patterns and personality. In P. Baltes & O. Brim (Eds.), *Life span development and behavior* (pp. 117–159). New York: Academic Press.

Elder, G., Nguyen, T., & Caspi, A. (1985). Linking family hardship to children's lives. *Child Development, 56,* 361–375.

Frankel, H. (1988). Family centered, home-based services in child protection: A review of the research. *Social Service Review, 62,* 137–157.

Garbarino, J. (1976). A preliminary study of some ecological correlates of child abuse: The impact of socioeconomic stress on mothers. *Child Development, 47,* 178–185.

Gecas, V. (1979). The influence of social class on socialization. In W. Burr, R. Hill, F. Nye, & I. Reiss (Eds.), *Contemporary theories about the family: Research-based theories* (pp. 365–404). New York: Free Press.

Gelles, R. (1980). Violence in the family: A review of research in the seventies. *Journal of Marriage and the Family, 42,* 143–155.

George, C., & Main, M. (1979). Social interactions of young abused children: Approach, avoidance, and aggression. *Child Development, 50*, 306–318.

Gersten, J., Langner, T., Eisenberg, J., & Simcha-Fagan, O. (1977). An evaluation of the etiological role of stressful life-change events in psychological disorders. *Journal of Health and Social Behavior, 18*, 228–244.

Gibbs, J. (1986). Assessment of depression in urban adolescent females: Implications for early intervention strategies. *American Journal of Social Psychiatry, 6*, 50–56.

Goodban, N. (1985). The psychological impact of being on welfare. *Social Service Review, 59*, 403–422.

Gore, S. (1978). The effect of social support in moderating the health consequences of unemployment. *Journal of Health and Social Behavior, 19*, 157–165.

Gray, S. S., & Nybell, L. M. (1990). Issues in African-American family preservation. *Child Welfare, 69*, 513–523.

Guttentag, M., Salasin, S., & Belle, D. (1980). *The mental health of women.* New York: Academic Press.

Halpern, R. (1988). Parent support and education for low-income families: Historical and current perspectives. *Children and Youth Services Review, 10*, 283–303.

———. (1990a). Community-based early intervention. In S. Meisels & J. Shonkoff (Eds.), *Handbook of early childhood intervention* (pp. 469–498). New York: Cambridge University Press.

———. (1990b). Parent support and education programs. *Children and Youth Services Review, 12*, 285–308.

———. (1991). Supportive services for families in poverty: Dilemmas of reform. *Social Service Review, 65*, 343–364.

Hess, R. (1970). Social class and ethnic influences upon socialization. In P. Mussen (Eds.), *Carmichael's manual of child psychology* (pp. 457–557). New York: John Wiley.

Horowitz, B., & Wolock, I. (1985). Material deprivation, child maltreatment, and agency interventions among poor families. In L. Pelton (Eds.), *The social context of child abuse and neglect* (pp. 137–184). New York: Human Sciences Press.

Huston, A., McLoyd, V. C., & García Coll, C. (1994). Children and poverty: Issues in contemporary research. *Child Development, 65*, 275–282.

Kamii, C., & Radin, N. (1967). Class differences in the socialization practices of Negro mothers. *Journal of Marriage and the Family, 29,* 302–310.

Kasl, S. V., & Cobb, S. (1979). Some mental health consequences of plant closings and job loss. In L. Ferman & J. Gordus (Eds.), *Mental health and the economy* (pp. 255–300). Kalamazoo: W. E. Upjohn Institute for Employment Research.

Kellam, S., Ensminger, M. E., & Turner, R. (1977). Family structure and the mental health of children. *Archives of General Psychiatry, 34,* 1012–1022.

Kessler, R., & Cleary, P. (1980). Social class and psychological distress. *American Sociological Review, 45,* 463–478.

Kessler, R., & Neighbors, H. (1986). A new perspective on the relationships among race, social class, and psychological distress. *Journal of Health and Social Behavi*or, *27,* 107–115.

Kessler, R., Turner, J., & House, J. (1987). Intervening processes in the relationship between unemployment and health. *Psychological Medicine, 17,* 949–962.

Kessler, R., Turner, J., & House, J. (1988). The effects of unemployment on health in a community sample: Main, modifying, and mediating effects. *Journal of Social Issues, 44,* 69–86.

Kriesberg, L. (1970). *Mothers in poverty: A study of fatherless families.* Chicago: Adline.

Langner, R., Greene, E., Herson, J., Jameson, J., Goff, J., Rostkowski, J., & Zykorie, D. (1969). Psychiatric impairment in welfare and nonwelfare children. *Welfare in Review, 7,* 10–21.

Langner, T., Herson, J., Greene, E., Jameson, J., & Goff, J. (1970). Children of the city: affluence, poverty, and mental health. In V. Allen (Eds.), *Psychological factors in poverty* (pp. 185–209). Chicago: Markham.

Lempers, J., Clark-Lempers, D., & Simons, R. (1989). Economic hardship, parenting, and distress in adolescence. *Child Development, 60,* 25–49.

Levinson, P. (1969). The next generation: A study of children in AFDC families. *Welfare in Review, 7,* 1–9.

Liem, R., & Liem, J. (1978). Social class and mental illness reconsidered: The role of economic stress and social support. *Journal of Health and Social Behavior, 19,* 139–156.

Longfellow, C., Zelkowitz, P., & Saunders, E. (1982). The quality of mother-child relationships. In D. Belle (Ed.), *Lives in stress: Women and depression* (pp. 163–176). Beverly Hills: Sage.

Makosky, V. P. (1982). Sources of stress: Events or conditions? In D. Belle (Ed.), *Lives in stress: Women and depression* (pp. 35–53). Beverly Hills: Sage.

Marshall, N. (1982). The public welfare system: Regulation and dehumanization. In D. Belle (Ed.), *Lives in stress: Women and depression* (pp. 96–108). Beverly Hills: Sage.

McAdoo, H. P. (1986). Strategies used by black single mothers against stress. In M. Simms & J. Malveaux (Eds.), *Slipping through the cracks: The status of black women* (pp. 153–166). New Brunswick: Transaction Books.

McLanahan, S. (1983). Family structure and stress: A longitudinal comparison of two-parent and female-headed families. *Journal of Marriage and the Family, 45,* 347–357.

McLeod, J., & Shanahan, M. (1993). Poverty, parenting, and children's mental health. *American Sociological Review, 58,* 351–366.

McLoyd, V. C. (1990). The impact of economic hardship on black families and children: Psychological distress, parenting, and socioemotional development. *Child Development, 61,* 311–346.

McLoyd, V. C., Jayaratne, T., Ceballo, R., & Borquez, J. (1994). Unemployment and work interruption among African American single mothers: Effects on parenting and adolescent socioemotional functioning. *Child Development, 65,* 562–589.

McLoyd, V. C., & Wilson, L. (1990). Maternal behavior, social support, and economic conditions as predictors of psychological distress in children. In V. C. McLoyd & C. Flanagan (Eds.), *New directions for child development. Economic stress: Effects on family life and child development* (pp. 49–69). San Francisco: Jossey-Bass.

Myers, H. F., & King, L. (1983). Mental health issues in the development of the black American children. In G. Powell, J. Yamamoto, A. Romero, & A. Morales (Eds.), *The psychosocial development of minority group children* (pp. 275–306). New York: Brunner/Mazel.

Neff, J. (1984). Race differences in psychological distress: The effects of SES, urbanicity, and measurement strategy. *American Journal of Community Psychology, 12,* 337–351.

———. (1985). Race and vulnerability to stress: An examination of differential vulnerability. *Journal of Personality and Social Psychology, 49,* 481–491.

Neff, J., & Husaini, B. (1980). Race, socioeconomic status, and psychiatric impairment: A research note. *Journal of Community Psychology, 8*, 16–19.

Ogbu, J. (1978). *Minority education and caste: The American system in cross-cultural perspective.* New York: Academic Press.

Olds, D. L., Henderson, C., Chamberlain, R., & Tatelbaum, R. (1986). Preventing child abuse and neglect: A randomized trial of nurse home visitation. *Pediatrics, 78*, 65–78.

Patterson, G. (1986). Performance models for antisocial boys. *American Psychologist, 41*, 432–444.

———. (1988). Stress: A change agent for family process. In N. Garmezy & M. Rutter (Eds.), *Stress, coping and development in children* (pp. 235–264). Baltimore: Johns Hopkins University Press.

Pearlin, L., & Johnson, J. (1977). Marital status, life-strains and depression. *American Sociological Review, 42*, 704–715.

Pearlin, L., Lieberman, M., Menaghan, E., & Mullan, S. (1981). The stress process. *Journal of Health and Social Behavior, 22*, 337–356.

Pelton, L. H. (1989). *For reasons of poverty: A critical analysis of the public child welfare system in the United System.* New York: Praeger.

Peterson, G., & Peters, D. (1985). The socialization values of low-income Appalachian white and rural black mothers: A comparative study. *Journal of Comparative Family Studies, 16*, 75–91.

Pierce, C. (1975). The mundane extreme environment and its effects on learning. In S. G. Brainard (Ed.), *Learning disabilities: Issues and recommendations for research* (pp. 111–119). Washington, DC: National Institute of Education.

Popkin, S. J. (1990). Welfare: Views from the bottom. *Social Problems, 37*, 64–79.

Portes, P., Dunham, R., & Williams, S. (1986). Assessing child-rearing style in ecological settings: Its relation to culture, social class, early age intervention and scholastic achievement. *Adolescence, 21*, 723–735.

Powell, G. (1982). Overview of the epidemiology of mental illness among Afro-Americans. In B. A. Bass, G. Wyatt, & G. Powell (Eds.), *The Afro-american family: Assessment, treatment and research issues* (pp. 155–163). New York: Grune & Stratton.

Powers, S., Hauser, S., & Kilner, L. (1989). Adolescent mental health. *American Psychologist, 44*, 200–208.

Radke-Yarrow, M., Richters, J., & Wilson, W. (1988). Child development in a network of relationships. In R. Hinde & J. Stevenson-Hinde (Eds.), *Relationships within families: Mutual influences* (pp. 48–67). New York: Oxford University Press.

Reddy, M. A. (Ed.). (1993). *Statistical record of Hispanic Americans*. Detroit: Gale Research.

Reese, M. (1982). Growing up: The impact of loss and change. In D. Belle (Eds.), *Lives in stress: Women and depression* (pp. 65–80). Beverly Hills: Sage.

Rollins, B., & Thomas, D. (1979). Parental support, power, and control techniques in the socialization of children. In W. Burr, R. Hill, F. Nye, & I. Reiss (Eds.), *Contemporary theories about the family: Research-based theories* (pp. 317–364). New York: Free Press.

Schorr, L. (1989). *Within our reach: Breaking the cycle of disadvantage*. New York: Doubleday.

Slaughter-DeFoe, D. T. (1993). Home visiting and families in poverty: Introducing the concept of culture. *The Future of Children, 3*, 172–183.

Steinberg, L., Mounts, N., Lamborn, S., & Dornbusch, S. (1991). Authoritative parenting and adolescent adjustment across varied ecological niches. *Journal of Research on Adolescence, 1*, 19–36.

Trickett, P., & Susman, E. (1988). Parental perceptions of child-rearing practices in physically abusive and nonabusive families. *Developmental Psychology, 24*, 270–276.

Turner, R., & Noh, S. (1983). Class and psychological vulnerability among women: The significance of social support and personal control. *Journal of Health and Social Behavior, 24*, 2–15.

U.S. Bureau of the Census (1992). *The black population in the United States: March 1991. Current population reports, P20-464*, Washington, DC: U.S. Government Printing Office.

Vaughn, B., Gove, F., & Egeland, B. (1980). The relationship between out-of-home care and the quality of infant-mother attachment in an economically disadvantaged population. *Child Development, 51*, 1203–1214.

Wald, M. (1988 Summer). Family preservation: Are we moving too fast? *Public Welfare*, 33–38.

Weinraub, M., & Wolf, B. (1983). Effects of stress and social supports on mother-child interactions in single- and two-parent families. *Child Development, 54*, 1297–1311.

William T. Grant Foundation Commission on Work, Family and Citizenship. (1988). *The forgotten half: Pathways to success for America's youth and young families.* Washington, DC: W. T. Grant Foundation.

Wilson, H. (1974). Parenting in poverty. *British Journal of Social Work, 4,* 241–254.

Wilson, W. J. (1987). *The truly disadvantaged: The inner city, the underclass, and public policy.* Chicago: University of Chicago Press.

Wolfe, D. A., Edwards, B., Manion, I., & Koverola, C. (1988). Early intervention for parents at risk of child abuse and neglect: A preliminary investigation. *Journal of Consulting and Clinical Psychology, 56,* 40–47.

Wolock, I., & Horowitz, B. (1979). Child maltreatment and material deprivation among AFDC recipient families. *Social Service Review, 53,* 175–162.

Wortman, R. (1981). Depression, danger, dependency, denial: Work with poor, black, single parents. *American Journal of Orthopsychiatry, 51,* 662–671.

Wright, K. (1982). Sociocultural factors in child abuse. In B. A. Bass, G. Wyatt, & G. Powell (Eds.), *The Afro-american family: Assessment, treatment and research issues* (pp. 237–261). New York: Grune & Stratton.

Zelkowitz, P. (1982). Parenting philosophies and practices. In D. Belle (Ed.). *Lives in stress: Women and depression* (pp. 154–162). Beverly Hills: Sage.

Zur-Szpiro, S., & Longfellow, C. (1982). Fathers' support to mothers and children. In D. Belle (Ed.), *Lives in stress: Women and depression* (pp. 145–153). Beverly Hills: Sage.

* * *

Round Table Discussion

Sameroff. Carl Dunst is doing some really interesting research now looking at belief systems and service providers. Clients seem to be sensitive to the attitudes of people who are providing services. And, if the people who are providing services don't believe that clients should be getting services, or believe they are evil people or angry people, clients are not very open to the kind of services they are getting. At one level, it's nice to say we should be changing some of these things, but there are really basic aspects of the psychology of the people in our society that, I think, in ways you referred to earlier that affect why we don't do these kinds of things. Why do we give people these roles? A second story is kind of a little tangential, but when Koch was Mayor of New York, he hired as head of social services a Ph.D. in Public Health who came in and rationalized the whole social service system, because they figured out why are social workers wasting all their time doing the enforcement things, doing the paperwork, clerks can do that for handing out the payments. And, the social workers should be out doing casework. So, they hired a bunch of clerks to do the paperwork, they freed up the social workers to begin to do the social work, and then there was a budget crunch. Where should the budget be cut? Well we can't cut the clerks, because they are doing all the paperwork. Now, we have this whole group of social workers, all they are doing is treating people. So, they dumped all the social workers. So, politics, real politics, interferes with so much of our best intentions, especially during the last 10–12 years of crunch times.

Lester. I am glad you mentioned the issue of beliefs. I just want to tell a little anecdote that is kind of relevant. We were doing a presentation a few weeks ago describing a comprehensive service delivery program that we put together for part of a multi-site study of cocaine-exposed kids. And, were doing a lot of services of providing transportation, primary pediatric care, substance abuse counseling, and things like washers and dryers. There were some snickers and comments from the audience composed of health delivery system colleagues and academic colleagues. "Gee, how can I get a piece of this, and maybe I should start using cocaine and I can get into somebody's services." And "Gee, do these mothers really deserve all of this." It's this basic attitude that people who are poor deserve to be poor and they don't really deserve to be much better. It is the concept of blaming the victim. We've had a lot of really terrific ideas today in terms of public policy and raised questions about why we can't seem to put these systems in place. I think one real obvious reason is that society just doesn't feel that poor people deserve these kinds of services. Thus, at the same time we think about public policy issues related to improving services, we need to think about doing serious work on changing attitudes.

Gasden. You probably noticed that there's beginning to be a campaign, I guess, to emphasize the human capital value of children, for that very reason. It's something that we have sort of been doing for awhile, but the slogan is that these are your social security. I keep hearing that floating around and I think that one of the ways we bring about an attitudinal change in society is to try to bring home to people that they have a vested interest in the children of the society growing up to be healthy, productive people. However you can go about getting that across is something that maybe has a change of having an impact.

McLoyd. I don't quite understand why in this country, how well children are doing economically, psychologically, and emotionally is not seen by the average person as a marker of the status and well being of society. So, people now are very concerned about how the U.S. compares to Japan on many indicators. But people don't think that one of the indicators that is relevant to the prestige of a society is the status of its children. I think that we need to do some public relations work in order to try to get people to understand that the well being of children is a legitimate marker of the level of the culture and development of society.

The other issue I think that people have to grapple with is the dubious interpretations of the comparative well-being of children in Europe versus those in the United States. In response to the high rates of poverty in the United States, compared to other Western industrialized countries, some people say, "Oh, but we have different kinds of poor people in the U.S. Part of the problem with poor people in this country is that they won't work." This is coded language to mask racist attitudes. I think that part of the ambivalence about doing things for poor people is because black people are disproportionately represented among the poor. I think the whole issue of poverty and race has to be put on the table and dealt with. Or else, I think the debate, the discourse, goes nowhere.

Randolph. One issue I would like to hear some more about is whether in fact when we constantly talk about the disproportionate representation of people of color, is to paint a picture of it's not my problem for a group of policy makers who are not that color. And, we haven't spoken about the Appalachian poor or the rural poor, or the inner city White poor, that constellation of poor that also includes people who are White who they may view as their future, or whatever. And, I think I spoke to it earlier by saying so goes America, when we talk about the problems of people of color. It's not until it becomes of crisis proportions or epidemic proportions that it becomes the policy makers' problems because they aren't viewing poor children as their children. But the very women who have embraced the notion of the feminization of poverty, or the divorced White mothers who find themselves out of income support, these need to be part of our public relations effort as well.

Zuckerman. I remember my other point. It goes to the point of attitudes when I think about welfare workers. Prior to the early 80s, the goal was to facilitate getting people who were on welfare into programs to meet their needs, it was conceptualized as a facilitative role. It got totally switched when Reagan came on board because of that image of the welfare mother with a Cadillac and the goal was to protect society from these people who were inappropriately getting these benefits. So, the workers were rewarded for identifying people who indeed were applying, were not eligible and they were graded that way. The whole thing on attitudes was to switch and was a barrier, and those attitudes, I think, are pervasive from the top down in a lot of ways. And, one of the things, the economic difficulties we are having now aside, I'd like to think that some of these attitudes will change. I think they have very pervasive, very important effects everywhere along the system to what people are rewarded for, what kind of work. And, that's one concrete example.

McLoyd. I think this issue of race and poverty has to be dealt with very carefully. I think that it is a double-edged sword. We really have to know what the goals are. I think that we absolutely have to expose the link between racism and poverty. I am not sure that there is anything to be gained by not making that linkage clear. When people say the causes of poverty are different in this country versus in Europe, they are speaking a coded language. Underlying their claim is the view that in America we have Black people who don't want to work, we have Hispanic folk who don't want to work. They don't have the work ethic. There was a series of back and forth editorials about this in the *New York Times* and I think that we can't just ignore this. But, at the same time, you don't want to encourage the perception that only Black people and Latino people are poor. Obviously, the majority of poor people are White.

CHAPTER 12

Policies for Children: Social Obligation, Not Handout

Aletha C. Huston

The statistics on children's poverty are by now all too familiar. In the United States, children are more likely than any other age group to live in poverty, and U.S. children are poor much more often than children in most other industrialized nations (Duncan, 1991; U.S. Bureau of the Census, 1990). In 1991, 21.8% of the children under 18 lived in families with incomes below the poverty line (U.S. Bureau of the Census, 1992). Children's poverty has increased over the last 20 years, and it remains seemingly intractable despite some major changes in social policies during that period (Huston, 1991; Korbin, 1992). The "liberal" policies of the 1970s did not cure the problem, and the "conservative" policies of the 1980s left children worse off than they had been before.

The major thesis of this paper is that successful policies for reducing poverty and its ill effects depend on challenging some fundamental assumptions underlying both liberal and conservative approaches. (1) Both assume that children's poverty is a result of parental inadequacy—that able-bodied parents ought to be able to support their children. Hence, the stated goal of most social programs for poor parents is self-sufficiency. (2) Both assume that responsibility for children's welfare resides almost entirely in the family, with little corresponding obligation of the community or the larger society. By comparison with most other societies, we emphasize individual responsibility almost exclusively, with the result that we have an imbalance between

parental and societal responsibility for children. (3) Many
decision-makers have an implicit belief that poor parents are
unworthy or inferior — a view fed by racism and class prejudice
that is often unspoken, but very real (Washington, 1988).

Why Children's Poverty Has Increased

Before considering each of these assumptions in more
detail, I will summarize briefly some of the major reasons for the
increase in children's poverty in recent years. First,
macroeconomic conditions have made it more difficult to earn an
adequate wage, particularly for young people and those without
post-high school training (Duncan, 1991; Wilson, 1987). The
average income of the bottom quintile of families with children
dropped from 1970 to 1988 (Congressional Budget Office 1988);
for families headed by young adults (less than age 25), earnings
dropped by 24% from 1973 to 1989. These changes have affected
middle-income families as well. Their earnings bought less in the
late 1980s than in 1970, and many maintained their standard of
living only by having two wage earners. By contrast, the incomes
of the top quintile increased in real value over the same period.
The result is a greatly increased gap between the rich and
everyone else (Congressional Budget Office, 1988; National
Commission on Children, 1991).

By the beginning of the 1990s, employment was no
guarantee against poverty (Garbarino, 1992). Many new jobs are
in service industries with low wages and few benefits. In 1991, a
person working full time at minimum wage received $8500, an
income well below the poverty threshold of $10,973 for a single
parent with two children (the average family on welfare) and far
below $13,812, the poverty threshold for a two-parent family
with two children. When benefits (e.g. food stamps) and costs of
employment (e.g., child care) are included, a single parent's
earnings remain below the poverty line. Even two parents
employed full time at minimum wage barely exceed the poverty
threshold (National Commission on Children, 1991; U.S. Bureau
of the Census, 1992).

Second, the number of children living with single mothers has increased considerably from the 1960s to the present, and single mother families are much more likely to be poor than two-parent families (Bane & Ellwood, 1989; Eggebeen & Lichter, 1991). In many cases, children of single mothers are supported by one wage-earner rather than two; women's wages are considerably lower than men's; and a single parents' ability to work is often limited by their child care responsibilities. Single parents are at a further disadvantage because families living in poverty typically spend 22% to 25% of their incomes on child care (Phillips, 1991).

A third cause for increased poverty is reduction in government benefits, particularly cash transfer programs. Although some of these reductions began in the 1970s, they were especially drastic after 1980. Fewer children were eligible for Aid to Families with Dependent Children (AFDC), and the value of payments to families declined (Huston, 1991). Between 1981 and 1984 alone, federal outlays for programs affecting children decreased by 11% (Garwood, Phillips, Hartman, & Zigler, 1989). Most analysts agree that these three factors: changing macroeconomic conditions, increases in single-mother families, and declining government transfers, were major contributors to the increases in children's poverty in the last 20 years. A reasonable approach to policy, therefore, should be based on dealing with these factors and their consequences. These analyses raise serious questions about the wisdom of programs that rely entirely on making parents self sufficient while at the same time assigning them almost sole responsibility for their children's welfare.

Self Sufficiency as a Goal

Self-sufficiency is such a strong value that it is almost sacrilege to question it as a goal. I certainly support the goal that all adults should be independent and assume responsibility for themselves and their families. However, individuals are not islands; our relation to society is interdependent. We all exist in a social and economic context which can make it more or less likely that efforts to assume family responsibilities will succeed.

Programs designed solely to make poor parents "self-sufficient" have little probability of making significant inroads on children's poverty so long as they focus only on changing those parents and not on their social and economic support systems. In *Poverty and Public Policy*, Morris and Williamson (1986) present a cogent case for the thesis that policies aimed at improving self-sufficiency of poor people, usually through education and training for jobs, have limited potential to reduce poverty because such policies require all of the following to happen: (1) participants must develop the motives and skills required for employment; (2) the model of skill training must be sound; (3) training must be sufficient to qualify the individual for non-poverty wages; (4) jobs must be available; and (5) graduates must have the ability and motivation to keep jobs once they get them. I would add a sixth: their life circumstances, particularly responsibility for care of children and other dependents, must allow them to work at a job. Hence, the success of these programs depends on making changes in individuals, on macroeconomic conditions, and on support systems such as care for children and other dependents.

The focus on individual change was a defining theme of the 1960s War on Poverty, and it emerged in the 1980s as a major thrust of federal and state welfare policy. Numerous education and training programs for parents receiving AFDC were implemented across the country in the 1980s. "Welfare-to-work" was made the centerpiece of the Family Support Act of 1988 with the creation of incentives for states to institute the Job Opportunities and Basic Skills (JOBS) program. In a summary of research evaluating these programs, often with reasonably well-controlled experimental designs, Gueron and Pauly (1991) concluded that a range of programs "can produce sustained increases in employment and earnings for single parents on welfare. . ." They go on to say that expectations should be modest, and increases in standard of living were limited. Although these programs helped, they produced relatively small gains (Gueron, 1987).

Direct assistance, according to Morris and Williamson (1986), requires that only two conditions be met in order to succeed in reducing poverty: the amount of assistance must be sufficient, and participants must receive what is due to them. Direct assistance can be income-based (e.g., public assistance), or social insurance, (e.g., paid parental leave for childbirth). The Uniited States has succeeded in reducing poverty among the elderly in part because major programs are social insurance. Social Security was credited with raising 34% of its recipients above the poverty line, a figure that contrasts starkly with less than 4% raised out of poverty by AFDC (Morris & Williamson, 1986).

In short, programs aimed at self-sufficiency through job training are insufficient to lift many poor families out of poverty. Many parents are unable to work; they have family obligations that makes work costly and difficult; when they do get jobs, they cannot earn non-poverty wages; jobs are not always available. Such programs are useful for some parents, but they need to be supplemented with continuing supports that represent the contribution of the society to its children.

Current policies aim at a level of self-sufficiency for the poor that we do not expect of more affluent families. Direct aid for families with children is built into the income tax system, but the benefits are generally greater for middle and upper income than for low income families. Federal tax regulations permit an exemption for dependents; in 1993, a parent's taxable income was reduced by $2300 for each dependent. For a family with no taxes owed, no benefit was received. For a family of modest income with a 15% tax rate, the benefit was worth $345 in taxes saved; for a high income family, it was close to double that amount.[1] These savings are even greater when state income taxes are taken into account.

Parents may also claim a tax credit for 20–30% of the costs of child care, up to some maximum amount. The credit is more equitable than an exemption because it is subtracted from taxes owed rather than from the income to be taxed. Therefore, the amount received does not vary with the individual's tax rate. Moreover, parents with low incomes can credit 30% of their costs, while those with higher incomes can credit only 20%.

However, parents receive the credit only if they owe taxes, and it is based on how much they paid for child care, so it is worth more for middle and upper income parents than for those who are poor (Garwood et al., 1989; National Commission on Children, 1991).

Two other forms of direct assistance are not limited to families with children, but do benefit middle and upper income families disproportionately. Direct housing assistance is given to home owners in the form of deductions for mortgage interest and property taxes. Subsidies for health insurance are provided by allowing employers to deduct their contributions to their employees' insurance.

These forms of family assistance belie the notion that individual parents should be entirely self-sufficient. We do not consider parents inadequate if they accept direct aid through the tax system; most people consider it reasonable compensation for the costs and responsibilities involved in raising a child. I turn now to the second major issue raised at the beginning of the paper: the imbalance of parental and social responsibility for children's welfare.

Balance of Parent and Societal Responsibility

Direct aid to parents is one manifestation of the community contribution to the rearing of its children. Such aid reflects the reasonable assumption that people who are raising children are making a contribution to the larger society which should be supported by all. The society has an obligation to and an interest in its children.

Relative to other industrialized societies, the societal contribution to rearing children in the United States is very small. We continue to assume that "other people's children" are not our responsibility (Grubb & Lazerson, 1988). Data gathered from seven other industrialized countries demonstrates that all but one of them have higher rates of direct transfers to families with children than the United States and that these transfers contribute significantly to their lower rates of child poverty (Duncan, 1991).

There are several moral and economic reasons for a societal interest and investment in other people's children. Economic survival and advancement depends on having an educated, skilled work force; that, in turn, depends on raising children who are physically and mentally healthy. The quality of life for everyone hinges not only on the earning capacity of future generations, but on their willingness to live in social harmony. When large numbers of children feel excluded from opportunity and satisfaction of basic needs, we establish a climate for crime, violence, and antisocial actions which affects everyone.

Classism, Racism, and the "Unworthy" Poor

Although the majority of poor children in the U.S. are European American, the stereotype in many minds is a single African American mother and her many children. It is certainly true that the risk of poverty is much higher for African American and Hispanic children than for other groups. African Americans are especially likely to live in persistent long-term poverty (Duncan, 1991). But even members of those minority groups do not all live in urban ghettos; many poor of all ethnic backgrounds live in rural areas and small towns.

I have already argued that poverty among young, able-bodied parents is assumed to be a result of parental inadequacy. When those parents are members of an ethnic minority, racism and stereotypes about that minority compound perceptions of inadequacy and make it easy for others in the society to see them as unworthy and undeserving. This subtext of racism is often ignored in policy discussions, but it may be better to acknowledge and address it directly. For example, programs for job training may well need to consider discrimination in hiring as a factor affecting the success of the program.

Universal or Needs-Tested Programs

My major argument in this paper is that policies designed to reduce children's poverty will have a chance to succeed only when there are changes in these assumptions about self-sufficiency, the balance of parent and social responsibility, and the undeserving poor. The most effective means of accomplishing these goals is to expand universal, non-income tested programs for children at both the federal and state levels.

Social programs can be broadly classified as income-tested or non-income tested, simply on the basis of whether eligibility depends on income. Non-income tested programs are sometimes referred to as universal programs although many are limited to certain categories of individuals (e.g., people over 65). Many non-income-tested programs are called social insurance—a term that may or may not indicate that beneficiaries contribute regularly through taxes (e.g., unemployment insurance). Virtually all of the social programs for children in the United States are income-tested[2] (Garfinkel, 1982).

Income-tested programs have several drawbacks that limit their effectiveness: Equity demands that direct aid to someone who is not working must not exceed or even equal the earnings of a working person at the bottom of the wage scale; therefore, benefits cannot be raised to a level that will lift people out of poverty. Second, income-tested programs are easy political targets because their constituents have little political power and because of the widespread view that poverty is the fault of the poor — a view that is exacerbated by class and race stereotypes. As result, the total amount of benefits is inadequate. For example, the real value of the average AFDC payment declined by about 1/3 from 1970 to the late 1980s (Duncan and Rodgers, 1991). By contrast, a large part of the population has a political stake in universal programs, making them difficult to eliminate or reduce (e.g., Social Security, home owners' deductions).

Third, a stigma often attaches to receiving benefits from an income-tested program, particularly if their use is public (e.g., food stamps). The amount of stigma depends on whether the beneficiaries of the program violate social norms (e.g., unmarried mothers), the proportion of the population covered, and the administrative nature of the program (Rainwater, 1982). Administration of such programs is not only complex, but demeaning to the participants. Current welfare programs are criticized by almost all parties involved for their tendency to destroy the self-respect of the participants and for their arcane bureaucracies.

Income-tested programs as they currently exist contain significant disincentives to work. Individuals who move from welfare to work pay an effective tax rate of over 60% on their earnings (National Commission on Children, 1991, p. 90). Moreover, they incur significant costs for child care, and they often lose eligibility for medical benefits under Medicaid while working in a job without health insurance coverage.

Although almost everyone agrees that single parents are at considerable risk of poverty, the current system also contains financial disincentives for marriage. When a single parent on welfare marries a person working full time, their combined income is reduced by about 20% (National Commission on Children, 1991). These disincentives might be reduced by tinkering with the current system, but it is unlikely that they can be completely removed without incurring other problems of inequity.

Equally important is the fact that many poor people are not served by the current income-tested programs. Approximately 40% of the poor get AFDC, and access to many other income-tested programs is hindered by lack of funds, or lack of availability (National Commission on Children, 1991). For example, in many rural areas, there are no physicians who accept Medicaid patients for obstetrical services (Kansas Action for Children, 1991). Two-parent working families are ineligible for most of the current programs except food stamps, although they receive some help through recent increases in the Earned Income Tax Credit (Ellwood, 1988).

Perhaps the best argument for non-income-tested, social insurance programs is that they work. They reduce poverty. Cross-national comparisons indicate clearly that the countries in which government transfers produce a significant reduction in poverty are those with universal programs, often supplemented by income-tested benefits (Duncan, 1991; U.S. Bureau of the

Census, 1990). These programs include child allowances, paid parental leave for childbirth, child care, and medical care (Kahn & Kamerman, 1983).

Within the United States, as already noted, we have been much more successful in reducing the poverty of the elderly than of children. From the 1950s to the 1970s, poverty declined for both children and elderly people; more recently, the downward trend continued for the elderly at the same time as children's poverty rose from a low of about 14% in 1973 to its current 21%. One major reason for lower poverty among the elderly is Social Security, a universal social insurance program with benefits indexed to inflation[3] (Morris & Williamson, 1986).

The main argument against non-income-tested programs is cost. Many assert that they would cost more and be less economically efficient than targeted programs in reducing poverty. If dollars were not increased, the poor would get less aid. After reviewing several economic analyses of this issue, Garfinkel (1982) concluded that differences in efficiency were not necessarily large, and that the poor would probably not get less aid because expenditures would increase. Non-income-tested programs are often simpler administratively, producing some savings. The overall conclusion of this analysis was that we should shift the balance toward more non-income tested programs than we currently have. One can also make a case that reduced poverty will produce long-term savings in expenditures for medical care, prisons, special education, and many other consequences of raising children in poverty, but it is difficult to calculate these savings exactly or to convince policy makers to invest more in children in the short run.

Universal Policies for Children

Given the complexity and seeming intractability of children's poverty, it is obvious that solutions are not easy. Changes in economic conditions are certainly important and have been addressed by Wilson (1987) and others. The part played in children's poverty by government policies concerning family and child support have been the subject of a number of recent proposals, all of which carry some common themes. One of those themes is universal non-income-tested programs. I will give two examples.

Refundable tax credits for children. The report of the National Commission on Children (1991), headed by Senator Jay Rockefeller, contains a comprehensive set of policy recommendations. The centerpiece is akin to a universal child allowance, but it is placed in the income tax system. Specifically, the commission proposed that the current exemption for dependent children be replaced by a refundable tax credit of $1,000 for every child. A refundable tax credit provides equal benefits for all children (unlike the personal exemption), and it is available even if parents do not owe that amount in taxes (unlike both the personal exemption and the ordinary tax credit). That is, if a parent does not owe the entire amount in taxes, s/he receives the difference between what is owed and $1,000 per child as a payment from the government. Using the tax system has some drawbacks in comparison to a monthly direct payment. It requires parents to file a tax return, and the payment may be received well after expenses are incurred. However, this mechanism is consistent with our current method of cash transfers to children through the tax system; therefore, it may be more acceptable to politicians and citizens than a monthly child allowance. Obviously, a universal $1,000 tax credit would cost the federal government more than the current system of exemptions. The Commission on Children estimated the cost at approximately $40 billion and provided a number of alternative proposals for financing it.

Child support assurance. The Child Support Assurance System is a proposal to assure child support to all children living with single parents (Garfinkel, 1992). It has three components: (a) a standard for child support awards—a numerical formula that establishes the amount of child support obligation a non-resident parent has, (b) routine income withholding of the child support from the wages of the non-resident parent, assuring that the payment will be made in full and on time to the resident parent; (c) an assured child support benefit that will be paid by government funds if it cannot be collected from the non-resident parent.

This program is designed to address some of the factors contributing to the high rates of poverty among children of single mothers. It provides guidelines to assure that courts make appropriate awards of child support, and it improves collection of child support. These two features were built into the Family Support Act of 1988 and are being gradually implemented across the states. However, adequate awards and improved collection will help only to the extent that fathers (the vast majority of non-resident parents) have the money to pay their obligation. Among minority families, in particular, many of the fathers are poor; so private child support awards will not lift their children out of poverty (Bane, 1986).

The assured benefit is not income tested, it would be available to all single parents. However, benefits would be taxable, so recipients would pay back some percent of what they received according to their tax bracket. Hence, benefits would be larger for low than for high income recipients. This component of the program has not yet been implemented.

The cost of the program would depend, of course, on the size of the minimum benefit and on the amount by which collections from non-resident fathers can be improved. Garfinkel provided estimates for benefits of $1,000, $2,000, and $3,000 in 1985 dollars. Assuming some improvement in collections (about halfway between mid-1980 levels and 100%), a $2,000 benefit would not change costs significantly (an increase of 0.1 billion dollars) because the costs of the benefits would be offset by savings in AFDC. It would reduce the poverty gap (the amount by which people's incomes are below the poverty line) by 17% and the number of people on AFDC by 20% (Garfinkel, 1992).

An assured minimum child support benefit might improve the lot of many single-parent families not only because of the added income, but because the benefit is paid on a regular and reliable schedule. One of the major complaints about the private child support system is the uncertainty about if or when payments will be made. There is an accumulating literature showing that many of the negative effects of poverty on children's socioemotional development are mediated by parental stress which leads to lowered nurturance and increased punitiveness (McLoyd, 1989; in press). Financial strain could be considerably reduced by having a predictable income, even if it is relatively small. The resulting reduction in psychological stress might leave a parent with more time and energy to provide attention and nurturance to her or his children.

Non-income tested programs like the refundable tax credit or Child Support Assurance are based on different assumptions about parental self-sufficiency and social responsibility for children than those guiding current programs. Income-tested programs in this country are usually defined as temporary; they are considered a "safety net" to help people get through periods of hardship. If individuals qualify for them over a long period, the program (and the person) are considered failures. Such individuals are "welfare-dependent." By contrast, most categorical, non-income tested, social insurance programs are expected to continue over a long period of time. Family allowances, personal exemptions in the U.S. tax system, and many other benefits are designed to last throughout the period of the child's dependency on the parent. Child-care tax credits are available as long as child care is used.

The goals of non-income-tested programs are to provide adequate and continuing support to families with children, not to rescue a failing parent. It is not assumed that poverty is a result of parental inadequacy which can be remedied by making the parent self-sufficient. It is assumed instead that all parents need and deserve support from others in their society who have an interest in and responsibility for children. Parenting is a contribution to society; at the very least, the society has a selfish interest in assuring that its children have the basics for healthy development. When programs apply to all, issues of stigma and race or class stereotypes also disappear.

Future Directions for Research

Public policy decisions about income maintenance have been informed over the past 25 years by some large-scale research efforts. The Income Maintenance studies in the late 1960s and early 1970s were experimental studies designed to evaluate a program that would provide a minimum income to all families with children. People in several parts of the country were assigned more or less randomly to experimental groups receiving different types of assured income benefits or to control groups who received only the benefits available in their area under existing programs (cf. Haveman, 1986). Similarly in the 1980s, several experiments were conducted to evaluate different types of education and training programs (JOBS) for welfare recipients (Gueron & Pauly, 1991).

What we need in the 1990s are some good evaluation studies testing non-income-tested programs like those proposed by the National Commission on Children. Although trials of the Child Support Assurance System were planned, the full system including the assured benefit has not yet been tried or evaluated (Garfinkel, 1992).

Large-scale social research of this kind needs a truly interdisciplinary team including, at the very least, people trained in economics, sociology, and developmental psychology. The major flaws in both the Income Maintenance experiments and the JOBS training experiments are their almost exclusive focus on economic criteria like earnings and labor market participation of parents. Even these data are often discussed without much consideration for their implications for the development of the children who are supposed to be the target of social programs. For example, the conclusion most often drawn from the Income Maintenance experiments was that such programs failed because adults reduced their labor market participation when they received guaranteed minimum incomes (Robins & West, 1980). In fact, a careful reading of these studies indicates that reduced participation was not universal, but occurred sporadically for some ethnic groups in some locations. Moreover, married women and adolescents were two groups who showed large reductions in labor market activity (Institute for Research on Poverty, 1976; Kershaw & Fair, 1976; Robins & West, 1980). One can make a good case that children may benefit when their mother can stay at home a little more, especially in a large family, and there is good evidence that extensive paid work time is a negative influence on the overall development of many adolescents (Steinberg & Dornbusch, 1991). From a psychological and social point of view, more time in the labor force is not always a desirable outcome.

Evaluation studies of this kind need to include measures of children's health and development as well as adults' economic activity. Some indicators of child development were collected in the Income Maintenance experiments, albeit rather superficially. An analysis of these data demonstrated that children whose families received income supplements showed improvement in nutritional status and educational progress (Salkind & Haskins, 1982).

A truly interdisciplinary approach to policy experiments would lead to measurement of psychological, social structural, and economic variables. It would also provide the possibility of interpreting the findings at different levels of analysis.

Conclusion

In the United States of the 1990s, it is unrealistic and unfair to expect that parents will be "self-sufficient" in the sense that they will be able to earn enough to support their families, pay for child care, and maintain adequate medical care. Many children are completely dependent on their mother's income; even a parent who works full time at minimum wage cannot earn enough to rise above the poverty level. Policies which provide some basic supports to parents, both economic and social, are needed. These policies should be based on the assumption that families need support throughout the child's life, and that need is not a sign of failure. The society has a strong selfish interest and a moral obligation to contribute to the development of its children.

NOTES

1. There are some compensations for these inequities in Earned Income Tax credits and restrictions on exemptions for very high income people, but these figures apply to the great majority of families.

2. The benefits conferred through the tax system are usually not listed as social programs.

3. By contrast, AFDC benefits are not indexed.

REFERENCES

Bane, M. J. (1986). Household composition and poverty . In S. Danziger & D. H. Weinberg (Eds.). *Fighting poverty: What works and what doesn't* (pp. 209–231). Cambridge, MA: Harvard University Press.

Bane, M. J. & Ellwood, D. T. (1989). One fifth of the nation's children: Why are they poor? *Science*, 245, 1047–1053.

Congressional Budget Office. (1988). *Trends in family income: 1970–1988*. Washington DC: Congressional Budget Office.

Duncan, G. J. (1991). The economic environment of childhood. In A. C. Huston (Ed.), *Children in poverty: Child development and public policy* (pp. 23–80). New York: Cambridge University Press.

Duncan, G. J. & Rodgers, W. (1991). Has children's poverty become more persistent? *American Sociological Review*, 56, 538–550.

Eggebeen, D. J. & Lichter, D. T. (1991). Race, family structure, and changing poverty among American children. *American Sociological Review*, 56, 801–817.

Ellwood, D. (1988). *Poor support: Poverty in the American family*. New York: Basic Books.

Garbarino, J. (1992). The meaning of poverty in the world of children. *American Behavioral Scientist*, 35, 220–237.

Garfinkel, I. (1982). Conclusion. In I. Garfinkel (Ed.), *Income-tested transfer programs: The case for and against* (pp. 495–523). New York: Academic Press.

—— (1992). *Assuring child support: An extension of Social Security*. New York: Russell Sage Foundation.

Garwood, S. G., Phillips, D., Hartman, A., & Zigler, E. F. (1989). As the pendulum swings: Federal agency programs for children. *American Psychologist, 44*, 434–440.

Grubb, W. N. & Lazerson, M. (1988). *Broken promises: How Americans fail their children*. New York: Basic Books.

Gueron, J. M. (1987). Welfare to work programs: Lessons on recent state initiatives. *Policy Studies Review, 6*, 733–743.

Gueron, J. M. & Pauly, E. (1991). *From welfare to work*. New York: Russell Sage Foundation.

Huston, A. C. (1991). Antecedents, consequences, and possible solutions for poverty among children. In A. C. Huston (Ed.), *Children in poverty: Child development and public policy*. New York: Cambridge University Press.

Institute for Research on Poverty. (1976). *The Rural Income Maintenance Experiment*. University of Wisconsin, Madison.

Kahn, A. J. & Kamerman, S. B. (1983). *Income transfers for families with children: An eight-country study*. Philadelphia: Temple University Press.

Kansas Action for Children. (1991). *Kansas Medicaid Availability Survey*. Topeka, KS: Author.

Korbin, J. E. (1992). Introduction: Child poverty in America. *American Behavioral Scientist, 35*, 213–219.

McLoyd, V. C. (1989). Socialization and development in a changing economy: The effects of paternal job and income loss on children. *American Psychologist, 44*, 293–302.

McLoyd, V. C. Jayaratne, T., Ceballo, R., & Borquez, J. (in press). Economic stress, parenting, and adolescents' socioemotional functioning: Mediational processes in female-headed African American families. *Child Development*.

Morris, M. & Williamson, J. B. (1986). *Poverty and public policy: An analysis of federal intervention efforts*. New York: Greenwood Press.

National Commission on Children. (1991). *Beyond rhetoric: A new American agenda for children and families*. Washington DC: U.S. Government Printing Office.

Phillips, D. A. (1991). With a little help: Children in poverty and child care. In A. C. Huston (Ed.), *Children in poverty: Child development* and public policy (pp. 158–189). New York: Cambridge University Press.

Rainwater, L. (1982). Stigma in income-tested programs. In I. Garfinkel (Ed.), *Income-tested transfer programs: The case for and against* (pp. 19–46). New York: Academic Press.

Salkind, N. J. & Haskins, R. (1982). Negative Income Tax: The impact on children from low-income families. *Journal of Family Issues, 3*, 165–180.

Steinberg, L. & Dornbusch, S. M. (1991). Negative correlates of part-time employment during adolescence: Replication and elaboration. *Developmental Psychology, 27*, 304–313.

U.S. Bureau of the Census. (1990). Children's well-being: An international comparison. *International Population Reports Series P-95*, No. 80. Washington, DC: U.S. Government Printing Office.

———. (1992). Poverty in the United States, 1991. *Current Population Reports, Series P-60*, No. 181. Washington, DC: U.S. Government Printing Office.

Washington, V. (1988). Historical and contemporary linkages between black child development and social policy. In D. Slaughter (Ed.), *New directions for child development: Vol. 42. Black children and poverty: A developmental perspective* (pp. 93–108). San Francisco: Jossey-Bass.

Weitzman, L. J. (1985). *The divorce revolution: The unexpected social and economic consequences for women and children in America*. New York: The Free Press.

Wilson, W. J. (1987). *The truly disadvantaged: The inner city, the underclass, and public policy*. Chicago: University of Chicago Press.

Wiseman, M. (1988). Workfare and welfare reform. In H. R. Rodgers, Jr. (Ed.), *Beyond welfare: New approaches to the problem of poverty in America* (pp. 14–38). Armonk, NY: M. E. Sharpe.

* * *

Round Table Discussion

Brooks-Gunn. If we could get all fathers to pay—because most of this is getting non-residential fathers to pay into the system—perhaps you get 10 percent. So, it kind of depends on how optimistic you want to be. One figure that's thrown around to get all kids who are on poverty currently above the poverty line, remembering that the poverty line is probably too low, would be $37 billion per year. So, $37 to $40 billion. And, that's a number that some of the economists have generated. But I think that by doing a universal system, even though the $1000 isn't going to change everything, the idea is to first start getting an idea of a universal entitlement system in place and then you can add onto it. Clearly mothers who aren't working would be getting AFDC. We aren't going to get rid of AFDC but it may be just a way, almost to promote attitude change the way Kathryn Barnard really was talking about, making the change in terms of values, to see children and the value of children in society.

Huston. Well, the other thing that it may do is to give enough of a boost so that people can earn income more easily, though the current AFDC system has a lot of disincentives in it for earning anything. An entitlement system in which you would receive these entitlements regardless of how much you earn doesn't have those kinds of disincentives in it, but it might give you enough to go on that you could find your child care, for example. Or be able to work part-time and supplement so that you kind of patch together these various things and have enough.

We don't know if self-sufficiency is going to do the job. Because, in fact, most of those families recover anyway. So, you could argue, if you want to play devil's advocate, the families that use AFDC as a safety net get off on their own anyway. Because the problem is that people who are on welfare for a long time are primarily those who enter as teenagers. They are about 75 percent of AFDC. So that's the group people are concerned about because it's taking the most money, even though it's a relatively small proportion. But to take the devil's advocate position; those people get off anyway, so why should we be doing any self-sufficiency training for people who are out of the work force for a couple of years just because of economic downturns in the neighborhood or something? Take the research on the education and training programs for example; all these big experiments are trying to see what are the effects of giving education and training to welfare mothers. They have also tried with men; it doesn't do any good for men at all. They are going to go back and get jobs when they can, is what it boils down to. The maximum effect that anybody has demonstrated is about 8 percent difference in the number of people who are on welfare. Well, what about the other 92 percent. You are right, there are a lot of other reasons why people are not earning enough money or not earning any money at all, but my argument is that self-sufficiency is probably unrealistic if we expect in our current economy for a lot of people with children to be able to earn enough money to cover the costs of raising a set of children outside the confines of poverty.

Gadsden. It's naive to assert that when you reach self-sufficiency you are self-sufficient for ever. No one expects the middle class to be self-sufficient forever. There are all kinds of things that happen. With the literacy effort the idea has been that we are going to get people competent enough to take care of their families, which often means for the people who are doing the planning that we would get people competent in literacy so that they can work in McDonalds.

Huston. And, that's not to say that some of these programs aren't worthwhile. There are certainly a lot of people who live in poverty who can benefit from programs to help them be more literate or to gain job skills. But, it's not going to solve the whole problem, or even the major part of the problem in my opinion. That's why I think that if we put it in the context of what we already do for the middle class, that it may help us to think a little bit differently. That we, in fact, do assume that people are entitled to some help in raising their families and we do it through the tax system. If we take that same concept of the tax system and say why don't we distribute that a little more equitably across society, it may have a better chance of being accepted in this country.

Kotelchuck. Where is the research data and the studies to show that universal entitlement would work?

Huston. Well, it's very clear if we look at the programs for the elderly that it works. Social security has done more to reduce poverty among the elderly than any other program.

Kotelchuck. That's not children.

Huston. It's the same principle though, that an entitlement program that is available to everybody reduces poverty by a lot.

Ramey. I think we have allowed this problem to be sloganeered with some of the most flawed language—language that is just devoid of substance. I don't know anyone who has argued outside of what people in the Enterprise Institute state that they won't ever try to solve any of these problems by throwing money at them. Now, there are a variety of programs that have been tried, including supportive employment, various ways to care for children combining workfare and childcare. Most of the funded programs in my opinion have been thinly conceptualized and implemented, back to the point where there was six month training for someone who had a tenth grade education. What could we expect to get out of such a program, particularly if we are not going to be caring for the children in some reasonable place. So, if you look at jobs and new changes in some of these programs, you had almost two streams never coming into contact: one is put them to work and forget their children; the other is to provide some childcare program and ignore the economics of the family. It just seems so obvious that one needs to think about the people who are at the bottom of the ladder. We need to think about the broad base of supports and we need to bring what I believe the Society for Research in Child Development community is able to bring, and that is serious tests of alternative models. Some are going to work and some are not.

    The bottom line is that we shouldn't be afraid to put together potent treatment programs that have multiple prongs to them, big packages, back to the fact that risk comes in big packages. And, we shouldn't be afraid, nor should we regard ourselves as failures if the programs don't work. That's a piece of information and, then, if you are in the pharmacological business, you'd put that compound aside and you spin out another one to say, how about this one? And, I think that we have just not allowed ourselves to develop the cumulative knowledge base that gets systematically synthesized and disseminated. And, I think, we need to do that.

Huston. Do you think what you are talking about is the layer that needs to go on top of this base that we don't have? And the base that we don't have is constant support for all of our kids. We cannot allow ourselves to define whether a program works, simply by whether the need for it disappears, which is what we do now with the poor. We don't do it with the middle class but we do it with the poor.

Kotelchuck. I have a slide in fact to show poverty rates among the elderly and among children in the last 20 years and it just suggests that it's a political decision in this country in some sense as to what levels of poverty we want to have or not have. We did make that difference for the elderly and they are not self-sufficient at the end; that is we gave them the money and they stay on it forever.

There's been a real effort recently to link the reimbursement systems, particularly AFDC, with health benefits and other benefits for families. Now, most people, I suspect, are not going to like them. You deduct money from people's income. What if the opposite was the case? What if we gave a bonus if your children were immunized as opposed to a penalty if you failed to get them immunized?

Huston. Interesting idea. I think there are just a whole lot of things if we stop thinking about this in a punitive way. As long as they remain conceptualized as programs for "those people", the poor, then there's always going to be this punitive feeling that, oh dear, we can't give it to them, they will misuse it.

CHAPTER 13

Toward Enhancing Knowledge about, and Service to, America's Poor Children: Models and Methods for Integrating Research, Policy, and Programs in Child Development Research

Richard M. Lerner

For the past 20 years, I have taken part in numerous scholarly symposia that were self-proclaimed as "historically un-precedented" events. The round table from which this book derived may or may not be an event of historical importance. But, many of the participants in the present event believe that these next four years represent a window of opportunity, certainly the first in more than a decade of our recent history, for actions on behalf of the needs of children.

Accordingly, in these brief remarks, I want to do more than just summarize the themes of the preceding presentations and discussions. I want to try to provoke us to new actions, ones that will help us, as scientists and as citizens, to address the needs of the poor children of our nation. Thus, with your understanding (and indulgence) of my intention to be provocative, let me begin by focusing on a recurrent theme in today's interactions.

The Politics and Science of Child Poverty

We cannot conduct our research as if it were independent of the political context, and of the power structure, that is invested in denying a different system of resource distribution in America (Hirsch, 1970, 1981, 1990; Hirsch, McGuire, & Vetta, 1980; Kamin, 1974; Lerner, 1986, 1992; Tobach, 1993; Tobach, Gianutsos, Topoff, & Gross, 1974). In other words, we must not ignore the fact that powerful groups in our society have a strong and deeply defended investment in maintaining the economic, class, and racial distinctions and divisions in our society.

This political and power structure will not readily provide entitlements to *all* children. They will not readily agree to take more resources from *their* businesses, families, and communities and to redistribute them to poor children. Their objections are often based on, and rationalized by, racism, by classism, and by sexism (Tobach, 1993; Tobach et al., 1974). Superordinately, a pervasive and pernicious Social Darwinism exists in these biases, a stance often legitimated by reference to what are labeled as "modern" biological theories such as behavioral genetics and sociobiology (Lerner, 1992).

In regard to the powerful institutions in America that maintain the status quo, let me note that the status attainment literature in demography indicates that the best predictions of a child's eventual social standing are his or her mother's SES or level of education (e.g., Featherman & Hauser, 1978). Correlations in the .7s, accounting for about 50% of the variance, are typical. These facts describe at least as much about our political world as they do about our sociological one.

I believe, then, that we should conduct our research in a way that incorporates the political context, and that integrates this level of organization with economic, social, and individual ones (Tobach, 1981, 1993). In other words, our research should involve not only multidisciplinary collaboration but also multiprofessional collaboration (Lerner & Miller, 1993; Lerner et al., 1994).

If we want these collaborations to have a chance to affect positively the life chances of poor children, families, and neighborhoods, we need to get their voices into the design and delivery of research and of the programs that, I hope, will be associated with our scholarship (Lerner, Entwisle, & Hauser, 1994). The people with whom we work—the participants in our research and "demonstration" programs—need to feel ownership of our research and outreach efforts, *if* community-based programs will build people's capacity *and* if these programs therefore can be sustained by the people themselves. Thus, we need community-collaboration as well.

Accordingly, what is required is at the least a new approach to our scholarship, if not in actuality a new paradigm. We need to share our power as scientists with poor people. After all, we are not poor and we know very little about what daily life is like, for instance, for a poor five-year-old living in a poor family in a poor neighborhood, one where poverty has existed for generations, where little hope exists for the future, and where this child confronts each day the reality of violent deaths, of family dissolution, of drugs and crime, and of seeing people on their streets whose lives are being irreparably squandered (cf. West, 1993).

Knowledge of what it is like to live like this does not reside with us. We need to recognize that the community has knowledge of "development-in-context;" and we must find means to incorporate this knowledge into our research, policies, and programs (Lerner & Miller, 1993; Miller & Lerner, 1994). Accordingly, qualitative research—ethnographies, focus group analyses—must become part of our methodological repertoire. And (since we are talking politically) we must demand that the results of scholarship based on such methods be published *regularly* in the pages of our research journals (and not relegated only to "Special Issues").

We cannot expect to enhance our science, or the outreach that we hope will be based on it, if we do not act creatively (and with some methodological courage) to better understand the real-life experiences of the poor children of our nation. Indeed, the quantitative measures we use in our research should be cast anew; they should be built upon the qualitative understanding of development-in-context provided by the participants in our research, our "partners," if you accept my notion of community-collaboration.

The measurement models we develop through this collaboration must be embedded in structural models that are more complex than many of the extant ones in use. This need is predicated not only on the fact that such models will be required, and will naturally emerge, when we bring multiple disciplines, multiple professions, and the community to the research-outreach collaborative "table." In addition, the models must be complex because simplistic, reductionistic, and disciplinary isolationistic models have, quite frankly, failed (McKinney, Abrams, Terry, & Lerner, 1994). It is not *just* eradicating illiteracy that will end poverty; it is not *just* doing better developmental psychological causal analysis that will prevent what Schorr (1988) labels the "rotten outcomes" of poverty; and it is not *just* refined or more flexible economic definitions of poverty that will substantially reduce the double digit increases in child poverty that America has seen over the last decade (Huston, 1992). We need all of these efforts. But we need them to focus on the *changing* relations among interactive, and in fact "fused," levels of organization (Lerner, 1991). It is crucial to understand why this scientific focus must emphasize diversity.

The Centrality of Diversity

Key facets of the integrated contextual and developmental model I am describing are change and diversity (Lerner, 1991; Lerner & Miller, 1993). Calling for change-sensitive designs and measures, and for longitudinally evaluating the outcomes of our policies and programs, may seem like "preaching to the choir" (cf. Baltes, Reese, & Nesselroade, 1977). Yet, most of our research remains cross-sectional, and few developmentalists worry about issues of measurement equivalence when they shift measures from one age group to another or from one racial or ethnic group to another (Baltes et al., 1977; Lerner, 1986). Furthermore, we remain, as a field, focused on means and on generic statements, and do not really treat, with sophistication, in our statistical methods issues of within and across time variation; of change scores; and of change trajectories or "growth" curves (Nesselroade, 1990; von Eye, 1990a, 1990b).

Moreover, our structural models have not adequately dealt with diversity. For instance, Hagen, Paul, Gibb, and Wolters (1990), in an analysis of the history of the publication record of *Child Development*, show that beginning in 1930 and continuing into this decade, more than 90% of the studies published in the prime journal of the Society for Research in Child Development have either assessed white, middle class children studied in laboratory situations, *or* have not even bothered to mention the race or SES of the participants in the study.

To put the problem that this situation produces in an admittedly provocative way, let me ask you to consider what percentage of the articles published in *Child Development* could be excised from the literature, and thus from our collective knowledge base, with absolutely no loss to the quality of life among the children of our nation. What percentage have been and are irrelevant to improving the quality of life of America's poor children? I will be the first to admit that in regard to my own publications, I would not score well in regard to these percentages.

But studying a more diverse array of racial and ethnic groups is not the only way to approach diversity. We need to recognize that diversity exists as well *within* any group. We need to do a better job of understanding the diverse life paths that exist within poor communities. In particular, we need to focus on the "success stories" that arise in these settings (Allison, 1993; Werner & Smith, 1982). What makes some children not only resilient to the risks they confront, but actually able to thrive in conditions and contexts within which other children succumb and fail? By focusing on these success stories we may be able to learn more about how to help communities build effective programs for poor children.

And it is these programs that represent one additional approach to diversity. We need to conceptualize programs and, I would add, policies, in a more diverse manner. From the perspective of the developmental contextual model I am describing, policies and programs represent more than just either social action or, what is often denigratingly labeled, as "applied research." Instead, I believe policies and programs can be seen to represent the interventions (or "manipulations") involved in *basic* explanatory research, that is, research designed to understand how development can occur in the real ecology of human development (Lerner, in press; Lerner & Miller, 1993; Lerner et al., 1994; Miller & Lerner, 1994). In other words, policies and programs are the "experimental tools" of the contextually and developmentally sensitive scholar. Such actions represent our theoretically-guided attempts to change the trajectory of human development; and the evaluation of these activities not only provides us with information about these endeavors but, as well, gives us quite basic information about how to enhance the life chances of diverse children.

Conclusions

Becoming more directly engaged with the development and evaluation of policies, with the professionals who make them, and with the people whose lives are affected by them, will help both our science and our service. This engagement will help us to demystify the policy development process or, at the least, it will help us overcome the sense of alienation that exists between the citizens of our nation—us, for example—and the people who set and organize policy. All members of state legislatures and, I think, of Congress, know that they will eventually lose their seats if they persistently act counter to the clear and pervasive wishes of their constituents. We, with the other members of our own professional and personal communities, must begin to participate in what are a burgeoning number of coalitions that act on behalf of children. In this context, we must not believe we are tainting our science if we act both as advocates for social action and as scientists (Tobach, 1993). To the contrary, if we believe that our science is important for society, we must act in ways that promote those aspects of society for which our science makes an important, and perhaps unique, contribution. For us, children are this contribution.

Finally, and to return to my initial point, the politics, policies, and power structures that promote the persistence of poverty, make poverty a non-random event for America's children (Huston, 1992; McKinney et al., 1994; West, 1993). This is a fact that cannot be ignored by any scholar hoping to use his or her talents to make life better for America's poor children. Many of us were children of the 60's. At that time, many of us used the phrase "power to the people." Now we are far from being children; as difficult as it may be for us to admit, many of us are seen as senior members of the child development scientific establishment. It is to me a historically pleasing irony to learn, therefore, that the exuberance of our youth was in a sense correct. By using our theoretical and methodological skills in a politically participatory manner, one that is inclusive of the people we seek to both understand and to serve, we can empower the children, and the future of America, to effectively pursue lives of hope, of opportunity, and of achievement.

REFERENCES

Allison, K. W. (1993). Adolescents living in "non-family" and alternative settings. In R. M. Lerner (Ed.), *Early adolescence: Perspectives on research, policy, and intervention* (pp. 37–50). Hillsdale, NJ: Erlbaum.

Baltes, P. B., Reese, H. W., & Nesselroade, J. R. (1977). *Life- methods.* Monterey, CA: Brooks/Cole.

Featherman, D. L. & Hauser, S. T. (1978). *Opportunity and change.* New York: Academic.

Hagen, J. W., Paul, B., Gibb, S., & Wolters, C. A. (1990). Trends in research as reflected by publications in child development: 1930–1989. Presented at the Biennial Meeting of the Society for Research in Child Development. Atlanta, GA.

Hirsch, J. (1970). Behavior-genetic analysis and its biosocial consequences. *Seminars in Psychiatry, 2,* 89–105.

———. (1981). To 'unfrock the charlatans.' *SAGE Race Relations Abstracts, 6,* 1–65.

———. (1990). Correlation, causation, and careerism. *European Bulletin of Cognitive Psychology, 10,* 647–52.

Hirsch, J., McGuire, T. R., & Vetta, A. (1980). Concepts of behavior genetics and misapplications to humans. In J. S. Lockard (Ed.), *The evolution of human social behavior* (pp. 215–38). New York: Elsevier.

Huston, A. C. (Ed.). (1992). *Children in poverty: Child development and public policy.* Cambridge: Cambridge University Press.

Kamin, L. J. (1974). *The science and politics of IQ.* Potomac, MD: Erlbaum.

Lerner, R. M. (1986). *Concepts and theories of human development* (2nd ed.). New York: Random House.

———. (1991). Changing organism-context relations as the basic process of development: A developmental contextual perspective. *Developmental Psychology, 27,* 27–32.

———. (1992). *Final solutions: Biology, prejudice, and genocide.* University Park: The Pennsylvania State University.

———. (in press). Diversity and context in research, policy, and programs for children and adolescents: A developmental contextual perspective. In G. K. Brookins & M. B. Spencer (Eds.), *Ethnicity and diversity: Implications for research and policies.* Hillsdale, NJ: Erlbaum.

Lerner, R. M., Entwisle, D. R., & Hauser, S. T. (1994). Editorial: The crisis among contemporary American adolescents: A call for the integration of research, policies, and programs. *Journal of Research on Adolescence, 4,* 1–4.

Lerner, R. M. & Miller, J. R. (1993). Integration human development research and intervention for America's children: The Michigan State University model. *Journal of Applied Developmental Psychology, 14,* 347–364.

Lerner, R. M., Miller, J. R., Knott, J. H., Corey, K. E., Bynum, T. S., Hoopfer, L. C., McKinney, M. H., Abrams, L. A., Hula, R. C., Terry, P. A. (1994). Integrating scholarship and outreach in human development research, policy, and service: A developmental contextual perspective. In D. L. Featherman, R. M. Lerner, and M. Perlmutter (Eds.), *Life-span development and behavior* (Vol. 12) (pp. 249–273). Hillsdale, NJ: Erlbaum.

McKinney, M. H., Abrams, L. A., Terry, P. A., & Lerner, R. M. (1994). Child development research and the poor children of America: A call for a developmental contextual approach to research and service. *Home Economics Research Journal, 23,* 25–41.

Miller, J. R., & Lerner, R. M. (1994). Integrating research and outreach: Developmental contextualism and the human ecological perspective. *Home Economics Forum, 7*, 21–28.

Nesselroade, J. R. (1990). Adult personality development: Issues in assessing constancy and change. In A. I. Rabin, R. A. Zucker, R. A. Emmons, & S. Frank (Eds.), *Studying persons and lives* (pp. 41–58). New York: Springer.

Schorr, L. B. (1988). *Within our reach: Breaking the cycle of disadvantage.* New York: Doubleday.

Tobach, E. (1981). Evolutionary aspects of the activity of the organism and its development. In R. M. Lerner & N. A. Busch-Rossnagel (Eds.), *Individuals as producers of their development: A life-span perspective* (pp. 37–68). New York: Academic.

———. (1993). Personal is political is personal. The Kurt Lewin Memorial Award: Invited Address to Division 9 (Society for the Psychological Study of Social Issues). One hundred first Annual Convention of the American Psychological Association, Toronto, Canada, August 20–24, 1993.

Tobach, E., Gianutsos, J., Topoff, H. R., & Gross, C. G. (1974). *The four horsemen: Racism, sexism, militarism, and social Darwinism.* New York: Behavioral Publications.

von Eye, A. (Ed.). (1990a). *Statistical methods in longitudinal research: Principles and structuring change.* New York: Academic.

———. (Ed.). (1990b). *Statistical methods in longitudinal research: Time series and categorical longitudinal data.* New York: Academic.

Werner, E. E. & Smith, R. S. (1982). *Vulnerable but invincible: A longitudinal study of resilient children and youth.* New York: McGraw-Hill.

West, C. (1993). *Race matters.* Boston: Beacon Press.

* * *

Round Table Discussion

Barnard. What do the sponsors of this round table hope to accomplish?

Fitzgerald. What we hoped to accomplish was the generation of perspectives for the future. What are the issues related to poverty that developmentalists should be attending to over the next ten years? How do we bring research issues, health care issues, and public policy issues to the same table so that all sectors have a sense of the interrelatedness of the issues? How do we bring the scientific community together with the other communities in order to effect change, and to get real work done? Where should our resources go? What are the real problems and are we addressing them? What impact does our science have on the problems of society? These are some of the issues and questions that motivated the organization of the round table. We also wanted to have an impact on the issues that members of SRCD believe to be at the front line, so we planned the first three round tables to focus on children of poverty, children of color, and children of addiction, respectively. There are many other topics such as children of divorce, foster children, rural children, etc., all of which provide opportunities for us to link research, health care, and public policy. Each of us knows how children in this most wealthy of nations are suffering; we know the statistics on child abuse and neglect, fetal alcohol syndrome, low birth weight, infant mortality and morbidity, learning disabilities, emotional and conduct problems, and juvenile delinquency. We know these problems aggregate in poverty, yet as behavioral scientists we have a tradition of ignoring SES by partialing it out of our analyses or controlling for it in our methodology. So, I guess one of the key goals of this round table is to confront poverty as a context, a context that has pervasive influences, not only on individual functioning, but pervasive influences at all levels of societal functioning.

Zuckerman. Given some of the issues brought up, and the importance of them, what should be the next steps, at least with respect to the Society for Research in Child Development?

Ramey. The SRCD is the premier organization in the country dealing with research about children in the broadest context, going across various disciplines, and as such, it enjoys tremendous respect and, potentially, tremendous power in Washington. I believe that we must be prepared to say that the organization, as one of its many goals, has to improve the quality of life for children and families in this country. There continue to be questions about the desirability and legitimacy of the SRCD being involved in public policy activities, although the people in this round table don't seem to have these concerns. I think that it's very important for this organization to find the appropriate way to say that the purpose of our doing research is to improve the quality of lives for children. Within that, we can embed any number of other activities, some of which will be directly relevant and some will not. But to not take that stance is, I believe, to cut away the muscle of this organization at the very time when the nation is crying out for sophisticated leadership of a scientific nature. So I think we ought to find ways to get the ambivalence off the table and to get the organization to say clearly, not only in areas of poverty, but in many other areas, that the purpose of doing the research—the public investment—is so that we will bring back something that will substantially benefit society.

Lerner. I would just add one friendly amendment, because I agree with everything you've said. Rather than society looking for scientific leadership, it is looking for scientific partnership. And what that means is that what society wants from us is not to go into communities and set the research agenda, but to develop partnerships so that we can begin addressing questions that matter to them about how life happens in their communities.

Ramey. I am in complete agreement. What I meant by leadership is that we have some scientific knowledge and skills which we need to bring as part of that partnership, and to exert leadership in what are important questions and how to address them adequately.

Kotelchuck. I agree with what you just said, but as one who has sort of stopped being very active in SRCD because I felt it didn't have enough applied research. It's been a struggle in SRCD to get social policy as one of the units for accepting papers. I just don't think we can train our students to think about these issues broadly. Granted, I'm in a school of public health. We require every doctoral student to add a chapter to their thesis on the implications of their research for the well-being of the public, in our case, we call it public health implications. Many of our students find this painfully difficult to write. Even our faculty find it painfully difficult. They do beautiful research, but if you ask them, "What does it mean?" they can tell you all these theories about teen-age smoking and how it fits this behavioral model and not that one, but they can't tell you what it means. I think that's not something that comes naturally, you know, because we train our students in a very different manner. They're brilliant at criticizing each other's studies, their designs are impeccable, but "What does it mean?" is something we don't train. While I can't say that I think anybody would support me on this, it may seem strange, but even in *Child Development*, we could ask for one paragraph at the end of our articles, or two paragraphs, on the meaning of this for the well-being of children. If you're using a criterion, could you cut it out if it didn't help the well-being of our children? For some articles, I can't picture how we'd ever write it, I'll be honest! But for other articles I can picture how we would write that, and I think that would do us a lot of good as a profession. It would get us thinking, it would move us to seeing that as part of our responsibility as scientists, because I do think we have the science to contribute.

Lerner. But we are preaching to the choir. I mean, people around this room are convinced of that. All of us are trying that, maybe not perfectly, but the best we can.

Kotelchuck. I wonder whether we're really pushing. I have to criticize myself now. Have I been pushing that in meetings that I attend, at organizational meetings in SRCD, on some of the caucuses? I mean, do I really ever say, "Let's do this institutionally, let's add a part"? People say oh it's just too much wasted paper, but I think these are important things to be advocating.

Lamberty. You can do so in the application for support money. For example, as part of the review process, require that investigators make a case for the significance of the proposed research for improving the lot of children.

Kotelchuck. To give MCHP credit, that action is a very important element in the review process. In some of the other fields that give us support, relevance is important, but we could up that a little bit in our assessment of grants.

Lester. Just in terms of the SRCD involvement, I think it's worth just letting people know, historically, a little bit, that when we were negotiating to put on this round table and to start this series over the next couple of years, we did this through the governing council, and we did it, basically trying to set up a continuing publication series. Part of what we wanted to do was to get SRCD to endorse the series and to be willing to have that written in the book, which they agreed to do. So they are going to be formally endorsing this particular round table, which I think is a reasonable statement. We also want to get a similar sponsorship and endorsement from other societies. But that's the way we approached this day and hopefully that will be some kind of statement on the part of the organization that they are willing to take this kind of thing more seriously.

Lerner. It's one thing to get an endorsement under the guise of academic freedom. They'll say, sure, we want all ideas to be brought to the table. It's another to get an endorsement in the realm of policy.

Lester. Yes, well, it's a step.

Barnard. The reason I asked this question is that I had hoped that maybe the organizers would take it a little bit further in terms of pressing the organization along the lines that have been discussed in the last few minutes. Number one, I think that Richard, your statement does embed the concept that part of the role of scholar and researcher really also brings with it some social responsibility. I don't think that's one that is widely accepted in the society at this point, and I think it's also one that is not well enough articulated in terms of graduate programs, in terms of developmental. So I hope that somehow we can bring the results of this round table back to the governing council and with the specific recommendation about scientific effort and defining the role of the scientist in child development and what its responsibilities are. And perhaps, I was thinking, there could be a position statement, we could ask for a special edition of *Child Development* to talk about this responsibility, that there is a way and illustrate people who are doing it. I think, actually, your idea about forcing people into the implications of their research, in terms of the well-being of children, would be an interesting experiment to take place and to ask *Child Development* to do it for a while. I think also the fact that this meeting is taking place is and should be a signal to the society that part of the proceedings of its work—really, its publications and its meetings—are not totally addressing the needs that need to be addressed. And so this format, in terms of bringing together information and social policy, maybe is a dynamic enactment of what should be happening in terms of this society's dealing with the social policy issue. I've gotten the feeling, belonging to the society for a number of years that social policy and changing people's behavior is kind of suspect. You know, that we should be "real scientists." Do our observational booth, do the little squares and little numbers, and you'll be all right. Pre-, post-test, and linear models, don't worry about what happens in the daily life of people.

Lerner. As some of you know, I feel very strongly about the link between being a scientist and being a citizen with social responsibility. I think the other side of the holocaust example that Arnie gave, which was unfortunately a telling one, I mean it was a very powerful example, was that one of the ways that people survived was just at the whim of these scientists who are medical researchers, who are making the selections on the ramp, who just happen to like the person's last name or like the particular profession, or thought there was something in them that would make them a good slave laborer. In a lot of the stories that people tell, you see the scientist who is devoid of social responsibility. I don't know if this is alarmist or what, but let me just put it out there: I think that we are at a point in society where if we as academicians do not move towards integrating our science with social participation, academics as we know it won't be here in twenty years. And as a citizen, I take off my hat as an academic, I say that's perhaps as it should be. I want my universities to be accountable for improving the lives of my kids and families and communities.

Houston. I agree. It seems to me that we might go farther in trying to do what we, I think, know how to do, and that is to write, but not to write the way we're used to writing. I like your idea of saying let's ask people to write a paragraph or two about what this all means. But we're all aware, I think, that when you write for policy makers or you write for public dissemination, you're writing in a very different form. You better be able to say it all in a page, it's best if you can have one-sentence bullets, and so on. And it strikes me that another thing that we as a society might undertake in a variety of ways would be to try to generate dissemination documents that do encapsulate what we think are important facts and information for people in the public, and that we might then also be training our graduate students in that form of writing, as well as the forms that are more typically the academic journalese that we now teach them. It's a different form of communication and we could be doing a whole lot more, at several levels, to promote that kind of communication of information which would, I think, do some of what we're talking about in communicating to the society.

McLoyd. I agree with you that we really need to be pressed hard to think about how our research can be used to help children and try to get the society to move in that direction, by way of endorsing that basic principle as well as the principle of social responsibility. The question I want to raise is whether it can be done in the absence of advocacy per se. I think that the society is very cautious about this whole issue of advocacy, because it has implications for all kinds of things, including the tax-exempt status of the organization. So there is that conservative bent here, and I think whatever statement is formulated has to be done either with a recognition of that restriction or to just say that restriction must go if the society is to be a viable organization that addresses the needs of the children in this country.

Lerner. I think it's important that we recognize the political realities of this society.

Zuckerman. To pick up on Richard's theme of the people in the sixties. We have a president who is a child of the sixties and he is disseminating a message about the importance of inter-dependence and caring. Applied research is being emphasized in Congress and I believe you will see the balance shifting between basic and applied research. Both are important but certainly in the past not enough attention and resources have been given to research that can have a direct impact on the lives of children. Every week you can read in the newspaper about some new, important medical information that has been published in the *New England Journal of Medicine*. Press releases regarding information that can be helpful to policy makers and parents in child development should also be disseminated in such a fashion. Research in developmental psychology is to understand children. Dissemination is an important and needed step. Part of the obligation should be to disseminate what you've learned, and not just to have it circulated among 5,000 professionals in this country. If you don't think it's more important than that, then it will become irrelevant.

Ramey. Well, it's not happenstance that the *New England Journal* and *JAMA* are out getting covered. What I believe the social and behavioral science community is naive about is that they have the model that somehow the reporter's going to come knocking on your door just as soon as the latest issue of *Child Development* comes out with something important to say. It requires straightforward old PR. I mean, the *New England Journal* doesn't get covered just because it's the *New England Journal*, and the SRCD won't be in a position to compromise its integrity, its tax-exempt status by saying here's important information. The public has provided support for this. We're giving back. And I agree with Richard completely, unless we are perceived to be part of the solution of society's problems, and it's not just in poverty, in twenty years our universities will be fundamentally different from what they are now, and we will have moved out into the contract shops; we will have moved out into the places that are willing to be relevant. The action that we want to be getting back, the scholarly products, the wide dissemination, that will become proprietary in the same way that we're seeing biotechnology become proprietary. I believe that this window of at least four years that we have is the reprieve to see if we, the children of the sixties, can get organized enough to be effective the second time around. And if we don't get organized enough in a relatively short period of time, which is going to require being courageous, stepping forward and taking some risks, that maybe we don't deserve to be the players that we are suggesting we can be when we gather and talk to fellow members of the choir.

Randolph. I just want to, I guess, understand, then, how we're moving it out of the choir and into the congregation and the preacher. I'm trying to understand. We've listed a lot of things that, I think, are steps for action, recommendations, even, for respective committees of SRCD, if not the executive committee, governing council, or whatever the leadership might be—and some that seem quite do-able and cost relatively little. I would hate to think they would hide behind the guise of 501 (c) (3) when there are lots of organizations that are doing advocacy in Washington D.C. I like the public relations piece, to let's make a recommendation to the publications committee, editor, whomever that goes to about the policy implications. A lot of those things can be done. Is there a mechanism that the organizers here, whoever has access to that we can put forth as some of these as things that came out of this discussion?

Kotelchuck. There's another thing that we can do, and this one came up in a conversation Richard and I had several years ago, which is that we have to be very aggressive in asserting that it's harder science to study people's real lives than it is to study them in the laboratory. People have been saying this for years, and every meeting I go to I make it very clear. In the world where you don't control anything, that is the hardest science. And in some sense, some of these social experiments we do are some of our most helpful science, because we really try to manipulate, we try to look, to do things in the real world and have a chance to learn from that.

Lerner. What we're doing is as basic as what you're doing in the laboratory—at least as basic, and it's harder.

Ramey. Interestingly, much of what is thought to be relatively hard science is moving in the direction that we are describing. You're seeing major changes in pharmacological research, moving out of tightly constrained subject characteristics, dealing with a broader range of treatment-drug interactions, you're seeing, at the very time when I believe we have won the battle of talking about having the necessity of describing dynamic interactive systems in developmental trajectories, we run the risk of the premier organization being a reactionary rear-guard organization and not capitalizing on what are the great breakthroughs that have been made. And so, if that occurs, I think that will be a strange paradox. If there was ever a time when Washington was saying, "Give me your best idea, give me your best dozen ideas," well, it is now.

Lerner. Just to underscore Craig's point, a discipline as far afield from the ones represented here is crop and soil science—people who study how you grow alfalfa, for example. What is happening with them, under the aegis of a major set of grants from the Kellogg Foundation, is what's called integrative farming, or sustainable agriculture. What they're saying is let's get those farmers away from planting their crops on the agricultural experiment station plots that exist on every land-grant university, and see if their ideas work in the real farming communities of the various states, to see if they can increase alfalfa yield, etc., out there in the real world as opposed to just on the ag. experiment station plots. That's exactly the point that Craig is making, that it's happening in crop and soil science. What I would like to recommend, though, is to ask the conference organizers, who have a tape of what we've said that has various action strategies. Why not do the following? Transcribe that, summarize it, see how many of us would be willing to sign our names to this list—you have the members of the audience, you have the folks around the table—and, in addition, commit ourselves to getting at least five people from our own institutions to also sign on, members of SRCD I would add, then have, if you will, a snowball sampling technique, in which we would then ask those five people to get five more so that when we write a letter to SRCD to enact the actual recommendations that we've all agreed to, there would be some power behind it. That would be one action strategy that could come out of this, as a way of being involved in the community coalition formation.

Fitzgerald. We certainly can move in this direction and since I see everyone nodding in agreement with your suggestions, we will try to enact your plan as part of our continuing agenda on children of poverty.

Author Index

Subject Index